THEORY IN ACTION

Studies in Critical Social Sciences Book Series

Haymarket Books is proud to be working with Brill Academic Publishers (www.brill.nl) to republish the *Studies in Critical Social Sciences* book series in paperback editions. This peer-reviewed book series offers insights into our current reality by exploring the content and consequences of power relationships under capitalism, and by considering the spaces of opposition and resistance to these changes that have been defining our new age. Our full catalog of *SCSS* volumes can be viewed at https://www.haymarketbooks.org/series_collections/4-studies-in-critical-social-sciences.

Theory in Action

Theoretical Constructionism

Edited by
Peter Sohlberg
Håkon Leiulfsrud

Haymarket
Books
Chicago, IL

Published in paperback in 2017 by
Haymarket Books
P.O. Box 180165
Chicago, IL 60618
773-583-7884
www.haymarketbooks.org

ISBN: 978-1-60846-834-8

Trade distribution:
In the U.S. through Consortium Book Sales, www.cbsd.com
In the UK, Turnaround Publisher Services, www.turnaround-uk.com
In Canada, Publishers Group Canada, www.pgcbooks.ca
All other countries, Ingram Publisher Services International, ips_intlsales@
ingramcontent.com

Cover design by Jamie Kerry of Belle Étoile Studios and Ragina Johnson.

This book was published with the generous support of Lannan Foundation
and the Wallace Action Fund.

Printed in Canada by union labor.

10 9 8 7 6 5 4 3 2 1

Library of Congress Cataloging-in-Publication Data is available.

Contents

Preface

Thanks to a generous project grant from The Norwegian Research Council, we have been able to establish a group of Nordic and North American sociologists working with theory and theory development. This has enabled us to meet, to have seminars, to offer joint PhD courses, and to develop a more explorative and creative approach to theory in interaction with master and PhD-students.

This volume is an outcome of a series of seminars in Trondheim, Bergen, Oslo and Tromsø with a focus on theoretical operations and theorizing. A second volume on concepts in action will be published in 2017.

On behalf of all the contributors to this volume we would like to acknowledge our gratitude to professor David Fasenfest as the editor of the series in which this work is published. In addition to David, we would also like to thank Marita Løkås for superb editorial assistance and to Theodore Pride for an excellent job with the index. It has also been a real pleasure to work with Rosanna Woensdregt at Brill and Prince Xavier at SPi.

Trondheim
22 August 2016

List of Figures

About the Authors

Göran Ahrne
is Professor emeritus at Stockholm University. His empirical research covers a wide variety of fields: class structure, organizations and social relations such as friendship and love. His main research interest is to integrate social theory and organization theory. His recent publications in English cover topics as meta-organizations; the significance of partial organizations and the organization of markets.

Mette Andersson
is Professor at the Department for Sociology and Human Geography at the University of Oslo. Her research interests are cultural and political sociology, focusing on issues related to migration, ethnicity, identity and the public sphere. Andersson's publications include articles, books and book chapters on the meaning of religion, elite sports, identity work and political engagement among ethnic and religious minorities

Willy Guneriussen
is Professor of Sociology at The Artic University of Norway in Tromsø. His main fields of research are modernization and globalization processes; traditions, paradigms and foundational problems in sociology/social science; social theory and the understanding of nature. He has written extensively on all of these issues.

Roar Hagen
is Professor of Sociology at The Artic University of Norway in Tromsø. His main focus of interest is theoretical sociology, especially theories of collective action, systems theory and functional differentiation as the principle of integration of modern societies. Hagen has worked with methodological issues under the label methodological constructivism. His publications include work on neo-liberalism in social science, rational solidarity and functional differentiation, and collective power.

Ragnvald Kalleberg
is Professor emeritus of Sociology at the University of Oslo. His research interests include organizations, history of sociology and theory of science. His most recent publications in English include extensive work on Raymond Boudon, Robert Merton and Adam Smith.

Håkon Leiulfsrud

is Professor of Sociology at Norwegian University of Science and Technology (NTNU), Department of Sociology and Political Science. Before coming to Trondheim, he worked at Stockholm University and Uppsala University. His research interests and publications are mainly in the fields of social class and social stratification, industrial relations, family, and in applications of sociological theory.

Willy Martinussen

is Professor emeritus of Sociology at Norwegian University of Science and Technology (NTNU). In addition to general sociology, his research interests are democracy and political participation, social inequality and welfare distribution, culture and religion. He has published books and articles on these subjects, as well as several influential textbooks in sociology.

Annick Prieur

is Professor in Sociology at Aalborg University, Denmark (COMPAS). She has introduced, developed and applied Bourdieu's work a number of areas, including Bourdieu's class model to a contemporary Danish context. Several publications from this study, published in *European Societies, Actes de la recherche en sciences sociales, Poetics* and *Scandinavian Political Studies,* have revolved around the significance of cultural capital.

Peter Sohlberg

is Professor of Philosophy of Social Science at Norwegian University of Science and Technology (NTNU). Before coming to Trondheim he has worked at Uppsala University and Stockholm University. His research interests are philosophy of science, with special focus on "knowledge-generating" research strategies in the social sciences and sociological theory. He has published within these fields, as well as in empirical sociology and social work.

Pål Strandbakken

is Researcher at Consumption Research Norway and Akershus University College of Applied Sciences. His main research interests are consumption research, household energy consumption, material culture and sociological theory. His most recent publication is Strandbakken and Gronow. eds. *The consumer in society* (2015).

Richard Swedberg

is Professor of Sociology at Cornell University, Department of Sociology since 2002. His two specialties are economic sociology and social theory. Before coming to Cornell, he worked at Stockholm University. His works include *Max Weber and the idea of economic sociology* (1998), *Principles of economic sociology* (2003) and *The art of social theory* (2014). Swedberg is also known for his work on social mechanisms and has written on many of the classics, including Weber, Simmel and Tocqueville.

CHAPTER 1

Theory and Theoretical Operations

Peter Sohlberg and Håkon Leiulfsrud

Introduction

The subject of this book is sociological theory in application and theoretical construction work. Analogous to the general treatment of method, we concentrate on the way in which the social world can be theoretically understood and constructed through the notion of theoretical operations.

This book aims to stimulate researchers and students in the broad, fragmented field of sociology to examine the theories and perspectives that guide our theoretical and sociological understanding of the world. Rather than presenting our version of a closed theoretical canon, we seek to generate theoretically based knowledge. From this perspective, our project aims to connect various potentially fruitful perspectives, thereby enabling theories to be used in practice. Rather than being advocates of one convergent perspective, we find it productive to allow for different voices and perspectives on theory understanding and construction. As a consequence, we have favoured alternative interpretations, allowing the reader to follow various lines of argumentation.

In our approach to theoretical operations, the theoretical craft consists not only of being informed about theory inscribed in classical sociology but also of extending beyond the conventional, passive use of theories. Several sociologists have referred to this ability to see beyond the conventional use of theories as a personal skill. In Charles Wright Mills' book, *The sociological imagination* (1959), it is the teacher (i.e., the author) who informs the reader (student) of how to use his/her mental faculties and imagination to actively apply sociological theories and concepts. In this case, sociological imagination is paired with practical advice on how to develop a professional attitude and a sociological identity.

Richard Swedberg's (2012) concept of "theorizing", as presented in this volume, is defined within a framework of developing personal skills and theoretical awareness and is paired with an ambition to better utilise the potential inherent in active theorising. In other words, the craft of theorising is more than merely a personal skill. Positioned at the core of theory and concept formation as such, theorising is thereby essential for the development of sociology as a craft.

Theories and Theoretical Operations

The Collective Heritage of Theory

The development of sociological theories and concepts for understanding society and social relations is seldom regarded as a collective effort or as part of a collective heritage. Instead, the focus is rather on the conflicts between perspectives, the problems with specific perspectives or the possible application of isolated perspectives. We also often take for granted the rich vocabulary of the sociological community and would have great problems imagining the "pre-conceptual stage" before the rapid development of social science in the 19th century. This development not only represented relatively comprehensive world views and assumedly true representations of society but also implied methods suitable for generating new knowledge, i.e., theoretical operations, as was the case with e.g. Karl Marx and Émile Durkheim.

In this volume, we will primarily concentrate on the positive contributions of the sociological tradition in understanding the social world. This approach does not imply that our presentation and discussion is uncritical but rather that we choose to focus on the ways in which alternative theoretical operations may help to construct and understand the social world.

The implications of Karl Marx, Max Weber or Émile Durkheim in their theoretical vocabulary, describing phenomena such as capitalism, economy, solidarity, labour or class are not only a matter of what these individuals wrote but also of where they found inspiration and how their findings may be understood in terms of alternative interpretations. For our purposes, we must consider how their work has been interpreted and understood by other researchers and how their findings might be potentially used.

Robert Merton, addressing the question of how to relate to theoretical tradition, distinguishes between the physical and life sciences and the social sciences:

> The record shows that the physical and life sciences have generally been more successful than the social sciences in retrieving relevant cumulative knowledge of the past and incorporating it in subsequent formulations. This process of obliteration by incorporation is still rare in sociology. As a result, previously unretrieved information is still there to be usefully employed as new points of departure.
>
> MERTON, 1968: 35

Merton's theoretical observation reminds us that sociology is not only rich in theory and concepts but also represents a wealth of underutilised potential.

In this project, we examine a number of potentially fruitful ways to actively use existing theory within sociology (cf. Marshall, 1990). We also aim to theorise and to broaden the theoretical vocabulary.

The Narrative of Sociological Theory

The Static Aspect

The background for our use of theories in different settings could broadly be identified in the narratives of sociological theory that are encountered in education and textbooks. The organisation of these narratives traditionally follows principles by which theories are presented in terms of "schools" or traditions and/or in terms of specific authors. For example, it is commonplace to refer to established theoretical units as, e.g., functionalism, marxism, and symbolic interactionism or to theoretical units as, e.g., Georg Simmel, Émile Durkheim, Dorothy Smith, James Coleman or Judith Butler. Potential intersections also exist between the approaches whereby Karl Marx represents the Marxist school, George Herbert Mead the symbolic interactionist school, etc.

When Jonathan Turner (2010) classifies theories in social science, he adopts a principal standpoint based on the theories' characteristics from a philosophy of science perspective. Under the umbrella concept of theorising, Turner's classification includes the following varieties: functional; ecological; stage-model evolutionary; biosocial; conflict; structural; micro-level interpersonal; cultural; and critical theorising (ibid). One could certainly discuss actual and potential overlaps in this typology, including e.g. overlaps among functional, ecological and bio-social theories. The advantage of this typology, however, is that the defining characteristics are a matter of theoretical structure, in which a specific theory has the potential to be transposable to different empirical settings.

Hans Joas and Wolfgang Knöbl formulate another typology of sociological theory in their textbook, *Social theory* (2009). This more conventional typology, which primarily addresses theoretical development after World War II, includes Talcott Parsons and elaborations on his approach; interpretive approaches; conflict theory, Jürgen Habermas; Niklas Luhmann; Anthony Giddens; Pierre Bourdieu; structuralism and post-structuralism; feminist theory; the "diagnostic" sociology of modernity; and neo-pragmatism (ibid: vii).

These are accordingly different descriptions of the theoretical field, even in its most elementary form – the cases of theoretical units. Substantial variety also exists in the interpretation of the specific characteristics of each of these theories. Although the identification of a meaningful common denominator is not a simple matter, one important feature is that the theories could all be structurally described as conceptual structures, i.e., clusters of interrelated concepts. In these structures and the assumptions connected with them we find the raw material for theoretical operations.

The Dynamic Aspect of Theory Development

The typologies of sociological theory described above are static representations, which do not account for the dynamics of theory development. To provide a completely coherent description of the development of sociological theory from the 19th century classics onwards is impossible, unless such a description is restricted to the most general terms. This development is certainly not a matter of convergence. Turner (2010) describes the development of sociological theorising as a matter of hyper-differentiation with a related decline in general theorising. The substance of this hyper-differentiation is a variety of theoretical approaches, which in the best case can be applied to various specific fields of empirical studies.

Parallel to the development of sociological theory since the classics, there has been a strong empirical tradition in the sociological community that is focused on inductive operations rather than "self-sufficient" and isolated theory. Interestingly, when Anthony Giddens updates his elementary textbook, *Sociology*, the structuring principle is primarily "empirical fields" such as environmental problems, the global financial crisis, new media technologies and new social unrest, and not the theoretical perspectives that Giddens earlier has formulated. The loose link to Giddens' previous theoretical contribution and theory development is striking (Giddens and Sutton, 2013).

One interesting observation concerning the narratives of theory development since World War II is that the narratives tend to rapidly become outdated. This phenomenon has nothing to do with the quality of the overviews. Does this rapid change in the definition of contemporary theory imply that the content of earlier narratives has been replaced by an easily identifiable theoretical content? The answer to this question is, again, the hyper-differentiation to which Jonathan Turner (2010) refers.

Thus, there appear to be no over-arching theoretical traditions analogous to the earlier Parsonian dominance or the (seemingly) anti-thesis to Parsons of the Marxist tradition. These structurally oriented traditions were, in their turn, opposed by the anti-thesis of micro-sociological perspectives such as symbolic interactionism and ethnomethodology. These areas of conflict between structural approaches and actor-oriented approaches subsequently met their softer anti-thesis in the form of synthetic approaches such as those of Giddens, Habermas and Bourdieu.

A major development in the theoretical landscape since the 1970s has been feminist theory, representing the anti-thesis of what is regarded as traditional, male-biased perspectives. Another major development since the 1980s has been the linguistic turn in social science, constituting an anti-thesis to the Marxist materialist perspectives, even if the former perspectives not necessarily are programmatically hostile towards the latter.

The ease with which the narrative of sociological theory is formulated in terms of the classic dichotomous structure of thesis-anti-thesis, suggests that much of theoretical belongingness has become a matter of positioning in the theoretical field. The crucial question is then: what factors determine theoretical position in this field of anti-theses? This question relates to the way in which we regard the function of social theory.

The Functional Aspect of Theory Use
The functional aspect of theory use is fundamental to a project that focuses on theoretical operations. Understanding the implications of concentrating on theoretical operations is facilitated by relating them to a variety of functions of theory. These functions could be divided into more narrow functions that are often discussed in the context of the philosophy of science, or in a broader sense, into functions related to the sociology of knowledge.

Well-established and formulated, theories could be used in a variety of overlapping ways in the everyday life of social scientists. In a narrow sense, these functions include theory as a reality description, an explanatory tool and a predictive device. These functions are generally regarded as manifest in Merton's sense.

From some realist perspectives, it would appear strange to ask questions concerning the function of theory. From a naïve realist perspective, the basic aspect of theory is that it represents actual reality. There are, of course, degrees of realism, and even opponents of naïve realism would adhere to a view according to which theories are intended to capture reality to various degrees. Few feminists, independent of their theoretical positions, would deny that there exists in reality an uneven distribution of resources, structured by gender. A rather conventional understanding would be to regard theories as explanatory devices, i.e., responses to the question of why something is the case. From a classical positivist perspective, the predictive value of theories is highlighted and regarded as closely linked with the explanatory capacity of a theory.

The more wide-ranging and often latent functions of theories must be related to the components of general sociological theories. By general theories, we refer to complex theoretical "architectures", e.g., Parsons or Foucault's theory, and even more complex traditions, e.g., social constructionism. The basic aspect of these types of theories or theoretical traditions is that they have the potential to offer a worldview. This viewpoint can, in turn, be divided into a philosophical worldview, including ontological and epistemological standpoints, and a "factual worldview", including assumptions regarding the social world.

This understanding of theory as a package of assumptions and premises invites membership into the "club", favouring the particular worldview offered by the theory or tradition. The choice of a specific theory is not generally made using truth as a criterion; instead, by adhering to a specific theory, one generally accepts the knowledge claims that are articulated within that theory. The use of a specific theory would then simply require adopting the concepts given with their interrelations and transposing these concepts to different historical and empirical settings. This approach would therefore employ theories as static nomenclatures without actually generating new knowledge and instead would simply rename the social world (see Mouzelis, 1995, for a sophisticated illustration of this problem concerning different uses of Parson's AGIL-scheme).

Theories regarded as "pure" conceptual structures, serving merely as nomenclatures that are applicable in a variety of empirical settings, tend to become more self-fulfilling, declarative statements than informative statements of the social world. Jonathan H. Turner describes the tendency for

> ...much theorizing in sociology to move into the philosophical clouds, undisciplined by research findings and indeed often unconcerned with stating ideas so that they can be tested, while empirical research continues to ignore a good part of sociology's theoretical canon because it is untestable.
>
> TURNER, 2010

The main problem with theory use in this broader sense becomes apparent when one employs theories as static icons that are transposable to every possible setting and immune to empirical variation. Openness to empirical variation is an essential aspect of abductive inferences, as elaborated on in the chapters by Richard Swedberg and Roar Hagen in this volume.

The Problem of Theoretical Icons and the Reification of Theory

The ambiguity of the concept of an "icon" fascinatingly addresses the ambiguity related to the approach to theory. One basic aspect and function of icons is that they can be objects of worship, which is certainly the case for particular theories in social science (Korpi, 1990). Worship is especially problematic in this respect when worship is associated with an uncritical acceptance of a specific worldview that is resistant to every possible anomaly.

An icon could be understood as a static representation of a human "object", as in the famous Russian art tradition. This static and stylised representation corresponds to a common and static use of theory when referring to Parson's theory or Giddens' theory of structuration as a type of fixed and closed entity, applicable to any system-universe or structure. In this static and "holistic" tradition, theories tend to become static nomenclatures considered to be more or less universally valid. For example, why could the "duality of structure" not be regarded as a potential empirical characteristic, open to variation?

Finally, in the world of computers, icons are simple graphical representations of complex computer programs and operations. In an analogous way, the substantial theoretical operationalisation processes based on some apparently simple iconic concepts could be complicated and fuzzy in practice. The simple label of discourse is a good example of an individual concept that covers numerous references of substantial complexity, theoretically and methodologically (cf. Foucault, 2002; Fairclough, 2010).

In positive terms, this fuzziness and complexity hidden behind the simple icons is one of the aspects that enable creativity in theoretical operations.

A central aspect of theories, independent of ontological and epistemological perspectives, is that theories depict or construct order and generally negate randomness in the social worlds constructed through them. Theories constitute cognitive gestalts by integrating, ordering and constructing different, otherwise non-existent or random aspects. Theories explicitly or implicitly exclude alternative worlds, as Göran Ahrne discusses in his chapter on counterfactual reasoning. Even the assumption of a universal contingency implies a general feature of reality. This structural and epistemological property of establishing otherwise non-existent or isolated phenomena is identical to their constructive potential.

As with perceptual gestalts, when regarded from the psychological perspective, the problem with theories as cognitive gestalts is that theories could construct order and continuity where there is none, i.e., if we accept some reasonable type of realism. If not, it would be impossible to have any corrective for theories; criteria of truth, fruitfulness or whatever criteria we would select.

The Non-closure of Theory Application

One rationale behind this publication is to relate to sociological theories without assuming the totality or closure of schools and authorships. This is a stance in strong opposition to the iconic approach to theory. By focusing on theoretical operations, we also make the interconnection between theories, methods and empirical analysis visible. Theories used as icons and closed units may contribute to the unfortunate division between theory and empirical study. As Bourdieu et al. (1991) relates to this division:

> ...those who pontificate on the art of being a sociologist or the scientific way of conducting sociological science often have in common the fact that they dissociate method, or theory (not to mention the theory of method or the theory of theory) from the operations of research (ibid: 2).

Most of the theoretical operations within the field of sociology are construction within specific theories, but theoretical concepts and operations are also travelling between different theoretical traditions. In this perspective, we often find a shift in the mission, function and connotations of ideas.

It is a strong ritualistic element in education as well as in research when we refer to the use of social theory. The standard model is to start with a collection of conceptual building blocks that by tradition are regarded as suitable for specific, well-known purposes. In this type of reasoning, some theories are by tradition and convention regarded as more suitable than others for specific purposes. Just to ask counterfactual questions; who would use functionalist theory in order to understand change or Giddens in order to elaborate on the importance of deterministic social facts or feminist theory in order to understand social change? Even though there are some examples of creative and surprising crossovers (cf. Lockwood, 1992), the tendency is that we habitually tend to use specific theoretical units for specific theoretical functions, with small variation. These habits by convention are a major obstacle for theoretical creativity.

Our approach where we not treat theories as closed totalities have the consequence that perspectives opposed in their totalities could have usable aspects in common. Bourdieu et al. (1991) criticizes e.g., what they call "spontaneous sociology" and "artificialism", where the idea is that private reflection and sociological common sense suffices for understanding the social world. They here find a common denominator among perspectives conventionally regarded as opposed in their totality:

> Durkheim's polemics against artificialism, psychologism, or moralism is simply the counterpart of the postulate that social facts "have a constant mode of being, a nature that does not depend on individual arbitrariness"...Marx was saying the same thing when he posited that "in the

social production of their life, men enter into determinate relations that are necessary and independent of their will"; and so was Weber, when he refused to reduce the cultural meaning of actions to the subjective intentions of the actors (ibid: 15).

This is merely one example where the theoretical de-contextualizing or re-contextualizing of theories, otherwise treated as closed and opposed totalities, could give way to unexpected and fruitful consequences.

We are thus not seeking *the one and only* construction in a convergent sense, but trying to give examples from different perspectives and traditions. A precondition for this approach is that theories not necessarily should be regarded as closed constructions always treated in their totality.

Varieties of Construction Work

Social science must consider the different layers of construction work. In this book we have discussed the complex relationship between everyday social constructions and the theoretical construction formulated in the vocabulary of social science. Willy Guneriussen elaborates on this complexity in his chapter discussing the relationship between everyday language and social science language.

The idea of social construction and the social construction of reality appears to have experienced a considerable renaissance in recent decades. Peter Berger and Thomas Luckman's *The social construction of reality* (1967) is commonly regarded as a departure for the "new" era of the social constructionist movement. Constructionist discourse has intensified since the publication of Berger and Luckman's work, and has become a constituting identity in the form of a social constructionist paradigm with numerous supporters. Similarly to other paradigmatic identities in social science, the result is a rather heterogeneous identity with a wide variety of traits.

Ian Hacking (2001) notes a significant number of titles referring to the social construction of a wide variety of phenomena, including phenomena as: authorship, danger, emotions, facts, gender, knowledge, nature, postmodernism, quarks, and vital statistics (ibid: 1). Contemplating all of these assumed social constructions, it is reasonable to ask the question: are there any phenomena that could be regarded as not socially constructed? Should the set of non-constructed phenomena be regarded as empty? In this respect, we could ask ourselves, what is the informative value of labelling a specific phenomenon as socially constructed?

When Hacking summarises the treatment of social construction in the literature, he primarily focuses on two aspects of social constructions, i.e., their contingent and normative character. As Hacking describes, identifying something as a social construction in the constructionist discourse generally implies that the construction is not a necessary and deterministic state of affairs. Furthermore, this state of affairs is not desirable and would be beneficial to change (Hacking, 2001).

In discussions on social constructions, there is widespread confusion concerning the distinction between theoretical and social constructions and their interrelation. In Hacking's discussion, it is trivial that theoretical constructions of social phenomena do not have the robustness of natural laws and, therefore, could be easily challenged. The ongoing conflict among different theoretical traditions in sociology provides ample evidence of this.

The situation appears to be fundamentally paradoxical. On the one hand, we have a discourse and tradition emphasising the notion that the social construction of phenomena is a non-trivial and radical position with profound implications for understandings of the social world and research methods. On the other hand, the notion that social life is socially constructed is an aspect of sociological common sense and hardly a distinguishing feature and theoretical position as such.

One way of understanding this paradox is that it concerns the problem of distinguishing between theoretical and social constructions. The complex relationship between social and theoretical constructions and the fact that these types of constructions cannot be absolutely differentiated on a conceptual level makes this ambiguity understandable. If not absolute, the distinction between these types of constructions is nevertheless important. This assertion relates to David Lockwood's allegedly artificial distinction between social and system integration:

> Whereas the problem of social integration focuses attention upon the orderly or conflictual relationships between the *actors*, the problem of system integration focuses on the orderly or conflictful relationships between the *parts*, of a social system.
>
> LOCKWOOD, 1992: 400

The distinction between the two types of constructions is important because of its reference to different types of social (and sociological) logics. When Lockwood makes his famous distinction between social and system integration, he is clearly aware of these different logics. If we apply the distinction between theoretical construction on the one hand and social construction on the other hand, *system* integration concerns the researcher's theoretical vocabulary and the abstract and theoretical quality of the system's functioning. *Social* integration, however, is the consequence of social actions perceived by the participating actors (cf. Merton's notion of manifest vs. latent functions). The abstract criterion of social constructions is that actors act upon them in social interactions, whereas theoretical constructions can be described as cognitive and theoretical devices for interpreting or explaining the (social) world. The distinction between theoretical and social construction is often forgotten or ignored because the vocabulary of theoretical constructions tends to be integrated into and acted upon in everyday life.

Class and gender are examples of powerful theoretical concepts once formulated as theoretical constructions that subsequently form the basis for social and political action, i.e., they are involved in social construction (cf. Leiulfsrud and Prieur's chapter in this volume). In another context, Ian Hacking describes theoretical entities of an "interactive kind". He states, "Interactive kinds interact with people and their behaviour...We can well understand how new kinds create new possibilities for choice and action" (Hacking, 2001: 130). The development of "new kinds" in Hacking's understanding is an example of theoretical construction work that offers the potential for subsequent social action, i.e., a transition from theoretical to social constructions. Hacking's example of a social construction of a new kind is when child abuse became an institutionalised phenomenon. Of course, this is not to say that the actual, concrete actions of child abuse not had occurred before its establishment as a theoretical construction; however, these actions were not understood and treated as child abuse before the theoretical construction.

Theoretical Construction Work

In the sociological tradition there is a strange difference concerning how to relate to theory versus how to relate to method. To understand the implications of working with theoretical operations, one can compare the approach to theory with the approach to method. Despite the immense variety of methods, one common denominator is the notion that methods are used to process some type of material, such as interviews, statistical data, observations or any other material. The consequence of this understanding of method is that methods typically generate knowledge, i.e., methods are applied to reveal something new or something that was not apparent before their use. The implication is that we do not generally regard the knowledge of methods as genuine sociological knowledge. Although this knowledge is instrumental and necessary to reveal findings and patterns, it is not substantial. This finding contrasts with how we typically regard theoretical knowledge.

What is conventionally regarded as substantial theoretical knowledge can be found in the following three separate fields: knowledge concerning a theory's concepts and interrelations; the philosophical worldview of the theory; and the way in which the theory "empirically" understands the social world. The mere knowledge of these aspects is in itself static and does not necessarily generate any new knowledge; in the worst case, it could be an iconic understanding by which adherence to a specific theory becomes a confession of faith. Even more serious is the case in which the theory dogmatically becomes an undisputed source of all knowledge. Therefore, in this project we focus on the generative potential of theoretical operations, whereby theoretical tools are used to process varieties of empirical material. There is no possibility of avoiding the theoretical operations necessary to make the analysis meaningful. In this sense, there is no unprocessed or absolutely raw material.

Theory Dependence of the Building Blocks of Theoretical Operations

Regarding theoretical constructions, the question of ontological or epistemological primacy has long been a crucial theme. This focus on "the elementary particles" of social science is partially dependent on the early dominance of the positivist tradition and its focus on objectivity, verification and intersubjectivity. The necessity of perspective and a conceptual framework, however, has been acknowledged even in the post-positivist tradition, and rival traditions have long formulated their basic units of the social world. Jeffrey Alexander emphasises the importance of the "basic components" in understanding the development of social science traditions in general:

> The problem is that people conceptualize these basic components in different ways. It is fair to say, indeed, that these different, often antithetical ways of conceptualizing the basic components of social science are exactly what contemporary theoretical debate is all about.
>
> ALEXANDER, 1987: 6

Regardless of whether we refer to social or theoretical constructions, one may ask the question *of* what, i.e., what are the basic units? There must be some basis or material *from* which the construction is made. Nils Gilje expresses this ontological assumption as follows: Human beings cannot create something ex nihilo but must to create it on the basis of some raw material (Gilje, 2011). How can we then describe the raw material to be used in theoretical constructions? This type of general metaphysical question tends to be treated in a dichotomous manner. The absence of absolute "rawness" or primacy is regarded as an argument that there is no dimension of "rawness". The complication, however, is that some phenomena could be relatively "raw" without being absolutely "raw". The existence of a group of humans, a dyad or triad, could be regarded as somewhat more "raw" than the existence of a social field. The existence of factories could be regarded as somewhat more "raw" than the existence of productive forces, etc. This argumentation builds using examples of intuitive evidence; it is likely impossible to principally identify a continuous dimension of "rawness" or primacy.

In the empiricist tradition, the search for epistemological primacy has had substantial implications for the development of the scientific method long since David Hume's distinction between impressions and the ideas based upon them (Hume, 2009). In social science, argumentation concerning what is more "real" or fundamental is not necessarily based on some type of perceptual primacy. Bourdieu, Chamboredon and Passeron (1991) illustrate this complexity when they formulate the principle of non-consciousness and criticise the notion that social science should be focused on "subjectivities". In the authors' words:

> ...the positive form of the principle of non-consciousness: social relations cannot be reduced to relationships between subjectivities driven by intentions or "motivations" because they are established between social conditions and positions and therefore have more reality than the subjects whom they link.
> BOURDIEU et al., 1991: 18

This hierarchical ordering of social reality in terms of ontological primacy demonstrates how theoretical construction begins at the very basis of capturing the social. If we accept a situation in which we cannot discover any non-constructed social reality, we must ask ourselves, what types of basic phenomena occupy the social world that can be embedded in theoretical perspectives?

Regarding the question of the degree of construction, Jeffrey Alexander describes what he calls a "scientific continuum and its components". The end points of this continuum are the "metaphysical environment" (related to "theories") and the "empirical environment" (related to "facts"). This continuum could be regarded as a dimension of the degree of theoretical construction work, whereby "observation" is the "rawest" methodological aspect (Alexander, 1987: 7). However, the clear-cut dimension of the degree of construction work becomes blurred, as even observations are "theory impregnated".

There is, however, a more pragmatic approach to the question of ontological or epistemological primacy – to articulate the (non-absolute) end point in terms of substantial examples and not in methodological terms. In a relatively basic form that is closely related to our everyday understanding, we have, e.g., actions, motives, social interactions, social situations, processes, social identities, various structures of positions and roles, forms of social organisation, social resources and their distribution, economic resources and their distribution, etc. None of these aspects can be observed in a "pure empirical form" without theoretical interpretation. In addition, these constructions are not entirely free creations of the mind, without reference to the external world. From an eclectic perspective, the interesting aspect here is that the phenomena listed are able to be "adopted" or embedded within different theoretical perspectives. This plasticity is a prerequisite for this project and its perspective on theoretical constructions.

The other side of this "pluralistic coin" is more generally observed. Namely, on this basic level of "social ontology", we find ourselves in a situation replete with various perspectives and conflicts. The conflicts concern the way in which to conceptualise basic components of social science, which Jeffrey Alexander refers to as the background for contemporary theoretical conflicts (Alexander, 1987: 6).

A basic cleavage in social science depends on the heritage, idealist and materialist, of philosophical traditions that lurks in the background and the consequent tensions between traditions focusing on definitions, ideas and discourses or on material resources and their distribution.

Examples of Theoretical Construction Work

There is no absolute demarcation between theoretical constructions and theoretical operations, and accordingly, there is no meaning in seeking the essence of these concepts. However, it may be convenient to use the concept of theoretical constructions for the more general theoretical structuring principles and that of theoretical operations for more restricted, piecemeal theoretical constructions. Every theoretical operation should, however, be qualitatively regarded as a type of theoretical construction, albeit a minor one.

A powerful example of construction work in social science is the theoretical and methodological principle "to treat social facts as things" (Durkheim, 1982).

For Durkheim, this approach implied that the theoretical constructions of the sociological universe have profound theoretical and methodological consequences. The theoretical assumption or starting point for Durkheim identifies structural features such as the division of labour, control, integration and solidarity as fundamental to understanding social life. Characteristic of Durkheim, as of all long-standing classics in sociology, is the dynamic relationship between theory and methodology with the lasting potential to generate new insights. Based on this methodological standpoint, numerous empirical fields could be investigated in which "data" should be selectively gathered using the criteria of being social ("aggregated") and not individual. For example, a methodological principle that aligns with this notion is that the social scientific language cannot be restricted to a vocabulary of individual social action; rather, from this perspective, we must use a vocabulary of systems.

Another example of principal theoretical construction work that could be employed in more specific theoretical operations is Marx's declaration in *Grundrisse*:

> Society does not consist of individuals but expresses the sum of interrelations, the relations within which these individuals stand. As if someone were to say, seen from the perspective of society, there are no slaves and no citizens: both are human beings. Rather, they are that outside society. To be a slave, to be a citizen, are social characteristics, relations between human beings A and B. Human being A, as such, is not a slave. He is a slave in and through society.
>
> MARX and ENGELS, 1978: 247

Several methodological principles follow from this isolated quotation. It does not suffice to locate what could be called social properties at the individual level. Even at the most basic and elementary level – "society" and its structure – becomes necessary for understanding social identities. We must then obtain an understanding and a vocabulary for this concept of society. If we did not know the materialist basis for Marx's understanding of society in terms of the relations of production and productive forces it would be an interesting counterfactual thought experiment to determine whether this quotation, without any context, would leave the interpretation open for a non-materialist understanding of society. Is it possible to accept the theoretical construction of the social structure without accepting the ontological basis of materialism?

A substantial and inspiring collection of examples of the interrelationship among epistemological position, theory and methodology can be found in

"*The craft of sociology*" (Bourdieu et al., 1991). Despite a somewhat polemical style, this book is a rich source of examples of the importance and implications of the theoretical construction of objects in social science. This book describes several examples of how theoretical constructions precede but do not replace the empirical study of social phenomena. We have attempted to provide examples in which this construction could be more or less complex without finding any absolutely "raw" or non-constructed social reality. The authors quote Max Weber to argue against the notion of "raw" objects, or naïve realism: "It is not the 'actual' interconnections of 'things' but the *conceptual* interconnections of *problems* which define the scope of the various sciences" (ibid: 33).

Note that the examples that we have selected are deliberately de-contextualised, taken out of their overall theoretical context, which comprises the following aspects; the total conceptual cluster of the theory; the sum of philosophical standpoints; and the sum of factual understanding of the social world based on the theory. This position is not equivalent to accept the theory in its totality. This permits the more pragmatic approach of theoretical operations. Although nothing hinders one accepting the entire theoretical package when using components of it for theoretical operations, the important point is that such total acceptance is not a prerequisite.

Contextualising Heuristics

To assess the fruitfulness of a project focusing upon theoretical operations, we must ask ourselves whether the objective of understanding the creativity of theoretical operations can be achieved in a systematised manner.

From a formal, descriptive and taxonomic perspective, we could draw upon previous attempts to derive systematic categorisations in the tradition of the philosophy of science. We could examine inductive inferences, deductive inferences or consider causal, functional and evolutionary explanations, etc. Despite the potential merits of this approach, we must ask ourselves, would this truly address the interesting and substantial aspects of the operations? Our answer to this question is no – and this answer is the very rationale behind this publication.

Concerning creativity deploying operations as a means of theoretical construction, it does not suffice to subsume them under descriptive categories meant to address the formal aspects of scientific reasoning, i.e., the context of justification. As an example, consider the case of causal explanations. The vast literature on causality in philosophy and the philosophy of science addresses formal and schematic aspects of causality, the notion being that if formal rules could be established for the correct or acceptable form of causal explanations, these rules would be applicable in all substantial cases of causal explanations. How these formal rules for causal reasoning could be established and how to validate them is a problem in its own right. Notably, formal rules have little bearing on the creative application of this type of (causal) reasoning.

Another approach when identifying some type of pattern in the possible location of theoretical operations would be to identify the intersection of nominally theoretical and methodological operations in the practice of everyday research. Above, we mentioned Jeffrey Alexander's description of a continuum concerning theory with the outer positions of "metaphysical environment" and "empirical environment". The steps along this continuum are substantiated by different aspects that could easily be interpreted as illustrating the intersection between theory and method. Certain steps that represent particular "hot spots" for identifying possible theoretical operations are models, concepts, definitions and classifications (Alexander, 1987: 7).

In a methodologically oriented application of the philosophy of science, Sohlberg and Sohlberg (2013) discuss various crossroads at which the choice of direction has implications for theoretical construction. These crossroads have a certain overlap with Alexander's continuum discussed above and are arranged according to complexity, including: descriptions, definitions, classifications, inferences, explanations and theories (ibid). These are possible fields in which strategies leading to diverse theoretical constructions are located.

These types of systematisations of the localisation of theoretical operations are fortunately never conclusive. The partial use of a theory in the form of a theoretical operation could, with respect to discovery, be entirely unpredictable, whereas once it is formulated, it becomes subject to the same procedural strictness as is generally accepted within the tradition. It is even possible that the partial application of a theory implies greater strictness than when relating to the theory as a whole.

For some, our pragmatic approach to the use of theory could be interpreted as superficial, eclectic or theoretical "cherry picking". It is not possible to provide a perfectly conclusive argument against this type of scepticism, and we would agree that in certain cases the use of de-contextualised and eclectic theoretical operations would be superficial. Even if the criticism of theoretical eclecticism and pragmatism appears to be reasonable, it has certain problematic implications that must be considered. One such implication of this criticism is that theories from a non-eclectic perspective are regarded as logically coherent entities in which the epistemological position follows logically from possible ontological standpoints and the methodology applied is a direct logical consequence of the epistemological position.

This strict logical prerequisite for principally excluding pragmatic theoretical operations is never fulfilled in practice for theories in social science. The theoretical structures of contemporary social theories are not logically coherent in this sense, which creates opportunities for theoretical operations of the type described in this volume. There is, however, no need to be less critical and tolerant of problematic theoretical operations than of the assessment of theories. The same criteria that are employed to assess the value of theories are applicable to theoretical operations, whether they are criteria of truth or other pragmatic and instrumental criteria. In this respect, it is also an open question whether a "pure" theoretical framework is necessarily more theoretically consistent or productive than a more eclectic one (cf. Lockwood, 1992; Mouzelis, 1995). With our focus on theorising as a form of "methodology", the research question, regardless of whether it is found within a specific theory, is what matters. This focus is also reflected in this volume, in which certain chapters tend to focus on research questions in a more closed theoretical context, whereas others are more generic and loosely coupled with specific theories.

In another volume, we will specifically discuss and demonstrate the use of concepts as a particular strategy for the creative theoretical construction of the social world. In this volume, we have collected selected examples of theoretical operations, most of which are not specifically confined to purely conceptual matters. Creativity, by its nature, appears not to be predictable and is difficult to conform to the restricted sphere of a systematic meta-language.

Contributions in this Volume

In organising the chapters, we begin with the foundations of science and the language on which to base and articulate the understanding of social life. We continue with different approaches to theorising. An interesting combination of theoretical approaches is addressed in the discussion of comparative case studies, counterfactual reasoning and abduction. We address the theoretical operation of explanation, which can be related to a diversity of research strategies in practical research. In a more specific sense of theorising, we discuss the potential of employing middle-range theory as a research strategy.

Chapter 2: Richard Swedberg: The notion that concepts are the foundation of scientific reasoning is obvious, and "science without concepts" (Blumer, 1998) would be absurd. Instead of arguing in abstract and detached terms about the role of concepts, Swedberg discusses their various heuristic roles in theorising in detail. In this chapter, we find an outline of a program for theorising in which theorising is regarded as a methodology and heuristic tool to formulate productive sociological questions based on sensitising concepts and everyday experiences.

Chapter 3: Willy Guneriussen: The value of a common-sense understanding of social life is a disputed topic in sociology. In this regard, Bourdieu powerfully argues for sociology to make a necessary break with our commonsensical understanding of the social world, which is permeated with ideology and power structures (Bourdieu et al., 1991). From this perspective, social reality as expressed by actors in everyday communication cannot be trusted as a correct description of social realities. Guneriussen problematises Bourdieu's position as being in a sense contradictory and highlights the importance of a social actor's language and social constructions. In line with this idea, Guneriussen suggests that theoretical operations should not be restricted to more closed and distanced theories formulated in the language of a social researcher but the language of actors and informants should be listened to and taken into account. Here, we have a contribution that suggests a close relationship between social and theoretical constructions.

Chapter 4: Pål Strandbakken: This chapter is an elaboration on Max Weber's concept and methodology associated with "ideal types". This essay is partially based on Weber's own program but is also an example of theoretical operations from Strandbakkens own research on religious movements and the protestant ethic in Norway. Although the discourse on ideal types is often oriented towards specific examples and their use, this chapter presents a broader approach that investigates their potential role as a tool in contemporary social science.

Chapter 5: Håkon Leiulfsrud and Annick Prieur: This chapter focuses on sociologically oriented class research in theory and practice, providing an example of how the traditional lines of demarcation between (Neo)Marxist and (Neo)Weberian class theory have gradually become increasingly blurred, and of a contemporary discussion that is more preoccupied with empirical than theoretical operations. To move beyond a class theory framed in a language of icons and fixed worldviews, we are asked to develop a broader theoretical operations of class that corresponds to contemporary societies and contemporary social issues.

Chapter 6: Ragnvald Kalleberg: This chapter provides readers with a discussion of a broad range of theory types and their possible implications. It also illustrates the problem operating with a rigid distinction between normative and factual research.

Chapter 7: Göran Ahrne: Thought experiments in social science are not codified to the extent that they deserve but are often used in the everyday scientific reasoning as a preliminary, non-codified strategy. A basic type of thought experiment is counterfactual reasoning. This chapter provides an example of how counterfactual reasoning may facilitate alternative questions concerning social processes. It also represents a more playful and experimental attitude toward the application of sociological theory in practice. In social science, as in science in general, post-hoc explanations are easily available for any specific historical trajectory, and counterfactual reasoning tests these explanations. By discussing counterfactuals, we broaden our understanding by seeking the mechanisms that influence the stream of events.

Chapter 8: Roar Hagen: When discussing the heuristics of social science, a universe of inferences that only includes induction and deduction is too narrow to address what actually occurs in everyday scientific activity. The vast majority of sociological writing adopts some type of abductive reasoning, which is theoretically integrated to varying extents to explain social phenomena. Hagen describes the concept of abduction as fuzzy, with numerous theoretical and methodological connotations. He makes a distinction between general theory and theories of society, and discusses the implications of this distinction for the methodology of social science.

Chapter 9: Mette Andersson: In this chapter, Andersson illustrates the interaction among research questions, theory and research methods in research projects in which she has been involved. Through Andersson's account of the past, we are informed about how the projects developed. In the more recent reflections of her past activity, we are informed about how the same results collected and analysed by the same researcher result in different interpretations because of a shift in theoretical operations. However, not all interpretations are equally valid or productive; instead, Andersson shows how additional or complementary theoretical foci may make the interpretation of the case more interesting. Andersson's paper draws from qualitative research methods in general and case study research in particular but is also an example of a theoretical reconstruction that is highly dependent upon theory.

Chapter 10: Willy Martinussen: This chapter presents a comprehensive overview of alternative explanatory practices in social science in general and sociology in particular. In the conventional discourse regarding the philosophy of science, explanations are habitually treated as isolated cases in their own right, e.g., causal, functional, evolutionary explanations, etc. In this type of discourse, what is explained (explanandum) is typically an isolated fact without a description of its relationships with actual research practices and strategies. Conversely, Martinussen's overview is related to a diversity of research strategies in actual research practice, used to understand social life. In this sense, the theoretical operations conducted in the explanations become substantial and sociologically meaningful.

Chapter 11: Peter Sohlberg: This chapter examines middle-range theory as defined by Robert K. Merton. The problems and possibilities of this approach are reviewed, and the danger of reification is discussed. A critical investigation of Merton's research strategies in practice, reveals creativity well beyond what is captured in his programmatic description of middle-range theory. A critical reflection is formulated concerning the paradox that the notion of middle-range theorising has been highly influential while simultaneously providing little instruction concerning how to practically conduct middle-range research. A close reading of Merton reveals rather a creative abductive approach than middle range theorising as Merton programmatically formulated it.

References

Alexander, J.C. (1987). *Twenty lectures: sociological theory since 1945.* London: Hutchinson.

Berger, P.L. and Luckmann, T. (1967). *The social construction of reality: a treatise in the sociology of knowledge.* London: Penguin.

Blumer, H. (1998) [1969]. *Symbolic interactionism: perspective and method.* Berkeley, L.A.: University of California Press.

Bourdieu, P., Chamboredon, J.C. and Passeron, J.C. (1991). Trans. R. Nice. Ed. B. Krais. *The craft of sociology.* New York: Walter de Gruyter.

Durkheim, É. (1982). *The rules of sociological method: and selected texts on sociology and its method.* London: Macmillan.

Fairclough, N. (2010). *Critical discourse analysis: the critical study of language.* 2nd edition. Harlow: Longman.

Foucault, M. (2002). *The archaeology of knowledge and the discourse on language.* London: Routledge.

Giddens, A. and Sutton, P.W. (2013). *Sociology.* 7th edition. Cambridge: Polity.

Gilje, N. (2011). "Epistemisk drift og vitenskapens etos. Vitenskapsteoretiske utfordringer i akademia", Eds. S. Andersen, I.B. Müftüoglu and F.I. Birkeland. *Humanioras fremtid. Kampen om forståelsen av menneske og samfunn.* ["Epistemic operations and science ethos. Science theoretical challenges in academia", Humanities future. The battle for the understanding of man and society]. Oslo: Cappelen Damm Akademisk.

Hacking, I. (2001). *The social construction of what.* Cambridge, MA. and London: Harvard University Press.

Hume, D. (2009) [1739]. *A treatise of human nature.* 2nd edition with text revised and notes by P.H. Nidditch. Oxford: Oxford University Press.

Joas, H. and Knöbl, W. (2009). *Social theory: twenty introductory lectures.* Cambridge: Cambridge University Press.

Korpi, W. (1990). "Om undran inför sociologerna", *Sociologisk Forskning.* ["Questions in the encounter with sociologists", Sociological Research]. 27(3): 2–10.

Lockwood, D. (1992). *Solidarity and schism: "the problem of disorder" in Durkheimian and Marxist sociology.* Oxford: Clarendon Press.

Marshall, G. (1990). *In praise of sociology.* London: Unwin Hyman.

Marx, K. and Engels, F. (1978). *The Marx-Engels reader.* 2nd edition. New York: Norton.

Merton, R.K. (1968). *Social theory and social structure.* Enlarged edition. New York: Free Press.

Mills, C.W. (1959). *The sociological imagination.* Oxford: Oxford University Press.

Mouzelis, N.P. (1995). *Sociological theory: what went wrong?: diagnosis and remedies.* London: Routledge.

Sohlberg, P. and Sohlberg, B.M. (2013). *Kunskapens former. Vetenskapsteori och forskningsmetod.* [Forms of knowledge. Philosophy of science and research methods]. Malmö: Liber.

Swedberg, R. (2012). "Theorising in sociology and social science: turning to the context of discovery", *Theory and Society.* 41(1): 1–40.

Turner, J.H. (2010). "Varieties of sociological theorising", Ed. C. Crothers. *Historical developments and theoretical approaches in sociology.* Vol. 1. Ramsey, Isle of Man: Eolss Publishers Co Ltd.

CHAPTER 2

On the Heuristic Role of Concepts in Theorizing

Richard Swedberg

Introduction

Concepts are central to sociology, and in this chapter I will focus on their role in theorizing. My argument is that at the stage of theorizing, concepts are primarily useful by being *heuristic*, that is, they help us to discover and make sense of what we are studying. They are tools of discovery. Their role in the final theory is quite different, namely to express or sum up some insight about social life in a clear and precise manner so that they also can be used in future research.

As we engage in a research project, we slowly make our way to the end. During this phase we use old concepts and sometimes try to create new ones. Whether the concepts are old or new, their main role at this stage is the same: to be heuristic or to help us discover and better understand what we are studying and trying to explain it (e.g., Swedberg, 2014a, 2014b).

One reason for focusing on *the heuristic role of concepts* is that most of the discussion of concepts that goes on in modern social science is about finding suitable empirical indicators and related methodological concerns (e.g., Goertz, 2006). While this type of issues are central and clearly indispensable to social science inquiry, they also need to be complemented and balanced by a knowledge and an understanding of the role that concepts play in theory and, related to this, in making discoveries.

The Naming of Concepts

Concepts have a name; and when you construct a new concept the issue of providing a name comes up. Hence the general importance of *naming*, when you discuss the role of concepts in theory as well as in theorizing.

There exist different approaches to naming. You can, for example, use existing words or invent new ones. It is also possible to start out from the name of an existing concept and add to it, creating a new concept in the process.

Max Weber took the position that it is usually best to use existing words.

> If we are not to coin completely new words each time or invent symbols, like chemists or like the philosopher Avenerius, we must give every

> phenomenon to which no term has yet been accorded the nearest and
> most descriptive words from traditional language and just be careful to
> *define* them unambiguously.
>
> WEBER, 2001: 63

As an example of this strategy, Weber mentions his own term inner-worldly asceticism. He also pointed out that most scientists dislike new terms (unless they are of their own making).

Sociologists sometimes use an existing concept and with its help, create a new one. Starting with the concept of role, you can get *role set* (Merton) and *role distance* (Goffman). Other examples of this way of proceeding would be *status contradiction* (Everett C. Hughes) and *greedy institution* (Lewis Coser). The advantage of naming a concept in this way, is that the concept gets firmly linked to other concepts and theories.

You can also invent new words for concepts, say, by using Latin or Greek, or just by giving a twist to some word that already exists in one's own language. Examples of this are such terms as *sociologie* (Comte), *colligation* (Whewell) and *quantomania* (Sorokin).

A variant of this approach is to take some obscure or forgotten term, and introduce it as a social science term. This is quite common, as indicated by such terms as *anomie* (Durkheim), *charisma* (Weber) and *habitus* (Bourdieu).

Charles S. Peirce, the American philosopher who was very interested in the process of theorizing, was a fierce advocate of using foreign names for new concepts. Philosophers should in his view not use everyday terms; and the reason for this is that philosophical terms must be "distinct and different from common speech" (Peirce, 1998b: 265). As examples from Peirce's own work, one can mention such terms as *abduction, retroduction* and *interpretant.*

In general, Peirce was fearful of the popularization of philosophical terms, something that in his mind would inevitably lead to a distortion of their meaning. One way to counter this, which he himself sometimes engaged in, was to create terms that are "so unattractive that loose thinkers are not tempted to use them" (Ketner, 1981: 343). As one example of this one can mention his term *pragmaticism.* Peirce did not like what William James and others had done to pragmatism; and this was one way of countering their ideas.

Peirce also believed that by choosing a new name you would be in a better position to control its meaning, than if you just chose an existing term. To some extent this is probably true, even if it also seems that all social science terms tend to lose some of their freshness and original meaning after a while.

It is also true that it is a mistake to introduce too many new terms. The reader of an article or a book will soon lose patience if too many new terms are introduced. The point, I would argue, is to draw attention to what is truly novel, not to create a whole new terminology.

To what has just been said, it should be added that you can run through a number of potential new names in your mind, not just to find the right one, but also to discover something new about the phenomenon the concept refers to. This is another example of the heuristic use of concepts, here applied to naming. Each name has a series of meanings and associations; and these may be worth exploring.

To Define a Concept

So far I have used "term" and "concept" interchangeably, but they are by no means identical. A term, for one thing, is less precise than a concept; for another, it does not need to be consciously constructed. According to Peirce, when you turn a term into a concept you make it more rational. A concept, he suggests, is "the rational purport of a word or a conception" (Peirce, 1998a: 332).

Introducing such a rational element can take many forms, including that of creating a definition or just giving a more analytical and economic description of something. Since efforts in this direction may have unanticipated and heuristic consequences, they should be encouraged.

But while it is important to create a concept, there are several steps to the process. Rushing into the creation of a definition is, in other words, not the best way to proceed when you do research; and there are many reasons for this. For one thing, the notion that you are pretty much finished with a concept, once you have produced a good definition, is wrong (Goertz, 2006: 3–5). Many tasks remain to be done.

The notion that you can somehow produce a definitive definition is also erroneous. When you define a word, as Wittgenstein has pointed out, you basically shift the problem to other words. "What should we gain by a definition, as it can only lead us to other undefined terms?", he asks (Wittgenstein, 1953: 26).

Most importantly, a rush to formulating a definition may be a rush to judgment. The reason for this is that a concept, like an explanation, can rarely be formulated at the beginning of the research process. It is often not possible to create a concept until the research is well under way.

It may be helpful with an example at this point. In *The Protestant ethic and the spirit of capitalism* Weber begins with a description, and not with the concept, of the spirit of capitalism. This is a deliberate move from his part; and he tells the reader that you cannot begin an investigation with "a conceptual definition" (Weber, 1930: 48). You should instead start with "a provisional description", Weber says; and "such a description is...indispensable in order to clearly understand the object of the investigation". "The final and definitive concept cannot stand at the beginning of the investigation, but must come at the end" (Weber, 1930: 47).

More by Weber on the Use of Concepts

Before you decide on a concept, you can let your imagination run free, and in this way come up with creative ideas (e.g., Weber, 1949: 94). But once this has been done, you need to tighten up the analysis, and for this you need a concept.

The concept, Weber also says, is "one of the great tools of all scientific knowledge" (Weber, 1946: 151). It allows us to proceed to the next stage of the research; and it does so through its capacity "to establish *knowledge of what is essential*" (Weber, 1975: 213).

In one of his writings Weber provides us with a description of the discovery of the concept. This account explains how useful a concept can be, but also how it can mislead:

> Plato's passionate enthusiasm in *The Republic* must, in the last analysis, be explained by the fact that for the first time the *concept*, one of the great tools of all scientific knowledge, had been consciously discovered. Socrates had discovered it in its bearing. He was not the only man in the world to discover it. In India one finds the beginnings of a logic that is quite similar to that of Aristotle's. But nowhere else do we find this realization of the significance of the concept.
>
> WEBER, 1946: 141

In the section that follows this mini-history of the concept Weber describes how the idea emerged in early Greek philosophy that if you could only come up with the right concept for some phenomenon, the problem of its true meaning would be solved. This idea was to have a profound impact on Western thought; and the tendency to look for the one right concept, in which all the different manifestations of reality can be expressed and summarized, still haunts social science.

Weber continues his mini-history of the concept as follows:

> In Greece, for the first time, appeared a handy means [viz. the concept] by which one could put the logical screws upon somebody so that he could not come out without admitting either that he knew nothing or that this

and nothing else was the truth, the *eternal* truth that never would vanish as the doings of the blind men [in Plato's cave] vanish. That was the tremendous experience which dawned upon the disciples of Socrates. *And from this it seemed to follow that if one only found the right concept of the beautiful, the good, or, for instance of bravery, of the soul – of whatever – that then one could also grasp its true meaning.*

WEBER, 1946: 141; *emphasis added*

Most of the rest of what Weber has to say about the way to use concepts in modern social science can be found in his discussion of *the ideal type*, a term he had picked up from a colleague and invested with his own content (e.g., Bruun, 2007). The ideal type, it should be noted, helps us to both construct concepts and to use them. And it does so in a very special way.

Much of what Weber says about the ideal type falls in the philosophy of science; and what he says is often hard to penetrate (Weber, 1978: 19–22, 2012: 124–137). In what follows I will bypass most of this material and instead focus on another task. This is to spell out how to construct and use ideal types in practical terms.

An ideal type, Weber says, is the creation of the social scientist. It is essentially a "mental construct" (*Gedankenbild*). All social science deals with meaning; and this is the case for the ideal type as well. In an ideal type you outline the action that a typical actor will take (or that make up a so-called order) and the meaning that answers to it. You also make the following important assumptions: that the actor has full knowledge, is fully aware of what he/she is doing, acts in a rational way, and commits no errors. You then confront this mental and ideal construct with the empirical reality you are studying and go from there.

An ideal type has a number of functions; and one of these is to provide terminological clarity and precision. Since reality is endlessly rich and contradictory, according to Weber, it is important that the ideal type is clear, simple and coherent. That an ideal type fulfills these criteria is helpful when you theorize, but especially important during the main study and when the results are presented.

The most important function of an ideal type, however, is something else; and it is precisely this quality that also makes it extra well suited for theorizing during the stage of the prestudy. It is to be *heuristic*.

The ideal type, Weber repeatedly says, is a "heuristic tool"; and this means that it should primarily be used to discover new aspects of a phenomenon (e.g., Weber, 2012: 116, 132). The ideal type "is a tool", Weber also says, "*never* an end [in itself]" (Weber, 2012: 126).

The ideal type can be heuristic in a number of ways. One of these is to help the researcher to come up with hypotheses. An ideal type "is no 'hypothesis' but it offers guidance for the construction of hypotheses" (Weber, 1949: 90). The way in which it does this is essentially as a result of being confronted with reality. The actor lacks full knowledge – why? The actor does not behave in a rational way – why? And so on.

Another way in which an ideal type can be heuristic, and which I have found quite useful, is the following. One of the purposes of an ideal type, Weber says, is to "serve as a harbor before you have learned to navigate in the vast sea of empirical facts" (Weber, 1949: 104). This means among other things that when you begin to study a complex phenomenon, it is useful to have an ideal type at your disposal.

If you want to study Japanese feudalism, for example, you may begin the research by using an ideal type of Western feudalism or alternatively, if no such ideal type exists, create one. With its help, you will then be able to focus in on certain aspects of Japanese history, while ignoring others, and in this way get your bearing. If you discover significant differences between the concept of Western feudalism and Japanese reality, you have to account for these, and perhaps also create a new concept. If not, you can keep the original ideal type.

It should finally be pointed out that Weber is not the only sociologist who has tried to create a theory of how to construct and use concepts. There is also Herbert Blumer and his notion of *the sensitizing concept* (Blumer, 1954). This type of concept, Blumer says, helps the researcher by guiding him and her towards certain aspects of social reality. Similar to Weber, Blumer stresses that no "definitive concepts" exist. You can improve a sensitizing concept, but it will never be perfect or complete.

More on Constructing a Concept

Let us now leave Weber and Blumer and look at some other ways for how to create a concept. What I first want to discuss is the situation when a social science concept grows out of some existing word and its use in everyday language. In this case, the meaning of the concept will typically change and fluctuate.

An example may illustrate what has just been said; and for this I will use the word "mobbing" (Agevall, 2008). Mobbing roughly means bullying in everyday language; while a social science definition reads a bit different: "one or more individuals are subjected to negative actions, on several occasions and over an extended period of time, by one or more individuals" (Agevall, 2008: 34).

The word mobbing was first used in 1969 by a Swedish medical doctor who was upset over the harassment of his adopted son. In using the word mobbing, he referred to Konrad Lorenz' theory of the inborn aggression of animals, and how violence can be directed by a group of animals against one of its member. The word immediately struck a chord with the Swedish public; and as it was used in the media its meaning was extended to a number of other phenomena. The term was, for example, given a legal meaning but also cast in the language of psychology. In an important book by psychologist Dan Olweus that appeared in 1973, the term mobbing was moved from the discourse of the group to that of the individual, and from the discourse of animal aggression to that of human behavior.

While Olweus mainly had schoolchildren in mind when he talked about mobbing, a decade later another Swedish psychologist extended its meaning once more. This time the actors were adults and the situation a workplace in which some people try to freeze out or otherwise harass and hurt an employee. Today the social science term mobbing also includes this type of behavior. Its current meaning, in other words, is a sort of sum of its history (cf. Somers, 1995).

But social science concepts can also come into being in other ways. One that is quite common is that a term that has been used for some time in social science is transformed into a full-fledged concept at a later stage. With Robert K. Merton we may call these terms *proto-concepts*. He has also described in an instructive way the way in which these differ from full-fledged concepts.

"Proto" means the earliest form of something; and "a proto-concept is an early, rudimentary, particularized and largely unexplicated idea" (Merton, 1984: 267). "A concept", in contrast, "is a general idea which, once having been tagged, substantially generalized, and explicated can effectively guide inquiry into seemingly diverse phenomena".

While proto-concepts, Merton says, "make for early discontinuities in scientific development", fully developed concepts "make for continuities by directing our attention to similarities among substantively quite unconnected phenomena" (Merton, 1984: 267).

As an example of how a proto-concept can be turned into a full-fledged concept, take the notion social mechanism. The term social mechanism can be found in the works of a number of early works by social scientists, but it was not much discussed by these, nor was it turned into a full-fledged theoretical concept. This did not take place until much later (e.g., Hedström and Swedberg, 1998).

Another example of a pseudo-concept that is in the process of becoming a full-fledged concept is that of theorizing. In sociology, the word theorizing made its first appearance around 1900, but as a search in JSTOR shows, it has had to wait for more than a century to be treated as a full-fledged social science concept (Small, 1896: 306; Swedberg, 2012).

It is not clear through what kind of cognitive processes a concept is constructed; nor how you consciously go about constructing one. Provisionally, you can perhaps say that when you go from observing something to turning it into a concept, you can proceed in two ways: you abstract and you generalize.

When you abstract, you remove details or, to use a metaphor, you move upwards and create one or more new levels. When you generalize, in contrast, you mainly move sideways. You do this by incorporating different kinds of phenomena, and finding things in common with these.

A sign of someone being an imaginative social scientist, according to C. Wright Mills, is precisely "the capacity to shuttle between levels of abstraction" (Mills, 1959: 34). Everett C. Hughes meant something similar when he said that a social scientist should also be able to see "likeness within the shell of variety" (Hughes, 1984: 503).

To run up and down the ladder of abstraction, and also to be able to stretch a concept through generalization, is something that you can learn to do through training. It is also an activity that certain individuals excel in. Among philosophers, Kierkegaard is in my view unsurpassed when it comes to the ease with which he forms new concepts and handles their different levels (see e.g., Kierkegaard, 1985). Reading through such sparkling texts as *Repetition* or *The present age* is not only very instructive, but also very inspiring when you try to create a concept.

Political Scientists on Concepts (Sartori, Goertz)

It is also possible to err in various ways when you run up and down the ladder of abstraction, something that has been especially discussed by Giovanni Sartori and a number of political scientists inspired by his work (e.g., Sartori, 1970; Collier and Gerring, 2009). A fine discussion of such notions as conceptual stretching, conceptual travelling and the like can be found in the work of Gary Goertz (e.g., 2005).

According to Goertz, you can extend the scope of a concept by reducing the number of central features associated with it; and vice versa, you can limit its scope by adding features. A concrete example may make it easier to understand Goertz' argument. You can define the concept of peasants in a minimalist way, as say "rural cultivators" (# 1). You can then add that they live in "peasant villages" (# 2); that they show "high levels of rural social subordination" (#3); and that they "control/own land" (#4; Goertz, 2006: 73).

Goertz notes that different theories have used different combinations of these features in their analyses of peasants. Advocates of the moral economy approach, for example, tend to define peasants as rural cultivators (# 1), who live in peasant villages (# 2), and who show high levels of social insubordination (# 3). Marxists would want to add that peasants also control or own land (# 4).

One point that Goertz is very careful to make, is that depending on the concept, you will end up with different populations. Merton has expressed the same idea, but extended it to observation more generally: "concepts, then, constitute the definitions (or prescriptions) of what is to be observed" (Merton, 1945: 465). From a heuristic perspective, you want to play around with different definitions and see what happens when this is done.

There also exist different ways to proceed when you want to operationalize a concept; and Goertz suggests that you should always try to minimize the distance between the definition of a concept and how it is operationalized. What Goertz does not say (but is perhaps implicit in his approach), is that by playing around with a concept along the ways that he suggests, you can also discover some new aspects of a phenomenon.

In fact, in his very important work on the construction of concepts, *Social science concepts* (2006), Goertz pays next to no attention to the way in which you create a new concept or, more generally, to the way in which you deal with concepts in the context of discovery. This is somewhat disappointing since it is clearly Goertz' ambition to cover all the major aspects of the use of concepts.

This does not mean that Goertz' work is not important for the way in which concepts are to be dealt with, in the context of discovery. On the contrary, a good knowledge of his work is essential as well as helpful for what takes place during the stage of theorizing.

Through a small slight of hand, it is also possible to turn some of Goertz' valuable insights in a heuristic direction. Take, for example, his insistence that when you map out the meaning of a concept, you should also decide what its opposite is. If you study war or revolution, you need to figure out what non-war and non-revolution means. And when you try to figure out the opposite of something, you may well end up with some new and interesting ideas.

Using Existing Concepts

So far in this chapter I have mostly talked about creating new concepts, but it is more common when you theorize to use existing concepts or a mixture of new and old concepts. You can either use existing concepts, without changing them, or you can tweak them a bit, like Weber often does. You can also use existing concepts as building material for new concepts, something that has already been mentioned and illustrated with the help of status contradiction among others.

The skillful use of existing concepts presupposes that the researcher knows quite a few concepts, so you have something to draw on and play around with. Some works in sociology are very rich in interesting concepts; and knowledge of these is therefore helpful.

One such work is Weber's *Economy and society*. This is especially true for its first chapter, which contains a presentation of what the author viewed as the basic concepts of sociology (Ch. 1, "Basic sociological concepts"; "*Soziologische Grundbegriffe*"). Weber carefully defines each of these concepts, and also tries to link them together, either in groups or by relating them to his central concept of social action.

That Weber builds all of his concepts in Chapter 1 in *Economy and society* on his notion of social action is worth emphasizing for the following reason. Sociologists are not so much interested in using and developing concepts as in using and developing *sociological* concepts. The difference is the following: while all concepts tend to focus on some aspect of reality and capture it, sociological concepts only do this for those aspects that are sociologically relevant (which means the relationship of some bit of reality to "society", "social interaction", "social action" or the like). Sociological concepts, in brief, direct and guide you to these particular aspects (e.g., Blumer, 1954).

While you may agree or disagree with the way in which Weber defines his basic concepts, his chapter is still very useful for anyone who wants to have a number of solid sociological concepts at his or her fingertips. You can also add to these concepts by reading the next three chapters in *Economy and society* (Ch. 2, "Sociological categories of economic Life"; Ch. 3, "The types of legitimate domination"; and Ch. 4, "Status groups and classes").

Also Georg Simmel's sociological writings are full of useful concepts, but these are more intuitive and less formal than Weber's. Simmel rarely defines a concept, nor does he try to relate them to one another. This may lower their value in one sense, but it also makes it easier for the reader to take them over and make them into his or her own.

Simmel was well aware of this particular quality of his concepts and actually cultivated it. Just before his death, he wrote in his diary that his ideas function like cash that you inherit. You can use it to buy whatever you want... (Coser, 1971: 198–199).

Simmel's writings also illustrate the point that it is not only useful to be familiar with works that contain a number of carefully constructed concepts, such as Weber's *Economy and society*, but also social science literature that is high on ideas. Of contemporary works in sociology that contain many interesting concepts, I especially have found the works of the following authors useful: Robert K. Merton, Erving Goffman and Everett C. Hughes. Merton's work contains many more concepts than most sociologists are aware of; and these have been as carefully crafted as those of Weber. The works of Hughes and Goffman are, in contrast, more like those of Simmel: very suggestive and easily made into your own.

Cognitive Science on Concepts

What makes it difficult to discuss the nature and use of social science concepts in a more satisfying way than has been done so far in this chapter, has much to do with the unclear status of the concept in modern science. What I am referring to is the important research that has been carried out by cognitive scientists, and according to which the so-called classical view of the concept is wrong (e.g., Murphy, 2002).

By the classical view of the concept is meant the theory, which originated in Antiquity and was famously advocated by Aristotle, that a concept covers a certain class of objects and has clear boundaries. Sometimes this is also called an essentialist definition of the concept; and it means that it is possible to enumerate the necessary and sufficient conditions for a concept (e.g., Goertz, 2006).

The problem with this approach is that people do not use concepts this way, according to cognitive scientists. Instead, they may use concepts as a kind of standard, which means that they see some phenomenon as embodying some concept, and others doing this much less (the so-called prototype view). A robin, for example, is seen as more of a bird than a penguin or an ostrich.

People's concepts are sometimes also centered around concrete examples, again in a way that goes counter to the classical view. If you grew up with a German shepherd, for example, this type of dog may be the archetypical dog for you (the so-called exemplar view). In all brevity, according to cognitive science, there exists quite a bit of ambiguity and lack of permanence in the way that people use concepts in their everyday lives.

Little effort has been made to spell out the consequences of this new and fuzzy view of concept formation in social science. It is however clear that you would end up with a new kind of social science concept if you followed the non-classical view (e.g., Goertz, 2006; cf. Ragin, 2000).

David Collier has suggested that under certain circumstances it can be useful to use non-classical concepts in social science or what he calls (inspired by Wittgenstein) family resemblance concepts (Collier and Mahon, 1993).

He defines these as concepts that just fulfill some necessary conditions but no sufficient conditions. Social scientists, for example, often define the welfare state as a state that fulfills some, but not all of certain conditions. A welfare state may be defined as a state that provides, say, two of the following three items: old age pensions, health insurance and unemployment compensation (Goertz, 2006: 59–60).

It is in my view clearly useful to know that it is possible to use two kinds of concepts: (1) those that fulfill both necessary *and* sufficient conditions (the classical view); and (2) those that just fulfill some necessary conditions but no sufficient conditions (the family resemblance view). It is not so clear, in contrast, that the latter type of concept captures what is new with the view of concepts that can be found in Wittgenstein and in cognitive science.

But it is, of course, also possible to make the argument that you should try to stay with the old view of social science concepts, even if it is true that people in their everyday lives use concepts in a different way. The reason for proceeding in this way would be that it is much more difficult to meet such criteria as clarity, economy and lack of ambiguity, when you use the view of concepts in cognitive science.

As an example of the old way of defining a concept you can take Weber's concept of "social action" in *Economy and society*. The term *action* is defined as behavior in which the actor has invested meaning; and the term *social* is defined as action oriented to the behavior of others (Weber, 1978: 4). Or to use another example, this time from Theda Skocpol's work: "social revolutions are rapid, basic transformations of a society's state and class structure; and they are accompanied and in part carried through by class-based revolts from below" (Skocpol, 1979: 4–5).

Regardless how this issue is decided, it is true that the new view of concepts in cognitive sciences does add ammunition against the old notion that you can somehow distill *the* true interpretation of a concept from the ways in which it is used. This is simply not possible, as Wittgenstein was the first to establish.

This view, according to Wittgenstein, is similar to the way in which we sometimes try to teach children the meaning of words (Wittgenstein, 1953). We point at an object, say an apple, and then pronounce the word "apple". To this view of seeing things, Wittgenstein counterposed his own theory of language games. The meaning of a word or a concept depends on the way that it is used or, more precisely, on the language game of which it is part.

Take, for example, the word democracy. When two ordinary persons discuss democracy it has one meaning; as part of a constitution, a second meaning; and as part of a social science analysis, a third. Or take love, which can mean the same as agape, friendship, and that you have zero points in a tennis game – all according to the context and how the word is used.

The current view in cognitive science of the unstable nature of a concept may also help to explain why it is so hard to fix the meaning of a social science concept and keep it intact. It is not only true that the world changes, and with it the meaning of words. Social scientists themselves also use concepts in the non-classical way when they talk, write and think.

The Clarification of Concepts

What is referred to as the clarification of concepts has attracted quite a bit of attention over the years in social science. Committees for this purpose have, for example, been created in political science, sociology and so on. But beyond publishing statements that contain definitions of concepts that the commit-tees recommend should be used (and which have usually been ignored), little seems to have been accomplished this way.

This should not necessarily be seen as an argument against having this type of committees. But their task may need to be changed. What is especially need-ed is conceptual clarification of a more fundamental type, and attempts in a Wittgensteinian spirit to clear up the various misunderstandings that create problems for social scientists when they use concepts in their research and their writings (Wittgenstein, 1953).

As mentioned earlier, new social science concepts tend to lose their original meaning after a while, another complication to keep in mind. One way that this may come about is through the diffusion of successful social science concepts into common language, via newspapers, television and so on. As examples of this you can mention charisma and serendipity (e.g., Merton and Wolfe, 1995).

Another way in which new social science concepts may lose their original meaning is through the way in which they are used by other social scientists than the ones who originally invented them. Peirce was particularly concerned with this issue and created an "ethics of terminology" to deal with it (Peirce, 1998b; cf. Oebler, 1981).

Peirce argued that a scientist who uses a concept in any other way than its original meaning, "commit[s] a shameful offense against the inventor of the symbol and against science, and it becomes the duty of the others to treat the act with contempt and indignation" (Peirce, 1998b: 265). No-one, so far, has tried to implement Peirce's ideas.

The unstable nature of the concept will also affect the attempt to operation-alize it. For a concept constructed according to the classical view, there will presumably be less room for different measures, than when a concept of the family resemblance type is involved. It is difficult to say much more than so on this particular issue.

But the topic of operationalization also raises some other issues that are important to mention. One of these has to do with the way in which measures of operationalization are related to a concept in the first place; and another with the different approaches to operationalization that can be found in quantitative and qualitative studies.

These two issues, as it turns out, are often related. Qualitative social scientists have a tendency to be quite interested in concepts and also in the issue of how these are related to data. Quantitative social scientists, in contrast, spend much less time with concepts; and what especially interest them are indicators and their relationship to variables.

An interesting discussion of these two issues can be found in a recent book by Gary Goertz and James Mahoney on the different cultures that have emerged around qualitative and quantitative studies in social science. In *A tale of two cultures* they write:

> For qualitative scholars, the relationship between a concept and data is one of *semantics*, i.e. meaning. These scholars explore how data can be used to express the meaning of a concept. For quantitative scholars, by contrast, the relationship between variable and indicator concerns the *measurement* of the variable. These scholars focus on how to use indicators to best measure a latent construct.
>
> GOERTZ and MAHONEY, 2012: 140

Finally, one aspect of operationalization that tends not to be mentioned in books on methodology is the heuristic one. To try to operationalize a concept also represents an opportunity to explore a phenomenon that should not be missed. You may not only discover some new aspect of a phenomenon, when you try to operationalize a concept, but also stumble over some new data set. This is especially the case at the early stage of the research.

Concluding Remarks

The main thrust of this chapter has been to argue that more attention needs to be paid to the heuristic role of concepts in sociology and social science. During certain stages of the inquiry, to summarize, concepts should be used for heuristic purposes so that they can help us discover new aspects of the phenomenon we are interested in. In the context of justification, in contrast, concepts should be treated in a different way. At this stage you want the concepts to be as stable and clear as possible, so that they can properly capture and express what you have found, and also relate this to the sociological tradition.

The inherently unstable nature of the concept often makes it hard to fashion concepts in such a way that they can play the role you want them to play in the final theory. At the stage of theorizing, in contrast, you can use the unstable nature of the concept to your advantage. It may well be true that for purposes of clarity, economy and logic, an attempt must be made to stabilize the final concept in various ways. When you try to explore a novel phenomenon or say something new, in contrast, to do so may well make it harder to reach your goal.

References

Agevall, O. (2008). *The career of mobbing: emergence, transformation, and utilization of a new concept.* Växjö: Department of Social Science, Växjö University.

Blumer, H. (1954). "What is wrong with social theory?", *American Sociological Review.* 19(1): 3–10.

Bruun, H.H. (2007). *Science, values and politics in Max Weber's methodology.* Expanded edition. Aldershot, England: Ashgate.

Collier, D. and Gerring, J. (eds.). (2009). *Concepts and method in social science: the tradition of Giovanni Sartori.* New York: Routledge.

Collier, D. and Mahon, J. Jr. (1993). "Conceptual 'stretching' revisited: adapting categories in comparative analysis", *American Political Science Review.* 87(4): 845–855.

Coser, L. (1971). *Masters of sociological thought: ideas in historical and social context.* New York: Harcourt Brace Jovanovich.

Goertz, G. (2006). *Social science concepts: a user's guide.* Princeton: Princeton University Press.

Goertz, G. and Mahoney, J. (2012). *A tale of two cultures: qualitative and quantitative research in the social sciences.* Princeton: Princeton University Press.

Hedström, P. and Swedberg, R. (eds.). (1998). *Social mechanisms: an analytical approach to social theory.* Cambridge: Cambridge University Press.

Hughes, E.C. (1984). "The place of field work in social science", *The sociological eye: selected papers.* New Brunswick: Transaction Press.

Ketner, K.L. (1981). "Peirce's ethics of terminology", *Transactions of the Charles S. Peirce Society.* 17(4): 327–347.

Kierkegaard, S. (1985). Trans. H. Hong and E. Hong. *Philosophical fragments. Johannes Climacus.* Princeton: Princeton University Press.

Merton, R.K. (1945). "What is sociological theory?", *American Journal of Sociology.* 50(6): 462–473.

Merton, R.K. (1984). "Socio-economic duration: a case study of concept formation in sociology", Ed. W. Powell. *Conflict and consensus: a festschrift in honor of Lewis A. Coser.* New York: Free Press.

Merton, R.K. and Wolfe, A. (1995). "The cultural and social incorporation of sociological knowledge", *American Sociologist.* 26(3): 15–19.

Mills, C.W. (1959). *The sociological imagination.* New York: Oxford University Press.

Murphy, G. (2002). *The big book of concepts.* Cambridge: The MIT Press.

Oebler, K. (1981). "The significance of Peirce's ethics of terminology for contemporary lexicography in semiotics", *Transactions of the Charles S. Peirce Society.* 17(4): 348–357.

Peirce, C.S. (1998a). *The essential Peirce.* Vol. 2. Bloomington: Indiana University Press.

Peirce, C.S. (1998b). "The ethics of terminology", *The essential Peirce.* Vol. 2. Bloomington: Indiana University Press.

Ragin, C. (2000). *Fuzzy-set social science.* Chicago: University of Chicago Press.

Sartori, G. (1970). "Concept misformation in comparative politics", *American Political Science Review.* 64(4): 1033–1053.

Skocpol, T. (1979). *States and social revolutions: a comparative analysis of France, Russia, and China.* Cambridge: Cambridge University Press.

Small, A. (1896). "Review of Arthur Fairbanks, an introduction to sociology", *American Journal of Sociology.* 2(2): 305–310.

Somers, M. (1995). "What's political or cultural about political culture and the public sphere? Toward an historical sociology of concept formation", *Sociological Theory.* 13(2): 113–144.

Swedberg, R. (2012). "Theorizing in sociology and social science: turning to the context of discovery", *Theory and Society.* 41(1): 1–40.

Swedberg, R. (ed.). (2014a). *Theorizing in social science.* Palo Alto: Stanford University Press.

Swedberg, R. (2014b). *The art of social theory.* Princeton: Princeton University Press.

Weber, M. (1930). Trans. T. Parsons. *The protestant ethic and the spirit of capitalism.* London: G. Allen & Unwin, Ltd.

Weber, M. (1946). Trans. and eds. H. Gerth and C.M. Mills. *From Max Weber.* New York: Oxford University Press.

Weber, M. (1949). "'Objectivity' in social sciences and social policy", Trans. and eds. E.A. Shils and H.A. Finch. *Methodology of the social sciences.* New York: The Free Press.

Weber, M. (1975). Trans. G. Oakes. *Roscher and Knies: the logical problems of historical economics.* New York: The Free Press.

Weber, M. (1978). Trans. E. Bischoff et al. *Economy and society: an outline of interpretive sociology.* Vol. 2. Berkeley, CA.: University of California Press.

Weber, M. (2001). Ed. D. Chalcraft and A. Harrington. *The protestant ethic debate: Max Weber's replies to his critics, 1907–1910.* Liverpool: Liverpool University Press.

Weber, M. (2012). Trans. and eds. H.H. Bruun and S. Whimster. *Collected methodological writings.* London: Routledge.

Wittgenstein, L. (1953). Trans. G.E.M. Anscombe. *Philosophical investigations.* New York: Macmillan Publishing.

CHAPTER 3

Sociology and the Power of (Ordinary) Language

Willy Guneriussen

Introduction

The pragmatic dimensions of language (use) have been of particular importance in sociology since the publication of Durkheim's study of religious sym-
bolism (Durkheim, 1976) and Mead's theory of significant symbols (Mead,
1934). Thereafter, Parsons made a fundamental contribution to this "symbolic
turn" in sociology (Parsons, 1977). The development of the speech-act theory
and the study of ordinary language use from the middle of the 20th century
have had a decisive influence on subsequent sociology, as attested by many
of the modern classics. Various aspects and functions of language have been
of interest for sociologists: language as a means/medium for *communication* (Luhmann, 1988; Habermas, 1981); as the all-important means for social-
interactional *rituals* and the definition of social situations (Goffman, 1967)";
and as means/media for the exercise of *power* and the construction of social
hierarchies (Bourdieu, Chamboredon and Passeron, 1991).

In this chapter, I will address certain issues concerning relationships between ordinary language and the scientific conceptions of social realities.
Bourdieu's critique of everyday language and common sense will be of particular importance. The chapter will suggest that although ordinary language and
everyday conceptions are inadequate as a scientific vocabulary, they are part of
the conditions for the existence of social reality. The "craft" of sociology must
combine insights into the constructive importance of everyday language and
the conceptions of various forms of scientific "breaks" with these conceptions.

Science and Ordinary Language

Sociologists must develop scientific concepts, theories and principles that are
not found in ordinary language. But can they completely dissociate themselves
from everyday concepts and linguistic practice? The logical empiricists developed the notion of a "universal" scientific language, cleansed of the impreci-
sion, vagueness and obscurity of everyday language. At the most fundamental
level, this language would constitute a common vocabulary and syntax for
all sciences, thereby ensuring unambiguous linguistic meaning and verifiable propositions. Bourdieu also insisted on a necessary break with ordinary

language (Bourdieu et al., 1991: 13 ff), not (merely) because of its vagueness and obscurity but primarily because of how ordinary language and linguistic habits function as a medium for or as an expression of underlying social forces and dominance. For this reason, sociologists must "challenge ordinary language and everyday notions" and break with the accompanying "spontaneous sociology" to generate a scientific discourse that is fundamentally distinct from "everyday opinion" (Bourdieu et al., 1991: 13). If not, they will become unwitting victims of and contributors to the power relations that they as sociologists should seek to disclose.

Bourdieu's arguments place him in an old tradition of suspicion regarding everyday language and beliefs – he mentions Durkheim's critique of the psychological explanations of social facts and Marx's theory of the social/material conditions of consciousness. The central point is that the notions of everyday language and actors' ideas cannot be trusted to be correct descriptions of actions and social realities. Based on modern speech-act theory, it is possible to argue against a generalised dismissal of ordinary language as a source of sociological knowledge. The concepts of everyday communications are incorporated into social realities and institutions. These concepts participate in the constitution of reality and are therefore also relevant for sociological analysis. The everyday experience of social life is already "sociological" in a basic sense because "...sociology itself is a commonly held skill of untrained people and, thus, an important feature of social life itself" (Lemert, 2012: 6; Giddens, 1984). Conceptual, theoretical and methodological operations in sociology are, in various ways, dependent on pre-theoretical conceptions in everyday social life.

Ordinary Language and Symbolic Power

Various types of social, cultural, economic and political power are mediated through elements and forms of everyday communication, as Bourdieu has demonstrated. The idea of symbolic power is fertile. Even the more extreme concept of symbolic violence can be employed in certain situations – e.g., the derogatory characterisations of minorities or the ritual denigration of low-standing individuals in various groups. However, if this conception is generalised as the only sociological theory of language, this may result in the neglect of certain basic constitutional functions of language use – primarily those of speech acts in ordinary social situations and institutions. There is also a blending of principally different forms of "force" or "power". The "deontic" force of various speech acts (their ability to create obligations among individuals and towards institutions) cannot (always) be explained as results of other types of non-linguistic power. Even if we accept that hegemonic powers and symbolic violence may be at work (and most often not recognised as such) in the majority of social situations, we can argue that ordinary interaction and communication presuppose some level of common meaning that is not merely the expression of (or the means for) other types of social power. Institutions are, of course, structures of power, but they can only function because the various actors have some common understanding of basic notions, actions, speech acts, institutions, obligations, duties and commitments.

Although this chapter concerns the ways in which language use is involved in the "production" of social realities, this focus does not imply that all of social reality is a linguistic phenomenon, even if it presupposes language. Making a promise is a linguistic act. Arriving at a designated place to satisfy that promise is an extra-linguistic, practical and material activity – although its meaning refers to the specific promise and its "illocutionary force", its ability to bind or commit actors to certain future courses of action (Austin, 1962).

The importance here ascribed to language is also not intended to deny the fundamental influence of material structures, technology and natural conditions. There is a wide variety of material "stuff" that renders society, social networks and associations durable and real. However, these material dimensions alone cannot explain social realities without including the constructive and constitutional influence of language (use). Society is both a material and symbolic reality. None of these dimensions can be reduced to or explained by another.

The Magical (?) Power of Words

In everyday communication and authoritative proclamations, we witness the power of language at work: promises given (and accepted), obligations stated, nominations declared, judgements passed, orders issued and so forth. All of these things affect actors and their actions in various ways. The words themselves and how the words are used in different speech acts appear to have causal power. They produce changes in activities and social relations. Whence does this power originate? What is its source? Is it something *internal* to language itself – a sort of linguistic magic? Does saying something make it real, or is the source of this "magic" external to language? Bourdieu argues against the notion of autonomous linguistic forces:

> ...looking within words for the power of words, that is, looking for it where it is not to be found. In fact the illocutionary force of expressions cannot

be found in the very words, such as "performatives"...The power of words
is nothing other than the delegated power of the spokesperson....

BOURDIEU, 1991: 107

On the one hand, Bourdieu accepts that words and language are involved in
the construction of social reality. The use of particular words influences how
actors experience their world and thereby contributes to the construction of
that world (ibid: 105–106). On the other hand, he argues that this constructive power is not located in language/words as such. Although they appear
to contain power – most visibly in formal rituals of coronation, passing sentences, appointing officials, etc. – this linguistic power is only "delegated", i.e.,
bestowed on the words/expressions/rituals through the power of "legitimated"
authorities – it "...depends on the social position of the speaker" (ibid: 109).
The apparently spontaneous acceptance of linguistic meaning is a product of
the *misrecognition* of the underlying relations of power, hegemony and even
symbolic violence. This is most effective when actors are oblivious to the true
forces behind and the real consequences of the so-called "illocutionary force"
of speech acts. A variety of social power is transformed and misrecognised
through communication and appears as pure relations of meaning.

> Symbolic systems owe their distinctive power to the fact that the rela-
> tions of power expressed through them are manifested only in the mis-
> recognisable form of relations of meaning (displacement).
>
> BOURDIEU, 1991: 170

Bourdieu suggests two opposing models or theories of language: an *"energetic"*
model that depicts the relations of force/power permeating social relations
and a *"cybernetic"* model that renders social relations as pure communication.
The cybernetic model is shorthand for widespread theories of language that,
according to him, are hampered by a sort of idealism: regarding language and
language use as a self-sufficient logical system of meaning-production in isolation from social power differentials and the socially delegated authority of the
actors involved. This critique is directed at positions as different as traditional
structuralist theories of language (Saussure (for the critique of Saussure, see
Bourdieu 1990: 32)), the speech-act theory (Austin) and Habermas' theory of
communication. Nevertheless, Bourdieu accepts that there is a moment of
truth in the apparent autonomy of language and communication. Therefore,
he attempts to reconcile the energetic and cybernetic models by demonstrating that this apparent autonomy is a result of "...transmutations of the different kinds of capital into symbolic capital". The illocutionary force of speech

acts (Austin, 1962) and the persuasive power of valid, rational arguments (Habermas, 1981) are the effects of symbolic power vested in the speaker/ interlocutors. This power is generated through the *transfiguration* of other types of power (based on economic, social, political and cultural capital), whereas these more fundamental dimensions of power somehow become (mostly) invisible in the apparently pure communicative effects of symbolic interaction. "Symbolic power, a subordinate power, is a transformed, i.e., mis-recognisable, transfigured and legitimated form of the other forms of power" (Bourdieu, 1991: 170).

Bourdieu cites Austin to demonstrate that even speech-act theorists implic-itly acknowledge that the words/utterances themselves are without the sup-posed "illocutionary force" ascribed to them by this theory. Austin (1962) men-tions an example of naming (baptising) a ship through the well-known ritual of cracking a bottle against the bow. This ritual in itself will not be effective unless the *right person in the right capacity in an appropriate situation* performs the act – the person *chosen or appointed* to do it. Thus, according to Bourdieu, the power of linguistic acts, their illocutionary force, lies elsewhere – in the social fields of power relations underlying or surrounding the explicit speech acts. "... one forgets that authority comes to language from without...Language at most represents this authority, manifests and symbolises it" (Bourdieu, 1991: 109).

Linguistic Power = Misrecognised Social Power?

An alternative operation to that of Bourdieu is to accept that institutions/ authorities confer power on linguistic acts but simultaneously demonstrate that there are ways in which linguistic acts have a force of their own that can contribute to the construction or change of social realities. A productive approach is to reveal how speech acts are connected to *deontic power* (Searle, 2010: 8 f). This concept refers to how interaction is influenced by actors' knowl-edge and recognition of rights, duties, obligations, etc. Various forms of deon-tic powers are necessary conditions for a wide spectrum of social phenomena and also underlie the most obvious exercise of other forms of social power (e.g., the economic power of investors, the cultural power of art experts, the political power of party leaders, etc.).

When a judge imposes a sentence on an accused person, we have an obvious instance of the ritual performance of social power and hierarchy that produces or changes social relations and realities. The judge is not able to achieve this in a personal capacity but rather in *the authorised status function of a judge in a court*. The accused is subjected to the authority of the institution and the judge. He may acknowledge the authority and bow freely or reluctantly to its proceedings and final verdict. Even without this acknowledgement, he remains subject to the court's authority/power because the judicial power is supported by the eventual use of "hard" power by the police. What function do language and words have in this respect and what is the origin of their force?

This scenario appears to be a clear instance of "transfigured" social power. The words produce nothing without the real force of the institutional order. Could speech-act theorists have missed this obvious point? They have not! Neither Austin (1962) nor Searle (1969, 1995, 2010) were that naïve. These researchers have highlighted the importance of the background and institutional setting for the performance of various speech acts. A distinction between "brute facts" and "institutional facts" has been commonplace within this tradition of action theory and speech-act theory since its beginnings (Anscombe, 1958; Austin, 1962; Searle, 1995: 31 ff; Searle, 2010: 10). In highly formalised and ritualised institutional proceedings, the force of specific linguistic acts is linked to how they are implicated in and legitimated by the institutional authorities (or the authority of the institution itself). It is the judge's duty/role to pass sentences and the destiny of the accused to accept these sentences. There is little latitude for any autonomous illocutionary force. In such instances of the ritual exercise of authority and "real" power, Bourdieu's strategy makes good sense: We should look out for the ways in which apparently neutral linguistic acts and symbolic meanings can be transfigured forms of underlying social powers. In this approach the concept of "institutional facts", as developed within an analytical theory of action and speech-act theory, is of no use because it appears to construct an image of institutional reality as a pure field of meaning cleansed of this type of social power and power differences.

One problem concerning Bourdieu's interpretations of symbolic and linguistic actions is that they primarily refer to two types of situations. In the first type, various forms of highly institutionalised, hierarchical, authoritative power are at work – political power, social power, religious power, cultural power, etc. (see Ch. 3 in Bourdieu, 1991). The other type of situation refers to the everyday use of gossip, slander, lies, praise, etc. – actions that are not necessarily formally regulated by institutional hierarchies but express power and subordination/superiority in everyday social life (Bourdieu, 1991: 105). The cases and examples are generally highly explicit illustrations of the type of "transfigured" power that Bourdieu is seeking. They appear to conform to the theory almost too well, and the linguistic actions somehow appear to be nothing more than prolongations of power-based social actions and relations. Bourdieu cites these types of empirical references (in conjunction with theoretical arguments) as arguments for a general theory of symbolic action and power in which there is no room for linguistic "idealism", that is, autonomous linguistic meaning and illocutionary forces. These are strong claims.

As a foundation for a strong version of the idea of the heteronomy of language and linguistic acts,[1] Bourdieu's arguments are unsatisfactory – empirically, methodologically and theoretically. Empirically, the arguments can be countered with questions concerning sampling. Does the sample cover all types of language use? Can we identify cases in which the theory does not fit or appears inadequate? Methodologically, we can question the form and foundation of the generalisation, the choice of cases and the form or interpretation of the material. Theoretically, we can question, among other things, a potentially self-defeating or self-contradictory analysis of language that may disqualify the writer from advancing arguments intended to convince readers of the credibility of the writer and validity of the theory. If all linguistic acts (including scientific argumentation) are merely expressions of underlying power relations and hegemony, why should we care about Bourdieu's *arguments*? The only interesting aspect would be his authority and power, not the validity of his propositions. If both writer and reader share this reductive view of communication, there would hardly be any logical sense in their arguing – except the quite common and "rational" motive of establishing or confirming hegemony. Screaming at one another or singing together could achieve the same ends were it not for the rules of academic competition and cooperation, which demand a *convincing appearance* of unforced meaning and the willingness to present and accept rational arguments.

To escape this self-defeating circle, Bourdieu must exempt himself from the logic of his own theory. One approach he has attempted to use is the following (see Bourdieu and Wacquant, 1992): Although ordinary communication is fundamentally programmed by non-linguistic social forces, certain forms of self-reflective academic communication can (partially) sunder the chains of power at work in the surrounding society. The members of a scientific community can challenge one another's arguments without succumbing to the all-too-human show of power.

---

1   This same heteronomy is found in Bourdieu's general theory of action – the "dispositional" theory of action (Bourdieu, 2013, also Bourdieu, 1977). This theory is contrasted with an intentionalist theory in which actors' conscious intentions are presumed to be the main cause of actions. Dispositional theory is closely connected to the concept of habitus. In this presentation, Bourdieu does not entirely reject influence from conscious intentions, although they occupy a subordinate role. Intentions come into play on the basis of (or within the boundaries established by) non-intentional dispositions and acquired habits/habitus.

There is something deeply unsatisfactory about this "exceptionality". Why can only (a special group of self-reflexive) scientists escape the fate of ordinary language users? This notion bears some similarity to the older theories of intellectuals as a cognitively privileged group who can rise above and withstand the impact of ideologies that influence other social strata. It is uncontroversial to accept Bourdieu's arguments that (reflexive) scientists are able (in certain instances) to relate to the *content or force of arguments* and not merely to the social power and authority of the speaker/writer within a field of research. Scientists (may) have exceptional knowledge and command of methods that can distance them from certain ideologies and biases involved in the everyday use of language. Bourdieu's analysis/theory of everyday communication is much more problematic and tends towards a position of *eliminative reductionism*: conceiving of linguistic action and expressions as nothing but transfigured social power.

Relying on alternative theories of language, it is possible to argue that ordinary, competent language users have the capacity for rational communication (to different degrees) in relation to various fields within their life-world (cf. Habermas, 1981). These users can make and evaluate statements, state facts, make promises, accept obligations, recognise rights, etc. without being merely victims or executers of non-linguistic, "real" social powers. This argument does not imply the denial of the causal importance of such social powers. However, it implies that there are levels and moments of communication in which linguistic meaning – both descriptive and normative – is at work "below" or "above" the play of non-linguistic power.

Institutions, Emergence and the Meaning of Actions

Let us return to the courtroom. As we have seen above, power and hierarchy are at work. However, they operate through linguistic actions that somehow hide and "transfigure" them such that they appear to have been created by the (magical) power of language itself. We have conceded this much: The form and effects of language use are of course deeply conditioned by the specific institution and the broader network of institutions, hierarchies and social powers (particularly within the structures of the state) in which language acquires its authoritative status. The judge would have had no power and her speech acts would have lacked illocutionary force if not for these conditions. Is this the end of the story? – "...authority comes to language from without..." (Bourdieu, 1991: 109).

There are various statuses at work in a criminal court proceeding, including the judge, the accused, the public prosecutor, the defence counsel, the jury, court servants and secretaries, police officers, witnesses, spectators, etc. The various roles are adjusted to one another, and their specific functions are defined by the statutes for this type of proceeding. The judge is appointed and her authority concerning the court process is created by other authorities. When the proceeding begins, all of her linguistic and non-linguistic actions take on meanings as defined by the institution. These are typical "institutional facts" as described by Anscombe and Searle. They are made possible by *constitutive rules:* X counts as Y in context C (Searle, 2010: 10). When she finally renders her judgement, her specific wordings count as imposing sentences on the accused, and the status of the accused is thereby *objectively* changed from being an accused person to becoming a convicted person, which is accompanied by changes in a range of social relations, the loss of (some) rights and the acquisition of new rights and obligations, etc. Through the judge's final speech acts, something is created other than the physical effects of sound waves – a new element is added to (this segment of) social reality, although the judicial system already has a store of a relevant *category* of elements, a standing role within this institution waiting for the right type of persons to "qualify" for it: the convict role. Although this change is small – only a movement of one specific person between predefined statuses – it exemplifies the real change that can be brought about through speech acts. The continuous stream of similar processes creates a change in social facts at one level (establishing various groups of convicts) and contributes to upholding institutional structures on a more general level – the judicial system and the various public institutions with which it is intertwined.

The different standing statuses and the order of the judicial system are in their turn also the consequence of (among other things) a variety of speech acts creating general institutional facts – for example, the function of the judge, the prosecutor, the accused and so forth. John Searle uses the concept of "declarations" to denote speech acts that have the capacity to "...change the world by declaring that a state of affairs exists and thus bringing that state of affairs into existence" (Searle, 2010: 12). This statement does not merely mean that the use of language has observable consequences (is a causal power) but also that the content and form of the speech act brings into existence the state of affairs that is declared to come about – for example, that the accused is ultimately convicted, that a person is declared (by the proper institutional authority) to be the judge, that this particular system is defined as the city court, etc. Declarations are essential to the construction of institutional reality, although the word "declaration" may not be used. The declarative moment may be implicit in the process. ("I therefore convict you to..." = I/we declare that you...). The main point is that the speech acts "have the same logical form as declarations" (Searle, 2010: 13). The more permanent statuses, the network of statuses, key actions, and procedures of course need not be declared into existence every day. They are permanent institutional facts that have meaning within the system, resting on what Searle calls "standing status function declarations". They are analogous to the rules of games, the body of laws, etc.

The various actors have rights and obligations vis-à-vis one another – generated through the use of power (primarily soft and silent but occasionally explicit and hard) within and around the specific institution and continually confirmed through the willing contribution by the actors to orderly, well-defined and meaningful interaction. The accused will most likely stand out because his obligations are not typically freely taken on – although when these obligations are conferred on him through the overwhelming power of the police and prison guards, he will nevertheless enjoy the rights that become his by virtue of his accused status. The court and its system of status functions are created from "above" through laws, decisions and prescriptions from various authorities. However, it is at every moment of its function also created, recreated or upheld from within, through the actions, speech acts and definitions of the situation by the actors. The coordinated activities in the network of roles contribute to the *emergence* of a social reality above each actor involved – the court as a functioning system and meaning-defining frame for the activities of all actors. We need not rely on "strong emergence" (cf. Elder-Vass, 2010: 28), i.e., the notion that "something comes from nothing" or that lower-level elements and their relations do not cause the institution. We can apply a "weak" version of emergence, or what Elder-Vass (2010: 38) calls a "relational theory of emergence": The elements *and their relations* bring about a reality that is not reducible to the elements and their properties. Conversely, the elements acquire new properties as a consequence of the emergent level.

This non-reducibility is also implicated by the formula for constitutive rules that generates "institutional facts" – "X counts as Y in C". A person acquires a specific status function in (and because of) a specific context/institution. Anna J. counts as (is appointed) judge in this court. All of the properties of Y (judge) are not to be found in X (Anna J.) – although Anna J. must have some properties or qualifications (some formal, others more personal) to be in a position to "count as Y in C". The lower level element (X – Anna J.) acquires institutional capacities that are not reducible to its individual capacities/properties. They are at most (part of) the necessary conditions for Y, but they are obviously not *sufficient* conditions. There are institutional realities over and above the individual level. A moderate version of holism is possible without relying on the metaphysical concepts of "Volk-Geist"/collective spirit or the assumption of strong emergence – creation ex nihilo. The emergent levels of institutions generate new properties in the institution's elements – new external, visible

properties connected to the roles or status functions and new internal properties, i.e., new intentions and motives for action on the part of the actors. Over
time these institutions will also contribute to the socialisation of individuals,
modifying or creating personality traits.

As new institutional facts and networks of actors develop and connect to
other institutional orders at different levels and in various ways, there may
arise institutional complexes and systems beyond the intentional horizon of
any actor. New actors may make these new orders the objects of intentional
actions (for example, through declarations). They may concern internal processes within the system or the general structure of the system as such. In this
way, we can see that society as a whole is neither an intentional product of any
(group of) actor(s) at any level nor a purely non-intentional objective system
beyond all actors and their manifold relations.

Speech Acts and Power

To summarise the arguments advanced thus far: There is no doubt that all language use may be "programmed", initiated, regulated, controlled and may function as a means for "real" social powers, hegemonic positions and authorities
to express or reinforce their power over persons in subordinate positions. The
"illocutionary force" of speech acts (e.g., promises) may then be nothing more
than appearance, a veil behind which the true forces are at work. An actors' linguistic power comes from elsewhere, from the authorities and the hegemonic
positions that are brought to bear on the situation. This may be the case in
numerous situations; the courtroom is one example.

However, this exercise of social power presupposes the reality of deontic
powers that are generated through speech acts and status function declarations: obligations, entitlements, rights, duties and so forth. By virtue of
language – in its performative mode (promising, agreeing, making appoint-
ments, etc.) – human actors have the capacity to create statuses and relations
that carry deontic power and bind (commit) them to certain future actions vis-
à-vis other actors. This situation occurs regularly in daily informal interactions
among peers without the use of external force. It can, of course, also arise because of power differences between individuals – I can force another to accept
an obligation as a result of my higher standing in the group with more social
and symbolic capital. The decisive point is that this creation of (new) realities
is possible without the threat of other types of force. I can commit myself and
call on my friend to commit himself to a future course of action. Together, we
construct new social realities – most often transient and small in scale.

The force of illocutionary acts does not operate unconditionally, irrespective of circumstances. It would make little sense to approach a complete stranger and promise him that I will meet him at the cinema in the evening so that we can watch a movie. There may be nothing wrong with the expression of the promise or the sincerity of my effort, although I might be considered quite disturbed for attempting to make a promise in this situation. The phrasing may be correct, but the situation and persons are wrong. It is not a question of a lack of social power but a lack of adequate relations. This is a ceteris paribus clause that parallels numerous areas of research and explanation: effects follow causes in a regular manner – provided "all other things are equal". If uttering a certain string of words will only create a normal effect when the situation is of the right type, this limitation does not mean that the speech act carries no force and that the power is exclusively attributable to the situation.

This ability to display illocutionary forces is also part and parcel of institutional processes – including highly ritualised actions and non-ritual practical interaction. As has been previously noted, these forces may be more or less controlled or programmed by the powers of various authorities. However, it is no coincidence that these powers (often) work though linguistic performances. The creation and existence of institutions presuppose actors' ability to make commitments, accept obligations, create relations and binding future actions, and construct and change "institutional facts" and fields of meaning – activities that are impossible without performing linguistic actions that carry illocutionary force. Many obligations may be forced on an individual, and one may submit to a superior power. However, the "art" of taking on obligations of all types is a capacity of social actors as competent language users. It is not exclusively created through non-linguistic social power.

In this chapter, I cannot venture into the conditions of human actors' capacity for linguistic practice – physical, biological or neurological processes. If we accept the notion of "weak emergence", we can argue that each level acquires some degree of autonomy in relation to its lower-level conditions and functions through level-specific causes, laws and principles (Elder-Vass, 2010). The principles of language, linguistic meaning and speech acts cannot be reductively explained as merely the effects of lower-level causes, although they depend on these causes and mechanisms (e.g., neurological conditions). However, these principles and workings of linguistic activities can neither be reductively explained by *higher-level* social forces, for example, the hegemonic powers at work in various institutions such as courts, schools, universities, military units, etc. These arguments support the contention that linguistic forces enjoy some autonomy despite Bourdieu's arguments concerning symbolic power/violence. They appear as necessary conditions for the display of power in various institutions. Non-linguistic power typically relies on the "infrastructure" of linguistic activity and its creative power. In a discussion of mechanisms and emergence in social science, Wight (2004: 284 ff) suggests:

> As such, not only may conceptual and semiotic systems have mechanisms, but they may also in themselves be considered some of the mechanisms that make the social what it is.

Concepts in Action

When human beings purchase items in shops, they act in the capacity of a customer, use money to pay for commodities in a building/premises defined as the shop, etc. They are defined by and acting out a system of institutional facts from the moment they enter the shop until they leave with the goods. Every actor (customers and staff alike) must have some minimum knowledge of the system to be able to act in meaningful ways that will count as being a "customer", "buying", "paying", and so forth. They must understand, in a practical sense, the concept of money, although they may have little knowledge of economic theory, the economic system at large or the complex function of money in this system. By acting as a customer, paying for commodities, etc., their practical knowledge and definitions of the situation contribute to reproduce the system, whereas the system-wide, long-term consequences of the totality of actions of all actors are most often beyond their horizon. Actors must know what money is (including a fairly complex system of activities and institutions) for money to continue to exist. If the majority of actors had no knowledge of money, no concept, no consciousness of and no intentional orientation towards money, there would be no money. The currency notes and coins would appear in their physical capacity as bits of paper and metal. "Institutional facts" may be defined from above, by powerful institutions and authorities. However, these facts must also be confirmed and recreated from below through actors' various speech acts and definitions of situations in a continuous stream of everyday activity.

Although concepts are, of course, not true or false, they may be included in propositions that can be true or false. Concepts may be judged not only as more or less useful but also as more or less fitting. However, concepts are not merely *of* things, events, actions, etc. They are also, in varying ways, incorporated *in* the social realities and actions to which they are referring. No such mechanism can be found in biology. A species does not incorporate our concept of the species and begin acting according to its meaning/definition.

However, this phenomenon is precisely what occurs in social life. An entire range of important concepts has become reflexive – they participate in the (constitution of the) reality they describe, including a wide range of artefacts. When I raise my arm to vote in a meeting, my body (including my mind) has incorporated and expresses the concepts of meeting and voting and the meaning of the overall situation. In this way, the activities of all participants (including the network of institutions and activities in which the specific meeting is located) contribute to reproduce the institutional fact – the meeting – and the institution as such.

We can extend these ideas to the analysis of perception: If the concept of "door handle" is incorporated into my actions, it is also simultaneously involved in my perception. I perceive the door and handle as I reach for it. I see with or through these concepts. It is not the case that first I apprehend an unorganised bundle of sense impressions and then subsume them under or categorise them with the help of concepts, and thereafter (construct a hypothesis that) I see a door and handle. Gestalt psychologists have long since characterised our vision as fundamentally holistic and ordered: Normally functioning humans spontaneously observe patterns, structures and ordered figures – not disjunctive impressions. This is deeply rooted in our biology and neurological processes. We do not first have to make "inferences" and then observe. When we become experienced in diverse social fields, our perceptual competence increases as we incorporate concepts from these fields into our perceptual function. We are able to perceive things, artefacts, persons, actions, interactions, symbolic units, relations, etc. without any intervention from conscious inferences. We may accept that our brain and central nervous system make continuous, swift and pre-conscious "inferences" (if we can call them inferences at all) such that we perceive things and holistic patterns. However, these processes are so rapid and unnoticeable that it amounts to the same thing – we spontaneously perceive things as ordered wholes. The possibility of perceptual mistakes is of course not excluded. The door and handle may actually be something else. We may even hallucinate.

A general philosophical implication of these arguments is that the distinction between epistemology and ontology will not be particularly important in this context. In the history of philosophy, conflicting views have been offered regarding the primacy of ontology or epistemology. Building on the analysis in this chapter, it is possible to argue that the ontic and epistemic dimensions are merged in social realities. The social ontology already includes epistemic dimensions – particularly actors' (practical) knowledge. Epistemological reflections on the condition of the knowledge of social phenomena already refer to and presuppose a social reality that is saturated with various types of knowledge – many of which the sociologist is himself familiar as a normal participant in social activities. This familiarity, this practical experience of social realities, is also an important starting point for sociological analysis. Without the normal/practical knowledge of family life, economic actions, schools, religion, politics, etc., the researcher could not begin her/his analysis. As a social actor, she/he is already able to identify basic traits of things/situations and institutions and to make distinctions that are built into the social realities, distinctions that are both necessary conditions for competent membership in various formal and informal social groupings and that constitute (some of) the building blocks of this social reality.

Members of the Hells Angels motorcycle club use various distinctions to draw borders between themselves and others, competing groups, enemies and associated groups called "prospects" and "hangarounds". What they perform is not merely a mental operation. It is a practical operation that defines and creates the reality of the groups thus designated and has real consequences for all. This operation is not merely fallible knowledge *of* things but constitutive conceptions in the construction of the groups. The argument does not imply that drawing borders and creating identities are straightforward and consensual matters conducted peacefully. Quarrels, conflicts and even violence have occurred to establish the current order and borders. The winners acquire the privilege and power to define. Physical, symbolic, economic and social forces have been and continue to be at work. However, this fact does not eliminate the force and effects of concepts in constructing social realities.

Another associated argument for "bypassing" the epistemology-ontology opposition is the approach to language employed in this chapter. It is not primarily the notion of language as a description of things, as true or false statements. This approach *positions the language user as an observer or spectator* attempting to cope with realities through observing, drawing distinctions and creating concepts. Our approach concerns the pragmatics of language use: the various forms of linguistic action and illocutionary force (Searle, 2010: 16). One of these types, declarations, is of particular importance for the construction of institutional realities. By participating in formal and informal networks displaying illocutionary force through speech acts, the language user is *posited as an interacting subject* – not merely an observer – contributing to the maintenance or creation of social situations and institutions.

Common Meaning – Reciprocal Misunderstanding

One implication of this analysis of language, knowledge and action is that we must assume some level of consensual, common meaning among relevant actors that share a way of life (cf. Taylor, 1971: 13). This is not a matter of "public opinion", widespread or overlapping ideas among individuals – for example how the majority of the public perceives the Hells Angels as a possible threat to society. Common meaning in this context concerns the concepts and interpretations that must be shared among actors to uphold or create the (part of) reality in which they are participating. Members of the Hells Angels must have some common understanding of their identities and relevant borders distinguishing them from "hangarounds" and "prospects" for these meanings to exist and for them to be members. Similarly, different actors participating in court proceedings must also have some common conception of roles and statutes. In the shop, both customers and staff share some common conceptions of "institutional facts" – e.g., money, commodities, payment, etc.

The idea of common meaning has, of course, been challenged in the social sciences. Likely the most famous – and now classical – opposition has come from the "school" of *ethnomethodology* (cf. Guneriussen, 2012: 16–17). Garfinkel (1984: 24–31) warned against the reification at work in assuming a stable, commonly recognised meaning of symbols and words and in the assumption of certain essential, natural forms of identity (e.g., "normal, natural female" – (ibid: 116–186)). He attempted to alert researchers to the chronically fluid character of meaning and suggested that common meaning was never clearly established and visible to all. A *sense* of common understanding is a result of various methods that individuals employ in communication processes. The commonality in meaning *does not have to be a reality*. It is enough that it is reciprocally assumed. This is a type of "reality work" in which individuals continually confirm and produce an *image or impression of unitary meaning*.

As an example, I will refer to a study that certain ethnomethodologists have used as support for their conception of meaning in communication. Skinner (1975) studied how doctors and patients communicated and were able to reach some common understanding regarding diagnosis, prognosis, the use of medicine and other treatment. Skinner interviewed patients and doctors separately after consultations to determine what each of them understood their agreement to be regarding illness, treatment, etc. The result was striking. Both doctor and patient believed that they had reached a common understanding. However, when questioned in greater detail regarding the substance of the agreement, it was obvious that what the doctor believed that the patient had said and meant and what the patient believed that the doctor had said and meant – in short, what each of them believed they had reciprocally agreed on – varied significantly. It was difficult to identify much "common understanding". However, they were both satisfied: an agreement had been reached and verbally confirmed by both. Leiter (1980: 154–155) employed this case as a premise for the conclusion that *no* common understanding (or meaning) exists.

Communication merely produces a sense of common understanding, and this sense – each actor's assumption that an agreement has been reached – is sufficient for the participants.

This situation is obviously a case in which the researcher breaks with actors' "spontaneous sociology". It is possible to identify unsubstantiated assumptions, misapprehensions and reciprocal misunderstandings. The sociologist must go beyond the actors' limited perspective because she knows better.

Does this case truly demonstrate a complete lack of common meaning? Actors, as has been shown, do misunderstand one another. They appear to make false assumptions regularly. However, are these misunderstandings all inclusive? The patient visits the doctor because he has an appointment at the hospital. He obviously knows (assumes?) that he is a patient visiting a hospital and that he will talk to a doctor about his illness, medical examination and treatment. The doctor must obviously know the same – and of course substantially more than the patient about the routines of the hospital and medicine. The patient knows substantially more than the doctor about his own life and experiences. However, a core of common knowledge, meaning or understanding must be present for the proceedings and actions to make sense at all: Why visit a house and a causal individual that were not known to be a hospital and a doctor for a medical consultation? This is the type of basic, common meaning that is the foundation for institutions and a host of institutional facts. At certain levels – within formal institutions and in life-world contexts – actors must possess valid knowledge concerning situations and institutional realities. There is knowledge *in* their actions and knowledge about action and institutions – knowledge that contributes to the constitution of the social realities in which they are acting and their identities and roles within these realities. The actors cannot be entirely mistaken.

Concluding Remarks

This line of argument may appear to presuppose a restricted conception of action: action and meaning as expressions of *conscious intentions*. The concepts of constitutive rules, institutional facts, institutions and construction all appear to imply a view of actions as released by deliberate intentions and explicit knowledge of situational meaning. Some version of an "intentionalist" theory of action and interaction is necessary to support the main line of argument. There must at least be moments and aspects of human activity that are (also) driven by explicit intentions and consciousness of goals, situations, relations, means and rules. Without such intention, we could hardly imagine a world of institutional facts. However, this is not the entire story. There is room for semi-conscious routines, preconscious habits and habitus in Bourdieu's sense. The rules of institutional facts may be incorporated and executed without a significant amount of deliberation. The notion of "standing status function declarations" does not presuppose that each instance of acting according to them must be a result of explicit decisions. It is possible to analyse patterns of action through the prism of a "dispositional" theory of action (cf. Bourdieu, 2013), provided that there is room left for intentional action. Unlike an intentionalist theory, a dispositional theory in Bourdieu's sense (see note 1) conceives of action as caused by a combination of external conditions (the actor's position in a social field of forces) and internal conditions (the actor's (socialised) habitus). We may even allow for subconscious forces in Freud's sense, provided that it is compatible with intentionality as described above: There may be deep biological instincts at work in the aggressiveness displayed in competitive sport while the actors must simultaneously intentionally relate to the institutional facts and social meaning of the activity. For example, the winner is decided by (actors applying) the rules of the game and not by the amount of instinctual energy.

Another implication of these reflections is that an "actor's point of view" is a necessary component of the sociological approach to social realities. More specifically, the researcher must reconstruct the meanings of institutional facts and illocutionary forces as they appear to actors in a first-person, performative mode, in other words, the way actors themselves cope with meaning and generate the institutional facts and realities that the sociologist seeks to analyse. Sociologists, however, need not remain in this mode. They must also extend (far) beyond actors' perspectives to grasp the various conditions of and influences on action, its consequences, its patterns and the encompassing social systems.

Sociologists must establish some distance from the situations and actors that are the subject of study. They must regularly break with everyday language and actors' understandings of situations – the so-called "spontaneous sociology" discussed by Bourdieu. If they do not, they will, according to Bourdieu, be caught up in everyday ideologies and misunderstandings and become unwitting victims and perpetuators of social powers and unable to conduct scientific research. This may very well be the case. However, the conclusion of this chapter is that ordinary language and "spontaneous sociology" are not particularly dangerous. Actors' everyday conceptions of social realities do not necessarily lead the sociologist astray. Moreover, at some basic level, the realities and meanings of social life are constructed through actors' everyday speech acts and conceptions. Sociologists must attempt to address the constitutive impact of these matters. Although they must construct scientific concepts, they should also always reflect on the (possible) relationships between their scientific vocabulary and everyday conceptions and speech acts. The "baggage" that sociologists carry from their own (non-professional) experience of social life makes up a necessary starting point for sociological descriptions and analysis in a variety of social fields. It is a resource for sociology, not a burden or constraint.

References

Anscombe, G.E.M. (1958). "On brute facts", *Analysis*. 18(3): 69–72.

Austin, J. (1962). *How to do things with words*. Oxford: Clarendon Press.

Bourdieu, P. (1977). *Outline of a theory of practice*. Cambridge: Cambridge University Press.

Bourdieu, P. (1990). Trans. R. Nice. *The logic of practice*. Cambridge: Polity Press.

Bourdieu, P. (1991). *Language and symbolic power*. Cambridge: Polity Press.

Bourdieu, P. (2013). "Manet-effekten", *Le Monde diplomatique*. [Manet effect]. December 2013.

Bourdieu, P. and Wacquant, L. (1992). *An invitation to reflexive sociology*. Cambridge: Polity Press.

Bourdieu, P., Chamboredon, J.C. and Passeron, J.C. (1991). Trans. R. Nice. Ed. B. Krais. *The craft of sociology*. New York: Walter de Gruyter.

Durkheim, E. (1976). *The elementary forms of religious life*. London: Allen & Unwin.

Elder-Vass, D. (2010). *The causal power of social structures*. Cambridge: Cambridge University Press.

Garfinkel, H. (1984). *Studies in ethnomethodology*. Cambridge: Polity Press.

Giddens, A. (1984). *The constitution of society*. Cambridge: Polity Press.

Goffman, E. (1967). *Interaction ritual: essays on face-to-face behaviour*. New York: Doubleday.

Guneriussen, W. (2012). "What is society", *Introduction to sociology: Scandinavian sensibilities*. Essex: Pearson.

Habermas, J. (1981). *Theorie des kommunikativen Handelns*. Vol. 2. Frankfurt a.M: Suhrkamp Verlag.

Leiter, K. (1980). *A primer on ethnomethodology*. Oxford: Oxford University Press.

Lemert, C. (2012). *Social things*. New York: Rowman & Littlefield Publishers.

Luhmann, N. (1988). *Soziale Systeme*. Frankfurt a.M: Suhrkamp Verlag.

Mead, G.H. (1934). *Mind, self and society*. Chicago: University of Chicago Press.

Parsons, T. (1977). *The evolution of societies*. Englewood Cliffs: Prentice Hall.

Searle, J. (1969). *Speech Acts: an essay in the philosophy of language.* Cambridge: Cambridge University Press.

Searle, J. (1995). *The construction of social reality.* London: Penguin Books.

Searle, J. (2010). *Making the social world.* Oxford: Oxford University Press.

Skinner, T.J. (1975). *The processes of understanding in doctor-patient interaction.* (PhD-Diss., Rice University).

Taylor, C. (1971). "Interpretation and the sciences of man", *Review of Metaphysics.* 25(1): 3–51.

Wight, C. (2004). "Theorizing the mechanisms of conceptual and semiotic space", *Philosophy of the Social Sciences.* 34(2): 283–299.

CHAPTER 4

Weber's Ideal Types: A Sociological Operation between Theory and Method

Pål Strandbakken

Introduction

Sociologists still read Weber, Marx, and Durkheim as part of learning the craft of their discipline. Sociology relates differently to the classics than natural science does, mainly because we employ different ideas about "theory". This does not necessarily mean that sociology fails to renew itself and change as a discipline, but it does mean that the classics remain important as common references and as sources of theoretical inspiration. This chapter takes a look at one of Max Weber's most famous concepts – "the ideal type" – and poses the following question: are Weber's concepts still relevant for theoretical operations in modern sociology, and if so, how might they be utilized theoretically and methodologically? This is not another text about Weber's concept of ideal types but is rather an attempt to determine how the ideal type may be used as a theoretical and methodological device. However, we first provide a brief account of the background of the concept (for a more comprehensive and in-depth overview, see Bruun, 2007; Swedberg in this volume).

The ideal type theme is addressed mainly by describing two different theoretical-empirical "uses" or operations. For the first, and by far the most important, I take one of Weber's most well-known ideal types – the *Protestant ethic* – out of its Calvinist/Methodist and mainly English context and apply it to a Lutheran Norwegian religious movement that was led by the lay reformer Hans Nielsen Hauge. By moving the theoretical object in time and space, we are compelled to reflect on what will happen when we transpose a specific ideal type onto a different space and time. This is the primary operation under discussion. In addition, I reflect briefly on the use of ideal type-like approaches in contributions from C. Wright Mills and Daniel Bell. These cases, or descriptions of theoretical operations, aim to elaborate the potential and possible limitations of Weber's concept and methodology.

The "ideal type" as an Analytical Construct

What is an ideal type? First, it is not "ideal" in any moral sense. As an analytical construct, it might just as well have been called an "idea" type. It was "extremely important for Weber to stress that the ideal type was *not* an ideal in the normative sense" (Bruun and Whimster in Weber, 2012: xxiv, italics in original). By deviating from common language, he wanted to create an intellectual space filled with meanings that were alternative to those that were associated with everyday language and common sense-based sociology (see also Swedberg's account of C.S. Pierce in this volume). With this theoretical operation, Weber invented both a concept and a heuristic device with methodological implications.

The following quote contains a number of key words and ideas:

> It is obtained by means of a one-sided *accentuation* of *one* or a *number of* viewpoints and through the synthesis of a great many diffuse and discrete *individual* phenomena (more present in one place, fewer in another, and occasionally completely absent) which are in conformity with one-sided accentuated viewpoints into an internally consistent *mental* image. In its conceptual purity, this image cannot be found anywhere in reality. It is a *utopia*, and the task of the historian then becomes that of establishing, in each *individual case*, how close reality is to it, or how distant from, that ideal image....
>
> WEBER, 2012: 125, italics in original

Weber's specifications in terms of "one-sided accentuation", "mental image", "viewpoints", and even "utopia" provide us with some clues to his conception of the ideal type. The ideal type is not a statistical generalization, but it does claim a degree of general validity. It should, in Weber's view, be a construction that we might recognize in historical-empirical reality as typical, albeit in condensed form.

It has been claimed that Weber presented two different ways to generate ideal types and that this approach reflected his attempt to create an in-between position on the German "Methodenstreit" in terms of the national economy and the struggle between Schmoller's historicism and Menger's more abstract and formal scientistic approach (Marshall, 1982: 28–29). It seems as though one class of ideal types was developed from a rather formal or nomothetic angle, whereas the other class was more grounded in specific ideographic historical analysis.

As examples of the first class, we might refer to Weber's types of rational action, the distinction between traditional, charismatic, and legal authority, or the model of bureaucracy (Weber, 2012). These ideal types are rather like generic concepts, which are defined by general features, and they have much in common with economists' models of "equilibrium" or "perfect markets". While an ideal type such as the *Protestant ethic* is historically situated and part of an explanation of a specific historical narrative, Bruun refers to the two models of ideal types as "generalizing and lean" versus "individualizing and fleshed out". His claim is that the shift in focus from a generic concept towards a more historic specific focus also reflects a change in Weber's thinking between 1904 and 1920 (Bruun, 2007: 42).

Whether we regard the two versions of the concept as compatible or not depends on how strictly we choose to define our terms and their relations (Andreski, 1984: 42–43). It is interesting, however, to observe how Weber's attempt at an intermediate position made him manoeuvre between generality and historical specificity. He moves in a landscape where both empirical-statistical generalization and theoretical conceptualization are employed to project some degree of order into a vast and fragmented empirical universe. The first aim is to provide explanations of certain phenomena. In these processes, we should not regard ideal types as ends unto themselves; they should be treated as heuristic devices that aid empirical research. The ideal type as a heuristic "tool" may help us to formulate hypotheses. It may also be of help in assembling and organising our initial thoughts, ideas or prejudices about a phenomenon (cf. Swedberg's chapter). The goal of generating and testing more or less general hypotheses, derived from even more general theories, appears to be a reflection of Weber's struggle with the two conceptions of social science. Inspired by Menger, Weber seemed to envision a social science that was a bit more nomothetic, leaning towards the logic of natural science rather than the singular study of history, even if he had learned and accepted the basic idea of historicism (Bruun, 2007: 127–130).

As stated above, the idea of using ideal types as tools to come to terms with complex and confusing empirical material and as "sensitizing devices" that indicate what to look for, seems to be most relevant. Rather than discarding them after the operation, we could develop and enrich them. As for developing hypotheses based on ideal types that were discarded in the process, it is not obvious if Weber ever took that approach. He did use his findings on specific Western forms of rationality as a type of yardstick when he analysed non-western civilizations, but whether he indeed constructed general theories based on hypotheses that were developed from heuristic ideal types is uncertain.

Social Science as Comparison

Whether we talk about statistical generalisations or about more theoretical constructs, ideal types are supposed to help us produce better comparative social science. The comparative method is often seen as a cornerstone in the development of social science (Durkheim, 1982). Max Weber's work serves as a good illustration of this. Initially he compared the economic development of areas that were dominated by Protestants to areas that were dominated by Catholics (Weber, 1992). Later, he compared Western civilizations, rationality, and religion to their counterparts in India (Weber, 1958) and China (Weber, 1951), and he also compared historical Judaism, which he described as a religion that was opposed to the use of magic – hence potentially "rational" – to its local competitors, which were mainly fertility cults (Weber, 1955). Comparison was his explicit approach to historical explanation.

Anthropological field studies regularly compare "they" to "us", and sometimes "they" to another "they", even if this often is done implicitly. Standard contemporary sociology compares social stratification in the US to social stratification in France. If we look at primary education in Norway, we employ an idea of how it could have been, even if we do not necessarily use the rhetoric of critical standards. Researchers might implicitly compare current issues in education with schools in the fifties. Counterfactuals (cf. Ahrne's chapter) are used to compare an observed situation to a situation that can be imagined, for example, Sombart's famous question about why there is no socialism in the US. When we remain within this comparative perspective in social science, we can conclude that the employment of ideal types is fruitful and meaningful to the extent that they help us to compare phenomena.

Comparing Theories or Ideal Types?

Cohen's (2002) *Protestantism and capitalism: the mechanisms of influence* aims to test Weber's claim about Protestantism's influence on capitalism by dividing the theory into nine main themes or hypotheses and 31 sub-hypotheses. For instance, under "Hypothesis IV: The rationalization of life", he formulates four sub-hypotheses, such as "Hypothesis IV d: The rational Protestant approach to life led Protestants to abandon traditional economic outlooks", or "Hypothesis V: Wealth and profit" and "Hypothesis V c: Protestantism approved of the acquisition of wealth" (Cohen, 2002: 19). Cohen's idea is that the truth of Weber's claims could be tested by answering these 31 hopefully testable statements and then by counting how many of them are supported by evidence and how many can be disproved. In his book, he attempts to test this impressive set of hypotheses against new material or data in the form of the diaries of two English Puritan merchants, Nehemiah Wallington and Elias Pledger.

Cohen's theoretical-empirical operation is designed to test Weber's theory in a hypothetical-deductive scheme. As such, it becomes a part of an interesting and ongoing Weber debate. My aim here, however, is not to assess Weber's theory from a "true or false" perspective but, rather, to assess the fruitfulness of transposing the ideal type – the *Protestant ethic* – into an alternative theoretical case as a historical-sociological theoretical operation. This is perhaps a more limited undertaking than a more comprehensive test of the theory, but it illuminates some of the limits and strengths of the straightforward theoretical and methodological operations of Weber's conception of ideal types.

Transposing the Ideal Type: The Protestant Ethic in Norway

A number of authors have tried to test Weber's perspectives with alternative data sources, e.g., Norman Birnbaum, who used the thesis to analyse Zwingly's Zürich (Birnbaum, 1971). The Norwegian religious movement that was led by Hans Nielsen Hauge has also been used as a case to illuminate the Protestant Ethic perspective (Jonassen, 1963; Kleivan, 1972; Sejersted, 1978; Molland, 1979; Strandbakken, 1987). This approach also illustrates the challenges in transferring one theoretical operation from one historical and social context to another.

In the text below, I rely heavily on three biographies (Bang 1910, Breistein, 1955 and Nordborg 1966, 1970) in addition to Hauge's collected writings (eight volumes 1947–1954) and his letters (four volumes 1971–1976).

The Norwegian Awakening

The religious movement that bears the name of its founder, Hans Nielsen Hauge, was an underclass- or peasant-based uprising in the absolutist Danish-Norwegian kingdom, starting at the end of the 18th century. It was inspired by, but also very critical of, Lutheran Pietism. It was even more critical of enlightenment theology. This mode of thought, which was dominant among the clergy at the time, tended to reduce Christianity to a type of abstract respect for the idea of a higher being. Folk religiosity was diminished by and alienated from this diluted philosophical preaching.

As with most Christian revivals, the movement was based on repentance and personal revelation, and it was apocalyptic and eschatological. Hauge's theology was nevertheless "worldly"; it tended towards emphasizing Christian responsibility and stewardship. He emphasized hard work in one's calling as a Christian duty. This was the movement's ideological basis, to which I return when I analyse the Norwegian variant of the Protestant Ethic.

In addition, both Hauge himself and a large number of his followers engaged in economic enterprise, and they were surprisingly successful. The movement initially became involved in large-scale economics when it needed to finance the printing of Hauge's religious pamphlets and books. At one point, all of the book printers in Copenhagen were busy printing his works. The printing was financed mainly by gifts from his followers and from sales of the books.

Later, Hauge established and ran a large trade company in Bergen, engaging in the custom of an old north–south exchange of fish for grain and other commodities. In 1800, he established a shipping company, initiated two paper mills, and arranged for the collection of used textiles for use as raw material for paper production in the technology of the time. He established a bone mill, a tannery, and a foundry and initiated a number of other endeavours. Hauge inspired many young farmers to go into trade. He persuaded a large number of young peasants to change their calling, and he helped them into trade and small-scale industry. He helped others expand their farms and modernise and run them more efficiently. He was able to convert parts of the peasants' savings into capital, and he used his religious network to spread and gain information about prices, local shortages, and other economic opportunities. Hauge's followers, or "friends", were disproportionally engaged in the early establishment of industry in Norway.

It is mainly this economic practice that led later commentators to identify the relevance of Weber's work. Instead of the indirect link between Protestant preaching and early capitalism in the original theory, with Hauge, we observe a much more direct appearance of the Spirit of Capitalism ideal type.

Weber builds the central part of his ideal type, his "change mechanism", on the idea of an indirect effect of the predestination dogma. In a culture in which the most important question was "am I among those chosen for salvation or not?", the tension of living permanently with this insecurity led to a gradual change in perception. The Puritans started to look for "signs" of being among the elected, and gradually, economic success came to be interpreted as such a sign. Weber never claims that Calvin said or wrote anything to that effect but that such a view is a degeneration or "perversion" of the original dogma.

A Lutheran Protestant Ethic?

How does Hauge's ethics, his theology, and his outlook on what it was to be a good Christian comply with the Protestant Ethic ideal type? What are the differences between Puritans and Hauge's followers, and to what degree are the differences interesting?

First, Hauge regarded the idea of predestination as a complete heresy. He insisted that God wants everyone to be saved and that Christians have a free will and may choose to accept or to reject the grace of God. In Weber's analysis, this dogmatic schism is the key to understanding the differences between Lutheran "traditional" Protestantism and the much "purer" reformed Protestantism of Calvin and his followers.

However, Hauge too is positive in his treatment of economic enterprise and profit-making, as it facilitates employment and provides a larger surplus to be shared. This approach, he argues, follows from the Lutheran idea of the duty of stewardship. Believers are supposed to act in this world, not withdraw from it. Hauge is always aware that wealth is a challenge that might lead people astray, but he insists that this is a challenge that Christians must face. As mentioned above, contrary to Calvin and the other reformed preachers, the Norwegian movement and its leader were directly involved in entrepreneurship and economic activity. Hauge refused to see economic success as a sign of God's grace and believed that God might both test Christians with hardship and bless them with wealth. Indeed, wealth could also be a challenge to believers. For Hauge, wealth was more a means to help the underprivileged than a sign.

Further, Weber holds the Lutheran idea of the "calling" as being more traditional than Calvin's, but in this Norwegian Lutheran movement, many followers were actually persuaded to change their calling to something more profitable. It also seems as though they were developing a work ethic that was more or less completely in line with the Puritan Protestant Ethic ideal type without justifying it through predestination dogma. These last observations suggest that Weber's argument was perhaps a bit too specific and elegant. It seems as though he underestimated Luther's concept of the calling, in addition to giving too much weight to predestination dogma. I will return to this idea below.

Both the Puritans and Hauge's followers were opposed to all forms of conspicuous consumption. Profit-making was accepted by both, but luxury was not. One of Hauge's followers, who happened to be one of the richest men in Stavanger, took the frugality or the simple lifestyle so far that Hauge felt he had to reprimand him for overdoing it. One of Weber's supposed mechanisms for explaining the connection between religious sentiment and practice, and subsequent economic success, is based on this relation between a positive valuation of profit-making and negative sanctions on consumption: Not all Christian entrepreneurs will succeed, but some of them probably will, and those who do have no choice but to reinvest.

Where the original *Protestant ethic-spirit of capitalism* ideal type claims a middle-class or bourgeoisie background for Protestant thinkers and their followers, the Norwegian movement was based on peasants and the underclass, even if Norwegian farmers at that time may have been more autonomous,

perhaps even richer, relatively speaking, than many of their European counterparts. This class difference is also reflected in intellectual styles. A preacher
such as Calvin belonged to the intellectual elite of Europe, whereas Hauge was
a Bible-reading amateur and layman, with no background in philosophy and
systematic theology.

Weber (1992) also claimed that the distinction Ernst Troeltsch introduced
on the difference between sects and churches was crucial for understanding
historical development. Persons were "born into" churches, but they had to
apply for and be accepted into sects. Thus, the sects were able to discipline
their members, and they only admitted persons after a thorough moral testing, while churches were geographically organised and included whole populations living in an area. Interestingly, Hauge's movement was something in
between: a sect-like awakening that never broke with the orthodox Lutheran
Norwegian state church. Hauge probably was, and remained more, tolerant of
other confessions than the Puritan preachers, but then again, he had not been
involved in the brutal religious wars that haunted Europe in the aftermath of
the Reformation.

Insights Gained through the Operation

"If Protestantism had no very profound connections to capitalism, then history
was indeed one damned thing after another" (Birnbaum, 1971). The Norwegian
movement, if we disconnect it from Weber's grand perspective, is basically just
an exotic story of an exceptional man achieving exceptional things in a pe-
ripheral country a long time ago. However, with the introduction of Weber's
perspective, it becomes an interesting part of our common European history
and of the story of modernization, capitalism, and the origins of Western su-
premacy, which is precisely what Weber wanted to understand. I suggest that
Weber helps us understand the Hauge movement and enables us to put it into
a more general perspective, with the additional thought that the movement
helps us more deeply understand Weber's thesis.

The transposing of the Protestant Ethic ideal type reveals a set of interesting
similarities and differences between the Puritans and Hauge's followers and
invites a comparison that points to some possible limitations and shortcomings of Weber's work. First, and most importantly, we should observe that it
was possible to arrive at the Protestant Ethic (and subsequently at the Spirit
of Capitalism) from a Lutheran perspective, which insists on man's free will.
Indeed, Weber was not unaware of this process. At least one of the sects that he
used to exemplify his ideal type, the Baptists, was opposed to predestination
dogma. In the posthumous publication *General economic history* (1927), Weber
devotes a chapter to the Protestantism thesis. There, he maintains his views

on the effects of religion on social change but fails to mention predestination altogether. As previously mentioned, Hauge's version of the Protestant Ethic was based on the dogma of man's free will and on the duty of stewardship. Further, Hauge's opposition to predestination dogma caused him to refuse to generally interpret economic success as a sign of being among the elect. If the Lord blessed one with wealth, a Christian should see this as a means to act in this world.

Second, Weber partly constructs his ideal type based on the perceived differences between Lutheranism and Puritanism. We have mentioned the one-sided accentuation of viewpoints as central to the method. As I see it, his prejudice against Luther probably made him underestimate the degree of Lutheranism's break with tradition. Hauge's preaching and practice shows how Luther's concept of the calling might be interpreted as dynamic. Weber tended to place economic agency in the urban middle classes, while he saw Luther basically as a peasant, preaching for fellow peasants. This is not necessarily a shortcoming, however, because, as we have seen, the status and the economic conditions of "a peasant" may be very different in the two contexts.

The ban on luxury and on conspicuous consumption unites Puritanism and "Haugianism", and for both groups, it contributes to an explanation of the observed mechanism of economic success through continuous hard work and reinvestment. The emphasis on reinvestment and discipline, however, also points to one of Hauge's shortcomings in terms of the Puritan ideal. In his economic practice, he was not quite able to live up to the ideals of orderly bookkeeping, financial discipline, and control. He expanded too fast, perhaps borrowed too much, was too impatient and probably lost control in a way that would have been scorned by proper Puritan merchants. However, even if we see that Hauge resembled Weber's "adventure capitalists", we should keep in mind that a discrepancy between what one preaches and what one practices is not uncommon. It is historically more important that Hauge preached the ideal type despite the fact that he failed to fully live it.

Ideal Type-Like Approaches: Mills and Bell

One writer who has actively incorporated ideal types in his theorizing is Charles Wright Mills. His concepts of "white collar workers", particularly "the white collar girl", and "the old office" and "the new office" are the type of abstractions and constructions that Weber employed (Mills, 1955) using precisely the kind of one-sided accentuation of one or a number of viewpoints that contribute to a definition. Similar to Weber, Mills developed his ideal types to come to terms with the great quantity of research that has been conducted on the cultural, economic, and psychological changes in the American middle classes. The typical American middle class position changed from individuals running small independent businesses to being employed by large organisations. Strangely, however, Mills never uses the term "ideal types" for the conceptualizations and operations that he undertakes in his book, *White collar*.

Further, Mills' concept of a "power elite" (1956) seems closely related to the idea of ideal types. We might perhaps even regard his concept of the "sociological imagination" (1959) as an ideal type and as a theoretical construct that can help us analyse, understand, and criticize the history and current practice of the discipline.

Fifty years after Weber's death, Daniel Bell published *The coming of post-industrial society* (Bell, 1973). Many of his operations lead to analytical constructs that "perform" in ways that seem quite close to those of Weber. As with Mills, Bell generously refers to Weber, but – also as with Mills – he does not refer to the ideal type method.

Bell's initial observation is that at some point between 1950 and 1980, the majority of the labour force was no longer employed in industry but was employed in what he terms the service sector. His narrative is based on describing this ongoing change from the ideal type "industrial society" to the ideal type "post-industrial society". Parallel to the way in which Marx used England as a utopia, a picture of the future for the rest of the world, Bell uses the economies of the US and Japan, analysing according to "how close reality is to it, or how distant from, that ideal image" (Weber, 2012: 125). He starts from labour statistics and uses them as a first indication of a switchover but refines his model by listing 11 dimensions that enrich and develop it (Bell, 1973: xvi-xix). The image of post-industrial society, which, as previously mentioned, is never referred to as an ideal type, is on a level of generalisation from which Bell is able to use it to assess liberalisation and social change in Czechoslovakia in the mid-sixties (Bell, 1973: 105–112), which, in our context, means that he has developed a transposable ideal type.

Further, when he identifies the typical industrial corporations of the first, middle, and last third of the 20th century as being U.S. Steel, General Motors, and IBM, respectively, he calls them the "paradigmatic" corporations (Bell, 1973: 26), Bell seems to be very close to Weber's notion of ideal types, as these corporations empirically represent a large number of other firms and corporations in the same period that resemble each other. Furthermore, still within an ideal typical line of reasoning, Bell contrasts what he calls the economizing and the sociologising "modes" of evaluating corporations and public policy (Bell, 1973: 274–289).

Both Mills and Bell employ a kind of semi-fictionalized concept or portrait in their theorizing to make sense of a vast number of details. They used these portraits to establish meaningful narratives as interpretations of their time.

Conclusion

Based on the material that is presented here, I have arrived at a dual answer to the question of the potential relevance of constructing and employing ideal types in contemporary sociology.

First, Weber's ideal types can be transferred to other situations; to move them in time and space may produce new sociological insights. In addition to the present transposing of the Protestant Ethic/Spirit of Capitalism ideal type, writers have compared his ideal type of bureaucracy to the writings of Kafka (Jørgensen, 2010). Weber's ideal types of charismatic, legal, and traditional leadership are frequently used and referred to in political sociology. There is a wealth of insights and fruitful perspectives in Weber's body of work that has not yet been utilized in a sociology that has still not superseded his perspectives.

Second, there are more recent contributions in macro-sociology or historical sociology that adopt approaches resembling Weber's, ones that perhaps even develop his method. The ideal type-like contributions from Mills and Bell appear to be on the same "level" as Weber's, historical macro-constructions that are employed for the analysis of social change. However, it remains to be seen if future histories of sociology and future theories of science will find it fruitful to define the concepts of Mills and Bell as ideal types. It is rather puzzling that two theoretically and methodologically aware and reflective writers such as these two avoid commenting on the relationship. However, discerning why they do not use the term is beyond the scope of this chapter.

References

Andreski, S. (1984). *Max Weber's insights and errors*. London: Routledge & Kegan Paul.

Bang, A.C. (1910). *Hans Nielsen Hauge og hans samtid. En monografie.* [Hans Nielsen Hauge and his time. A monograph]. Christiania: Andersen.

Bell, D. (1973). *The coming of post-industrial society: a venture in social forecasting*. New York: Basic Books.

Birnbaum, N. (1971). "The Zwinglian reformation in Zürich", *Toward a critical sociology*. New York: Oxford University Press.

Breistein, D. (1955). *Hans Nielsen Hauge. "Kjøpmann i Bergen". Kristen tro og økonomisk aktivitet.* [Hans Nielsen Hauge. "A Bergen merchant". Christian belief and economic activity]. Bergen: Grieg.

Bruun, H.H. (2007). *Science, values and politics in Max Weber's methodology.* Aldershot: Ashgate.

Cohen, J. (2002). *Protestantism and capitalism: the mechanics of influence.* New York: A de Gruyter.

Durkheim, E. (1982) [1895]. Trans W.S. Halls. Ed. S. Lukes. *The rules of the sociological method.* New York: The Free Press.

Jonassen, C.T. (1963). "Etiske systemer og økonomisk atferd", *Tidsskrift for Samfunnsforskning.* ["Ethical systems and economic behavior", Journal for Social Sciences]. 4(2): 57–72.

Jørgensen, T.B. (2010). "Weber og Kafka – det glasklare og det gådefulde bureaukrati", Eds. R. Antoft, M.H. Jacobsen and L.B. Knudsen. *Den Poetiske Fantasi – om forholdet mellem sociologi og fiktion.* ["Weber and Kafka – The crystal clear and the enigmatic bureaucracy", The poetic imagination – the relationship between sociology and fiction]. Aalborg: Aalborg Universitetsforlag.

Kleivan, R. (1972). "Hans Nielsen Hauge. Individ i historien", *Sosiologi i Dag.* ["Hans Nielsen Hauge. An individual in history", Sociology Today]. 4: 3–27.

Marshall, G. (1982). *In search of the spirit of capitalism: an essay on Max Weber's protestant ethic thesis.* New York: Columbia University Press.

Mills, C.W. (1955). *White collar: the American middle classes.* New York: Oxford University Press.

Mills C.W. (1956). *The power elite.* London: Oxford University Press.

Mills, C.W. (1959). *The sociological imagination.* New York: Grove Press.

Molland, E. (1979). *Norges kirkehistorie i det 19. århundre – Bind 1.* [A history of the Norwegian church in the nineteenth century]. Oslo: Gyldendal.

Nordborg, S. (1966). *Hans Nielsen Hauge. Biografi 1771–1804.* [Hans Nielsen Hauge. Biography 1771–1804]. Oslo: Cappelen.

Nordborg, S. (1970). *Hans Nielsen Hauge. Biografi 1804–1824.* [Hans Nielsen Hauge. Biography 1804–1824]. Oslo: Cappelen.

Sejersted, F. (1978). *Den vanskelige frihet 1814–1850, Cappelens Norgeshistorie.* [The difficult freedom 1814–1850, Cappelens Norwegian history]. Bind 10. Oslo.

Strandbakken, P. (1987). *Protestantisme, kapitalisme og sosial endring. En historisk-sosiologisk studie av haugevekkelsens økonomiske aspekter i lys av Webers teorier om den protestantiske etikk.* [Protestantism, capitalism and social change. An historic-sociological study of the economic aspects of the Hauge movement from the perspective of Weber's theories on the protestant ethic]. (Masteravhandling, Diss., Universitetet i Oslo).

Weber M. (1927). Trans. F.H. Knight. *General economic history.* New York: Greenberg.

Weber, M. (1951). Trans. and eds. H.H. Gerth. *The religion of China: Confucianism and Taoism.* Glencoe: The Free Press.

Weber, M. (1955). Trans. and eds. H.H. Gerth and D. Martindale. *Ancient Judaism.* Glencoe: The Free Press.

Weber, M. (1958). Trans. and eds. H.H. Gerth and D. Martindale. *The religion of India: the sociology of Hinduism and Buddhism.* Glencoe: The Free Press.

Weber, M. (1992) [1905]. Trans. T. Parsons. *The protestant ethic and the spirit of capitalism.* London & New York: Routledge.

Weber, M. (2012). Trans. H.H. Bruun. Eds. H.H. Bruun and S. Whimster. *Collected methodological writings.* London: Routledge.

Additional Sources

"Hans Nielsen Hauges skrifter". ["The writings of Hans Nielsen Hauges"]. Ed. H.N.H. Ording, 8 volumes, 1947–1954, Oslo.

"Brev Frå Hans Nielsen Hauge". ["Letters from Hans Nielsen Hauge"]. Ed. I. Kvamen. 4 volumes, 1971–1976, Oslo.

CHAPTER 5

Class Operations and Measures

Håkon Leiulfsrud and Annick Prieur

Introduction

Why do so many social scientists still insist on the relevance of class analysis? For some, the answer to this question may be trivial, i.e., it continues to be a crucial dimension that shapes living conditions, life chances, and how we perceive the world. For others, mainly those who are preoccupied with issues of class distinctions and social recognition, their research interest may instead lie in demonstrating how class is a part of social identity or public discourse. Particularly in Britain, where social class continues to trigger wide public attention, class is still integral to discussions of symbolic power, lifestyle, and social hierarchy (Charlesworth, 2000; Sayer, 2005; Devine and Savage, 2005; Skeggs, 1997, 2012). A third reason for the continued interest in class analysis may be the professional satisfaction of combining theoretically informed research with internationally validated measurements, large data sets, and advanced statistical tools. In this respect, class analysis is a research area that adheres to the established scientific phases of observation, hypothesis, testing, theory, and observation. (see e.g., Evans, 1992; Rose and Harrison, 2010; Mills, 2014).

In this chapter, we provide a brief outline of classical sources of inspiration for contemporary class analysis. This includes a discussion of class as a proxy of how society is designed and of actor-based class approaches. The second part addresses the challenges of class complexities and units of analysis as examples of underdeveloped theoretical operations. In the third part, operations of class are discussed with reference to mainstream comparative survey research that is grounded in an employment and work relations (work contracts) perspective as well as research that focuses on cultural and symbolic distinctions. In the final part, we conclude that operationalisation of class is ultimately a matter of the questions that are asked.

Class as a Function of How Society is Designed Versus Actor-Based Approaches

Despite the fact that Karl Marx neither invented the idea of analysing class in terms of social divisions and social conditions nor developed a fully-fledged class theory of his own, he stands as the standard reference for anyone who is interested in class theory. Marx's (1961) own writing on social class is brief and tentative, particularly in his *Capital* (Vol. III, Chapter 52). This text differs in emphasis from *The eighteenth Brumaire of Louis Bonaparte*, which has a more explicit focus on political mobilisation in a concrete historical context, and from his and Fredrich Engels' *The communist manifesto*, which contains more universalistic class propositions and predictions. However, Marx continues to be a standard reference due to the questions that he asked and his theoretical idea of social class as a general analytical concept that addresses social structure and social change and that can also be used as descriptive term for actual social divisions in concrete societies. In Marx's view, social class is ultimately seen as being based on conflicting economic interests and exploitation and not merely as a "natural" order in which wealth is distributed. In this respect, Marx is opposed to political economists such as Adam Smith, Adam Ferguson, and David Ricardo, but he is also opposed to the claim made by Friedrich Hegel (1967) regarding the harmony and integration of "estates" (Calvert, 1991).

The concept of class in the Marxist tradition refers both to class relations and to class structure. Class relations are more or less seen a priori as socially and historically embedded, whereas class structure mainly mirrors the overall economic organization of society and demographic shifts in the composition of power and authority relations. Marx is primarily concerned with class relations in terms of class interests, class conflicts, class consciousness, and class formation, i.e., as ways to promote a more egalitarian society. He builds on the idea that there is a functional fit between class structure and the way that people and actors think about and express their social identity, interests, and way of life. To what extent and how this fit may appear is an open question and will vary both between societies and historically, but it is nonetheless believed to represent a systemic tension of class interests that in the long run will erode capitalism. Although Marx refers to classes in terms of the value of labour power sold by free wage-workers to capitalists, it is not restricted to the added value as such but to the total value of the entire product that is created by labour.

As Marx himself used the concept of class frequently, without a clear-cut theoretical operation, numerous class operations have been suggested over the years. Most of them include at least one of four theoretical building blocks: (1) property and possession brought about by labour; (2) the functions of employment or capital; (3) types of work relations (high- or low-skill labour, or "manual" versus "intellectual work"); and (4) control of a production process. In standard discussions of class analysis, Marx's notion of social class is typically operationalised in a theoretical vocabulary of social relations of exploitation to map class structure (Carchedi, 1977; Wright, 1985). Most scholars in the

Marxist tradition, however, are still more interested in how class relations play out in terms of how societies are organized and institutionally shaped than in class nomenclature per se (Wright, 2005: 14).

The same problem of a tentative and sketchy outline of social class is found in the work of Max Weber. Even if he is less concerned with class than Marx, it is still part of his theoretical vocabulary in his empirical studies of the agrarian population in Prussia and in his later critique of Marx(ism) for the interpretation of history as a never-ending class struggle. He agrees with Marx that class is important for understanding power and social divisions but does not see it as a fully encompassing perspective. In Weber's (2010) analysis of power, classes are mainly understood in terms of property rights and market freedoms (market/property); established values and honour (communal); and organizational hierarchies that are found in corporate and state bureaucracies (authority). In Weber's account, these three dimensions form socially and historically different class configurations in which we may determine both the distribution of power relations and the life chances of individuals and families (cf. Pakulski, 2005: 161). Unlike Marx, it is not a theoretical framework that will "necessarily correspond with the ways in which social relations form, social clustering occurs, social divisions appear, and social antagonisms arise" (ibid: 161). For Weber, it is an empirical question whether a society should be described as a "status" or a "class" society. His theoretical framework has an open outlook as to how individuals, families and social clusters of actors organize, identify, and distance themselves relative to the dominant systems of meaning. From this perspective, class relations are not seen as primarily concerned with class categories as such but with the class situations and inherent opportunity structures (probabilities) that lie within and between different classes (Smith, 2007).

Emile Durkheim's classical text, *The division of labour* (1964), echoes Adam Smith's notion of the division of labour. Like Smith, but unlike Marx, Durkheim attributes property to a "sacred" status and therefore as essentially legitimate. In Durkheim's view, the division of labour is mainly to be understood in light of an ongoing modernization process, where rank, guilds, and social classes fragmentize and decompose collective interests. Occupational groupings (such as labour unions) are not unable to mobilize collective power struggles, but class solidarity is in the long run incompatible with the principle of social differentiation and solidarity engendered in organic bonds. From this perspective, values that are embedded in social groupings and individualism, with an emphasis upon the development of individual rights, are highlighted instead of class formation and conflicts.

Due to his more narrow focus upon social differentiation, solidarity, and social organization, Durkheim's contribution to class analysis has mistakenly been regarded as less important than Marx's and Weber's contributions. Even if interpreted in a theoretical language of social cohesion rather than of inherent class conflicts, there are numerous examples of theoretical applications where norms and value systems are analysed in terms of symbolic power (Bourdieu, 1984), ideology, or "hegemonic ideas" (Gramsci, 1957; Laclau and Mouffe, 1985) or are seen as a necessary addition to a more traditional production-oriented model of class and social stratification. One of the best examples of the latter, translated into a Marxian theoretical framework, is life form analysis (Højrup, 1983), in which social classes correspond to ways of life in terms of how people orient themselves in the world, make priorities, and organize working life and family life. This approach implies an explicit focus on the core values and meaning systems with which actors identify, cherish, and cultivate but also on the ways of life from which people want to disassociate and distance themselves. Comparing the traditional class research of the 1970s and 1980s with that of today, it is probably fair to say that while most research focuses on levels of living and life chances, there is currently an increased interest in questions of class distinctions and social recognition.

It is increasingly difficult to label contemporary class theory as neo-Marxist, neo-Weberian, or neo-Durkheimian in terms of the theoretical operations that are made. It is not primarily the empirical operations and description of classes that differ but the questions that are asked and the way in which we make sense of social class as an analytical and descriptive tool.

Theoretical Operations – Initial Challenges Linked to Unit of Analysis and Research Questions

The unit of class analysis within the Marxist tradition is typically a question of social movements and political alliances that contribute to and are affected by ongoing class and power struggles. As presented in Engels' work, this may also include families and households as class units, but if so, there is a focus on the historical roles and functions of the family institution in different societies (see e.g., Seccombe, 1995; Therborn, 2004).

The typical unit of class analysis in the Weberian tradition is one of families and households. Its perspective on social stratification and life chances, which includes probabilities of mobility closure in class structuration, is also linked to processes that are manifested at the family level (Smith, 2007).

Durkheim's contribution to class theory is less obvious in operational terms, as he is more interested in norm and solidarity structures of communities and actors than power struggles as such. Nevertheless, several commentators see Durkheim's *Division of labour* as supplemental to traditional class theory (Lee, 1994). Grusky and Galescu (2005) suggests that Durkheim's notion of occupational communities may be seen as a functional equivalent to that of class interests, as it is recognized and sponsored by the state and closely linked to major reward systems. Pierre Bourdieu's contribution to class theory, however, shows that Durkheim's notion of power-based norm and solidarity structures can be applied to a wide range of objects – to elites, organizations, households and gender relations and to studies of field differentiation (see below).

Almost regardless of theoretical legacies, the class researchers who are primarily concerned with class as positions in a social structure must solve a number of tricky questions. A first and obvious question is how to address the complexities of "real class relations" as opposed to theoretical constructions of class. A second question involves what is to be included once we have designated individuals and families in various class positions.

The typical response to the first question is to accept that, at best, social class can be partially measured. In sociological terms, class can be understood neither in terms of individual attributes nor as a matter of all social relations but as specific class relations within social relations. It is also a theoretical operation, in which it is a priori assumed that people make choices, act, and participate in ways that are systematically structured according to class positions and class interests. In other words, there is assumed to be a correspondence between structural class position and agency, i.e., how people live their lives compared to others, even if few researchers expect to find a perfect fit. In this respect, social class can at best be seen as a proxy of "the rights and powers people have over productive resources" (Wright, 2005: 14) and of how such rights and powers are manifested in systematic inequality and opportunity structures.

To designate class positions, we must decide both on which aspect of class structure interests us and on the number of theoretically meaningful class positions. If we are primarily concerned with questions of symbolic power, it makes more sense to highlight the theoretical dimensions of cultural capital at the expense of economic capital. If we are primarily concerned with work and market relations, it makes more sense to develop theoretically based class schemata that either focuses upon key aspects of exploitation or power and/or dominance relations within the realm of the capitalist labour process and/or the labour contract. This approach may be used for studies on the more intensive utilization of labour, including the relevance of workers' knowledge, skills, and the increased demands of personal involvement, for our understanding of norms that govern contemporary labour relations, or for different types of labour contracts (Thompson, 2010: 10).

Class Measures – Wright Versus ESeC

In the Marxian class model developed by Erik Olin Wright, class is operationalized in terms of (1) *ownership* (owners versus employees), (2) *hierarchy* (managers versus non managers), and (3) *skills* and/or *expert credentials* (low- and high-skill labour), in which employers and the self-employed are distinguished from employees in working class positions (non-managerial and low-skill) and middle class positions (managers, supervisors, experts).

The class operation that was initially made by John H. Goldthorpe and incorporated in the European Socio Economic Classification (ESeC) is at first glance not unlike that of Wright, but it relies to a greater extent on the characteristics of the occupations, in which criteria such as ownership, hierarchy, skills and/or expert credentials are primarily used to differentiate between the service class (upper and intermediate middle class), workers, and a growing share of employees in "mixed" working contracts (neither typical workers nor typical service classes in terms of work contract, wage, or class interests).

Both class operations are examples of conceptual constructions of class positions and employment relations, i.e., not of persons. The translation from theory to data in ESeC is performed by an

> ...algorithm that maps occupations and employment statuses on the schema's categories...to create this algorithm we require data on employment relations for each combination of occupation by employment status within the matrix. Only then can we allocate people to the empty places and subsequently validate the classification.
>
> ROSE and HARRISON, 2010: 15

In the case of Wright, the allocation of class positions is based ideally on theoretically based measurements of hierarchy and skills and/or credentials, opening up for stricter or more inclusive definitions of, e.g., the working class (Wright, 1985, 1997); however, even in this strand of research, we find examples of protocols of how to standardize employment status and occupation based on algorithms (Wright, 1997; Leiulfsrud, Bison and Solheim, 2010).

Albeit handy in empirical analyses, the class algorithms and protocols above are always based on a number of explicit and implicit assumptions and justifications. Some of these assumptions are directly linked to class theories (e.g., the nature of the work contract, the idea of contradictory or mixed class positions, and the importance of different types of organisational capital). Some are based on empirical assessments of how to best group and classify in-between categories in mixed employment contracts (e.g., clerical and technical workers or lower supervisors). This may be illustrated, for example, in terms of probabilities of having work autonomy or skills in different occupations, but such probabilities are hardly ever fully applicable to the actual work situation of all individuals (Rose and Harrison, 2010). In the same vein, for work-centred models, there is always the challenge of how to allocate those who have never been employed or those who no longer are in the labour market. An additional challenge is what to do with those who are unemployed (even if there are several practical strategies for how to allocate these individuals into their previous or probable class positions, as in the case of children into their parents' class).

The agency dimension of class is clearly more challenging to determine than the structural dimensions of any of the two class schemes above. It is nonetheless interesting to observe that neither Goldthorpe nor Wright approach classes as "pure" theoretical constructions, but they are instead interested in the sociological complexities of dual class positions. In the case of Wright (1978, 1997), this is translated into a theoretical framework of "contradictory class positions" in which the middle classes are torn between labour and capital and are seen essentially as a heterogeneous and fragmented class grouping. The same applies to Wright's theoretical operation of self-employed and small employers who are difficult to distinguish on the basis of either capital or labour alone. In the case of Goldthorpe (and ESeC), with a more explicit focus upon the work contract and the typical class situations that are associated with it, it is the growth of "mixed" labour contracts (neither corresponding to traditional workers nor to owners and management) that is highlighted.

The strategy of addressing, but in practice avoiding, the problem of "contradictory class positions" or "mixed class positions" has also lead to an underutilization of class analysis in the research on post-industrial work relations and various claims of new types of production and employment regimes. Instead of asking what would be the possible consequences of growing numbers of people in neither typical-worker nor middle-class jobs, the standard procedure among class researchers continues to be one of merging roughly equal groupings. This may make sense if we want to create an impression of order, but it is problematic for anyone who is interested in "sociological ambivalences" (cf. Merton, 1976). The same strategy can also be found in previous discussions on the appropriate unit of class analysis when class relations at the household level often tend to be mixed. Standard operations in which this problem is overcome by designating the dominant class position to the family unit may seemingly reduce complexity but are also a good illustration of how other relevant questions of power and living conditions are systematically ignored.

Class as Icons or Exploratory Devices

Class analysis, as shown above, has primarily relied on theoretical frameworks that aim to make sense of class relations in different types of social contexts. Almost regardless of their merits, they are essentially theoretical constructions that face a critical test of measuring existing class relations or those aspects of class that are the focus of their investigations.

The European Social Survey (ESS) is a good illustration of data that were designed to facilitate the use of different versions of Wright's and Goldthorpe's class schemes and ESeC. It is a goldmine in terms of data, and the countries that were included combined with a broad range of attitude data are state of the art in survey research. The ESS is also a data archive that provides expert advice on issues such as how to operationalize class based on a number of core variables. Regardless of the choice of class model, SPSS-syntaxes are provided by the ESS consortium and associated experts to be utilized by prospective researchers. This may at least potentially contribute to a higher degree of standardization of class measures and modelling than in the past, but it also comes with a risk of not asking or questioning the basis of how these class syntaxes were made.

Although ESeC is a good example of a class model that has been exposed to rigorous empirical testing and validations, it is nevertheless the case that surprisingly few researchers openly discuss the methodological problems that are involved in the operationalization of class positions in the first place. It is consequently rarely discussed in scientific journals how small changes in operational criteria may have larger consequences for the measurement that is used than those that are based on theoretical differences between competing class models. For example, small shifts of emphasis on dimensions of skill in Goldthorpe's class scheme have contributed to a substantially higher percentage of workers in ESeC than in earlier versions of Goldthorpe's class scheme (Leiulfsrud et al., 2010).

It is also of interest to ask why class analysis a priori must be based on individuals or households rather than aggregate outcomes of, for example, wage struggles or voting, in which classes are manifested in more floating interest groups with a major impact on the class formation of a society (Lewin, 1972).

Class schemes, once they are established, tend to live a life of their own. They may also serve as a case in which class is seen as a social fact, something to be taken into account because we assume it serves as an important explanatory variable. To treat something as a social fact, however, is not limited to a discussion of class as an outcome. It is also a question of why class matters.

Class as Cultural Distinctions

An alternative operation to the definition of class as what people do at work is to focus on the subjective or discursive aspects of class that both reflect and sustain objective, distributional structures.

In softer versions of class research, this approach has been discussed in terms of a blurred or muted discourse on class in different Western societies, with an emphasis on how class emanates from boundary drawing on cultural or moral grounds, on how classes are formed through negative rather than positive identifications, or on disidentification with class categories. As shown in Bourdieu's (1984, 1987) operations, it may also be formulated in a stronger research programme, in which class is seen as being at the core of symbolic and distributional differences but where social groups that are formed on the basis of common interest are rare. For Bourdieu, classes do not exist as such. What exist are distributional differences, which the researcher may label class differences, thereby creating classes on paper. Only at rare moments may such groups become classes by regarding themselves as groups with common interests.

Subjective classes have been analysed sociologically in a series of different ways, in Marx (1999) or Marcuse (1968) as *class consciousness,* in the tradition of British cultural studies as *structures of feelings* (Williams, 1958), or in Hoggart's (1958) and Thomson's (1963) accounts of the working classes as lived *everyday experiences* and as *cultural practices.* These works paved the way for a stream of research regarding class first and foremost as experiences and feelings: experiences of affinities or alienation, feelings of sympathy or antipathy, or bodily located feelings of being in one's right place like a fish in water or in the wrong place like a hair in soup.

Such encompassing operations on class proliferate today in works such as Langston's (2004) and Charlesworth's (2000) ethnographies or Monteiro's (2008) emphasis on class as *bodily inscriptions.* Reay (2005) included *feelings* that are involved in class, e.g., "ambivalence, inferiority or superiority, visceral aversions, recognition and the markings of taste" (Reay, 2005: 911), and stated that they all contribute to a whole "psychic economy of class" (ibid: 911) (cf. Reay, 2008). Likewise, Sayer (2005) drew attention towards how "people experience class in relation to others partly via moral and immoral sentiments or emotions such as benevolence, respect, compassion, pride and envy, contempt and shame" (Sayer, 2005: 3). Such feelings are not necessarily experienced as having to do with class, but they are instead about certain people being perceived as strange, snobbish, rude, narrow-minded, sympathetic, or attractive. Thus, class may be experienced as many other things than the ones upon which are usually focused in traditional class analysis.

Class is not only social division, but it also encompasses the effects that these divisions have on other areas of life. Bourdieu's concept of *habitus* encompasses practices, experiences, and feelings, as well as distinctions and the drawing of boundaries. Specific forms of habitus fit to specific life conditions and trajectories and are expressed in material and cultural consumption as well as in political and moral orientation, and as much in condemnation as in preference. As Bourdieu (1984) states:

> In matters of taste, more than anywhere else, all determination is negation; and tastes are perhaps first and foremost distastes, disgust provoked by horror or visceral intolerance ("sick-making") of the taste of others.
> BOURDIEU, 1984: 56

Therefore, class identity not only concerns who one is but also who one is not.

Analysing both men in elite positions and working class men in the United States and in France, Lamont (1992, 2000) challenges Bourdieu with a claim that moral boundaries are more important than cultural boundaries, especially in the American case (cf. also Sayer, 2005). Lamont and Sayer may underestimate the importance that Bourdieu actually attributed to ethical, moral, and political class differences in *Distinction*, in which they systematically accompanied cultural and economic distinctions. Nevertheless, it still seems to be justified to question whether the forms of high culture that played such an important role in class distinctions in Bourdieu's study of France actually play such a strong role in other societies (cf. e.g., Bennett et al., 2009; Prieur and Savage, 2011, 2013).

Bourdieu's shift of emphasis from affirmation and belonging to *negation and distances* has been taken up in other studies (e.g., Savage, 2000). Devine and Savage's (2005) reading of Bourdieu's identification implies differentiating oneself from others in a field, making class *identity* a relational claim to other players in the field. Thus, attention is drawn towards the interplay between position and *practices of positioning*, which demand a degree of reflexivity from the agents. The complexity of this interplay is not fully explored by Bourdieu, who concentrates on cases of fits between positions and dispositions in *Distinction* (Bourdieu, 1987). The rare misfits that are described are in cases of social mobility, when the *habitus* of a former or an imagined future position may be traced in current dispositions. His later work, *The weight of the world* (Bourdieu et al., 1999), contains numerous portrayals of misfits. These misfits are seen as a lack of adaptation of the habitus to new social conditions that are imposed by the decline of industrialism, with little attention paid to the issue of reflexivity.

In a study of a group of women who, according to all sociological criteria would belong to the working class but stubbornly resist this label, Skeggs (1997) came to question Bourdieu's assumptions about fit between positions and dispositions. Skeggs regarded such *disidentifications* or *misrecognitions* as reflexive identity constructions because to be working class offered the interviewed women no kind of positive identification. Studying working class men in United States and in France, Lamont (2000) shows a similar dissociation of socioeconomic status from moral worth at a subjective level, thereby revealing the reflexive reworking of the social hierarchy.

Thus, in the literature presented here, class is expressed in indirect ways, through judgments and categories that are not explicitly about class. Class appears as a lived, everyday experience, which translates to feelings and is expressed through the drawing of boundaries towards others, and more clearly as negative rather than positive identifications. The subjective identifications that are related to class do not necessarily fit with objective positions, as categorizations are reworked reflexively.

Significantly different concepts are employed in the literature on class, and a question may be raised about how well they fit together. A habitus exists at the subjective level, while it reflects intersubjective entities such as cultural representations or shared schemes of perceptions, evaluations, and categorizations. The pair that is formed by *habitus* and *representations* corresponds to the poststructuralist vocabulary's pair of *subjectivities* and *discourses*, but the former conceptualization offers a greater impact on the unconscious and nonverbal expression than the latter does.

Discussion and Conclusion

Despite the differences in historical and theoretical origins, we currently observe a strong tendency towards convergence between competing class schemes in conventional class research. This is clearly the case if we compare the operational criteria that are used in the class schemes of Goldthorpe and

Wright. It is also interesting to observe that their initial focus on work relations (and, in the case of Goldthorpe, combined with market power) is used as an attempt to investigate a broad range of questions beyond social distribution and welfare research, including questions of class identity and class consciousness as well as cultural consumption.

Both Goldthorpe and Wright tend to give the employment contract a key role in their class operations. In this respect, they appear to follow in the footsteps of much previous labour theory, even if none of them accept Marx's value theory. Notably, not even Marx attributed such an encompassing role of class relations to labour power as in Goldthorpe and Wright's class schemes. In line with Marx, the term "class relations" refers to more than just "socially necessary abstract labour"; it also refers to other aspects of class and stratification in any society.

From most researchers in the tradition of Bourdieu, Bourdieu's theoretical operation of class is seen as an alternative to conventional class research and in direct opposition to rational action theory (Weininger, 2005). His concept of "habitus" as systems of dispositions that orient our thoughts and actions is both more socially bounded and preoccupied with the symbolic system and boundaries between classes than in traditional class analysis. It is a perspective in which class cannot be reduced to economic struggles but is seen as interwoven with symbolic struggles, not unlike Weber's idea of status differentiation (cf. Weininger, 2005: 84). It is also a theoretical framework in which Bourdieu repudiates the idea of class as something that is given or functions as a theoretical icon. In Bourdieu's view, this is not a question that we can answer theoretically – it must be grounded in the basic sociological question of collective experiences that take place in society. Classes are manifested empirically in the way that collectives of people tend to live their lives. The research programme in *Distinction* is not merely intended to map systematic differentiations of lifestyles but also to study another crucial aspect of distinction, i.e., that of discrimination and social closure vis-à-vis other social groupings.

Although Bourdieu's own theoretical program and operation of class may share a number of commonalities with traditional class research in practice – for example, in the operational criteria that are used to measure economic and cultural capital – it is nonetheless also a productive departure for analyses of intersections among gender, class, and ethnicity.

For those who are preoccupied with class as lived experiences, we also see a possible third operation of class research that is neither expressed in conventional class theory nor fully covered by Bourdieu. We may label this as subjective class but with a more explicit focus on everyday life, social identifications, and identity politics than in classical accounts. Class is expressed in indirect

ways, through boundary drawing, judgments, and categories, and objective positions do not necessarily fit with subjective identifications as categorizations
are reworked reflexively. How this translates into everyday experiences is a key
question for future class research that is concerned with class as agency and
not merely as social structure.

Complexities in class relations, such as cross-class families, class travel
across generations, and class heterogeneous networks, are examples of where
subjects like class identity, class voting, and identity politics are of particular
sociological interest. To understand the social mechanisms at work in these
complex situations, it is vital to bring in subjective class but also to reflect upon
the contexts in which subjective class takes place, the organization and demographic structure of social ties, and the relevance of social space in formations
of their habitus (Bourdieu, 1984: 107 ff).

Alternative operations of class in terms of intersectionality also bring in a
whole range of "class links" to gender, race, ethnicity, and generation that may
help us understand both class complexities and enduring inequality structures. There are surprisingly few class researchers who incorporate theory
and discussions from feminist or ethnic research. Doing so could mean a less
a priori and more open theoretical operations of both the role and functions
of the family unit and changing class and gender relations, for example (cf.
Skeggs, 1997). It may also potentially re-introduce questions of how subordination translates into social identities and everyday practices as well as how
social privilege may prevent us from addressing critical questions at the core of
class theory. In this respect, class research is not only a question of how other
people live their lives but also how social scientists tend to view the society in
which they live from their class-privileged point of view (Charlesworth, 2000).

Although the question about the existence of classes in contemporary societies is an empirical one, it cannot be answered without a theoretical reflection
on what a social class is. What should one look for? A sociological discussion of
classes may make references to economy, education, mobility, work relations,
characteristics of occupations, lifestyle, identity, and attitudes – ranging from
economic distribution to feelings and corporeal inclinations. This may seem
confusing, and the sociological debate about class participants frequently
breaks down because all parties do not talk about the same thing. From one
standpoint, one may declare that classes do not exist, as people do not easily
identify with class categories anymore, and from another standpoint, one may
respond that classes exist as long as economic inequality exists. Both parties
may have a point, but they understand class in very different terms. It is, however, difficult to deploy the insight about the magnitude of manifestations of
class as concrete guidelines for empirical research.

In a Bourdieu-inspired study in Aalborg in Denmark, it was suggested that class in a Nordic context should focus on class as distributional differences (primarily economic and cultural resources); class as habitus (experiences, corporeal sensations, etc.); class as the drawing of symbolic boundaries; class as conscience and identifications; and class as structures of (symbolic) domination (Faber, Prieur, Rosenlund and Skjøtt-Larsen, 2012, 2014). Because there is a strong public belief in Nordic countries that classes do not matter so much anymore, to operationalize class in this cultural context is also to address provocative questions rarely asked, and thus, these questions are often ignored in both public and sociological debates.

Almost regardless of how well the measures used may work in empirical research, it is ultimately an adjudication of multiple (as opposed to singular) manifestations of class relations that has to be addressed. This includes class operations of what takes place among individuals and groups, but it must also be supplemented with an interest in the economic system and "meta-actors" (such as the upper echelon of the 1% richest). Without asking these types of questions, we easily forget that even the most economic egalitarian countries on paper (such as the Nordic countries) tend to have powerful financial elites in terms of ownership, wealth, and capital gains. They may be few and hard to map in conventional survey research, but are nonetheless crucial if we want to do meaningful analysis of the economic dynamic driving class relations in any developed market economy (Piketty, 2014).

While this chapter has argued for a broad understanding of class, it is important to warn against the risk that the attention to cultural distinctions and moral boundaries together with the emphasis on hierarchal dimensions other than class (e.g., gender, race, ethnicity, sexuality, sexuality) come to overshadow the "old" issues of economic inequalities, which in today's societies are as real as ever. An advanced sociological understanding of class should grasp how the different forms of inequalities sustain each other. This argument is in line with Breen and Rottman (1995) who remind us that that is far easier to establish empirical correlations between social inequality and class on a number of outcomes, but it is more difficult to understand the sociological mechanisms contributing to such empirical associations.

References

Bennett, T. et al. (2009). *Culture, class, distinction.* London: Routledge.
Bourdieu, P. (1984). *Distinction: a social critique of the judgement of taste.* London: Routledge.

Bourdieu, P. (1987). "What makes a social class? On the theoretical and practical existence of groups", *Berkeley Journal of Sociology*. Vol. 32. Berkeley: Berkeley journal of
sociology.

Bourdieu, P. et al. (1999). Trans. P. Parkhurst et al. *The weight of the world*. Cambridge:
Polity Press.

Breen, R. and Rottman, D. (1995). "Class analysis and class theory", *Sociology*. 29(3):
453–473.

Calvert, P. (1991). *The concept of class: an historical introduction*. London: Hutchinson.

Carchedi, G. (1977). *The economic identification of social classes*. London: Routledge
and Kegan Paul.

Charlesworth, S.J. (2000). *The phenomenology of working-class experience*. Cambridge:
Cambridge University Press.

Devine, F. and Savage, M. (2005). "The cultural turn, sociology and class analysis", Eds.
F. Devine, M. Savage, J. Scott and R. Crompton. *Rethinking class: culture, identities
and lifestyle*. New York: Palgrave Macmillan.

Durkheim, É. (1964) [1893]. *The division of labor in society*. New York: Free Press of
Glecoe.

Evans, G. (1992). "Testing the validity of the Goldthorpe class schema", *European Sociological Review*. 8(3): 211–232.

Faber, S.T., Prieur, A., Rosenlund, L. and Skjøtt-Larsen, J. (2012). *Det skjulte klassesam-
fund*. [The hidden class society]. Aarhus: Aarhus Universitetsforlag.

Faber, S.T., Prieur, A., Rosenlund, L. and Skjøtt-Larsen, J. (2014). "Nye tider – nye
klasseskel?", Ed. C.S. Hansen. *Socialt rum – symbolsk magt*. ["New times – new class
divisions", Social space – symbolic power]. Copenhagen: Hexis.

Gramsci, A. (1957). *The modern prince and other writings*. New York: International
Publisher.

Grusky, D. and Galescu, G. (2005). "Foundations of a neo-Durkheimian class analysis",
Ed. E.O. Wright. *Approaches to class analysis*. Cambridge: Cambridge University
Press.

Hegel, F. (1967) [1821]. *Hegel's philosophy of right*. London and New York: Oxford University Press.

Hoggart, R. (1958). *The uses of literacy*. London: Penguin.

Højrup, T. (1983). *Det glemte folk: livsformer og centraldirigering*. [The forgotten people:
life forms and centrally planning]. The Copenhagen: Dept. of European Ethnologi-
cal Research and Danish Building Research Institute.

Laclau, E. and Mouffe, C. (1985). *Hegemony and socialist strategy: towards a radical
democratic politics*. London and New York: Verso.

Lamont, M. (1992). *Money, morals and manners: the culture of the French and the
American upper-middle class*. Chicago: The University of Chicago Press.

Lamont, M. (2000). *The dignity of working men: morality and the boundaries of race,
class and immigration*. New York: Russell Sage Foundation.

Langston, D. (2004). "Tired of playing Monopoly?" Eds. M.L. Andersen and P.H. Collins. *Race, class and gender: an anthology*. United Kingdom: Thomson and Wadsworth.

Lee, D. (1994). "Class as a social fact", *Sociology*. 28(2): 397–415.

Leiulfsrud, H., Bison, I. and Solheim, E. (2010). *Social class in Europe II: European Social Survey*. Trondheim: Norwegian University of Science and Technology (available at http://www.svt.ntnu.no/iss/ClassSyntaxes.html).

Lewin, L. (1972). *The Swedish electorate 1887–1968*. Stockholm: Almqvist and Wiksell.

Marcuse, H. (1968). *One dimensional man*. London: Routledge & Kegan Paul.

Marx, K. (1961) [1894]. "Chapter 52", *Capital: the process of capitalist production as a whole*. New York: International Publishers.

Marx, K. (1999) [1852]. *The eighteenth Brumaire of Louis Bonaparte*. Marx/Engels Internet Archive (marxist.org).

Merton, R.K. (1976). *Sociological ambivalences and other essays*. New York: Free Press.

Mills, C. (2014). "The great class fiasco: a comment on Savage et al.", *Sociology*. 48(3): 437–444.

Monteiro, B. (2008). "Dimmed sights, poisoned feelings and ineffable injuries: some aspects of the working class everyday life in times of 'crisis'", *Paper*. SCUD meeting Sæby, Denmark.

Pakulski, J. (2005). "Foundations of a post-class analysis", Ed. E.O. Wright. *Approaches to class analysis*. Cambridge: Cambridge University Press.

Piketty, T. (2014). *Capital in the twenty – first century*. Cambridge: Belknap Press.

Prieur, A. and Savage, M. (2011). "Updating cultural capital theory: a discussion based on studies in Denmark and in Britain", *Poetics*. 39(6): 566–580.

Prieur, A. and Savage, M. (2013). "Emerging forms of European cultural capital", *European Societies*. 15(2): 246–267.

Reay, D. (2005). "Beyond consciousness? The psychic landscape of social class", *Sociology*. 39(5): 911–928.

Reay, D. (2008). "Psychosocial aspects of white middle-class identities", *Sociology*. 42(6): 1072–1088.

Rose, D. and Harrison, E. (eds.). (2010). *Social class in Europe: an introduction to the European socio-economic classification*. New York: Routledge.

Savage, M. (2000). *Class analysis and social transformation*. Buckingham and Philadelphia: Open University Press.

Sayer, A. (2005). *The moral significance of class*. Cambridge: Cambridge University Press.

Seccombe, W. (1995). *Weathering the storm: working class families from the industrial revolution to the fertility decline*. London: Verso.

Skeggs, B. (1997). *Formations of class and gender: becoming respectable*. London: Sage.

Skeggs, B. (2012). "Feeling class: affect and culture in the making of class relations", Ed. G. Ritzer. *International encyclopedia of sociology*. Oxford: Blackwell.

Smith, K. (2007). "Operationalizing Max Weber's probability concept of class situation: the concept of social class", *British Journal of Sociology.* 58(1): 87–104.

Therborn, G. (2004). *Between sex and power: family in the world 1900–200.* London and New York: Routledge.

Thompson, E.P. (1963). *The making of the English working class.* Harmondsworth: Penguin.

Thompson, P. (2010). "The capitalist labour process: concepts and connections", *Capital & Class.* 34(1): 7–14.

Weber, M. (2010). "The distribution of power within the community: classes, stände, parties", Trans. D. Waters et al. *Journal of Classical Sociology.* 10(2): 153–172.

Weininger, E.B. (2005). "Foundations of Pierre Bourdieu's class analysis", Ed. E.O. Wright. *Approaches to class analysis.* Cambridge: Cambridge University Press.

Williams, R. (1958). *Culture and society.* London: Chatto and Windus.

Wright, E.O. (1978). *Class, crises and the state.* London: New Left Books.

Wright, E.O. (1985). *Classes.* London: New Left Books.

Wright, E.O. (1997). *Class counts: comparative studies in class analysis.* Cambridge and New York: Cambridge University Press and Maison des Sciences de l'Homme.

Wright, E.O. (2005). "Foundations of a neo-Marxist class analysis", Ed. E.O. Wright. *Approaches to class analysis.* Cambridge: Cambridge University Press.

CHAPTER 6

Question-Driven Sociology and Methodological Contextualism

Ragnvald Kalleberg

Introduction

A research design can be conceptualized as consisting of four operations: asking, data collecting, theorizing, and answering (Kalleberg, 1992: 14–16, 1996: 2–35). *Data collecting* and *theorizing* are often discussed among sociologists, and there is a great deal of literature on methods and theory. However, there has been much less of a collective focus on the two other basic operations, the *asking* of research questions and the argumentation *pro et contra* in the process of *answering*. This imbalance is surprising because it is widely accepted that the most important single element of research design is the question, which provides direction to the other elements.

This chapter focuses on questioning and theorizing, on their characteristics as operations, and how the basic operations influence each other within research design. This contribution is located within the overlapping fields of the sociology of science, the theory of science, and the sociology of knowledge. In these fields, published books and articles are routinely used as empirical material. I incorporate a few classic articles on theoretical sociology by Robert Merton as part of my data material. Using evidence-based sociology and the theory of science, I focus not only on Merton's theory of science and recommendations but especially on his actual research practice. Merton presupposed in his theory of science that normative questions were external to sociology as a science. However, in his research practice, he actually discussed and answered normative questions in interesting ways.

"Theory": Terminological Unity and Conceptual Diversity

"Theory" is a central word in sociological vocabularies. It has a wide variety of meanings. We have one word, but there is a multitude of different concepts associated with that word. This has been the situation for a long time. In 1945, Merton observed that the term "sociological theory" was used to refer to the products of several related but distinct activities carried out by members of a professional group called sociologists (Merton, 1968: 140). In an article in the *American Journal of Sociology*, he noted "six types of work often lumped together as comprising sociological theory". They are still with us today: (1) "Theory" often refers to methodology – work that focuses on research design and the general logic of scientific procedure. (2) Merton provides an example of "general orientations toward substantive materials" in Durkheim's advice that the "determining cause of a social fact should be sought among the social facts preceding it" (ibid: 142). (3) Merton also notes that sociologists talk about "theory" when they refer to the analysis, revision, and formation of sociological concepts. (4) *Post factum* sociological interpretation is another type of activity that is often referred to as "theory", for instance, interpreting official statistics that have been collected for practical purposes. (5) Merton distinguished sociological interpretation from empirical generalization. According to Merton, these operations should not be labelled "sociological theory" but instead characterized with words that are closer to each operation, such as concept formation and generalization. (6) Merton regarded "theorizing" as it could and should be practiced in the development of sociology into a science. In his article "On sociological theories of the middle range" two decades later, he presented the same idea:

> ...the term *sociological theory* refers to logically interconnected sets of propositions from which empirical uniformities can be derived...One speaks of a theory of...the formation of social norms just as one speaks of a theory of prices, a germ theory of diseases, or a kinetic theory of gases.
>
> MERTON, 1968: 39–40

This was, and is, the standard scientistic, or positivistic, interpretation of "theory" in social science (Kalleberg, 2009). Examples from the natural sciences are used as illustrations. Boyle-Mariotte's law refers to a law of nature. The law of nature makes it possible to explain and predict outcomes of operations. If a temperature is constant and the volume of the gas is halved, the pressure is doubled. We say that the cause brings about the effect. Scientistic theorists of science generalize such laws and claim that it is the basic task of all scientific disciplines to causally explain phenomena. Merton agrees with this and accepts the feasibility and desirability of causal explanation of not only diseases and gases but also of norms and prices. He adhered to this understanding of theory 6 throughout his career. If sociology is to become a full-fledged science in the future, we must produce theory 6, as has been done in the natural sciences.

In this scientistic vision of sociology as a future science, it is often said that the discipline should be *theory-driven*. Hypotheses about the invariant relationships between causes and effects should be derived from hypothetical-deductive theories and tested against what is actually happening in social reality. Such tests can be the basis for confirmation, modification, or rejection of hypotheses. Research is theory-driven in that the sociologist asks questions to fill the gaps in the hypothetical-deductive system (e.g., Galtung, 1969: 451–490). The evolving hypothetical-deductive theory is a core value in this vision of a future sociological science.

The enthusiasm for theory 6 in modern sociology was at its most intense during the middle third of the 20th century. However, this interpretation of social science has a longer history, stretching back to Auguste Comte and John Stuart Mill and to social theorists in early modernity, such as Thomas Hobbes. It still influences sociological theorizing but now mainly as an implicit kind of theory of science. After centuries, however, there is still not a single example of it in social scientific research.

This vision of the future of social science distorts our understanding of scientific tasks. In an examination of contemporary "theories of social change", Boudon documents several of these distortions, such as the influence of an implicit "nomological bias" (1986: 61–89) that lures social scientists away from a focus on concrete historical and social contexts as they seek to discover general laws that are independent of contexts. Boudon summarized a central argument as follows: "In the social sciences, Laplace's demon is still whirling about, even though he is no doubt a harmful rather than a useful fiction" (ibid: 154, 75).

Merton's typology is still useful. All six uses of the word "theory" can be found in discussions and publications by contemporary sociologists. In an article that I wrote two decades ago, I took inspiration from Merton's typology and introduced eight additional meanings based on how the single word "theory" was actually used by researchers and graduate students in sociology (Merton, 1996: 56–57). The word could also refer to the following different kinds of operations: (7) providing an overview of the existing literature in a research field; (8) engaging in general social theory and social-philosophical analysis, for instance, a la Giddens (structuration theory) and Habermas (theory of communication); (9) discussing classics such as Weber and Durkheim; (10) building models and ideal types; (11) developing general insights on the basis of ordinary experiences, such as Merton's article on self-fulfilling prophecies (1968, Ch. 13) or Habermas' analysis of everyday rationality and communication (1984: 8–42); (12) practicing the philosophy of science; (13) synthesizing knowledge and insights in a field, for instance, in organization theory (as Mintzberg, 1979) and democratic theory (as Dahl, 1989); or (14) developing explanations for puzzling phenomena (as Boudon, 1998).

To distinguish between these different conceptions, I order them from 1 to 14 and refer to "theory 6" or "theory 14". This more extensive typology is of course not exhaustive. Theory 15 could refer to the activity of developing typologies, such as distinguishing between different types of institutions, theories, and types of rationality. Theory 16 could be the one that is used by Ritzer (2008: 2): sociological theories "have a *wide range* of application, address *centrally important issues*, and have *stood the test of time*". A standard example is Marx's analysis of class struggle and social change. Theory 17 could refer to the articulation of general analytical frameworks for sociological description and analysis, such as Mills' (1959) conception of sociological imagination, or different perspectives to explain social change by means of material ("Marx") or cultural ("Weber") factors.

In summary, in the field of sociology we have one word, "theory", which expresses a wide range of different ideas (or concepts) and refers to several different tasks, operations, and corresponding scholarly products. Much valuable work has been done within the frameworks of these different conceptions of "theory", and they have all stimulated interesting questions. Some of these conceptions are closely related, for instance, theory 10 and theory 13. Others have little or almost nothing in common, such as theory 6 and theory 4, or theory 7 and theory 12. In such instances, we are not comparing apples with apples, nor even apples and pears, but rather apples and squirrels.

Ambiguity and polysemy is a common phenomenon in our everyday world and in several scientific fields, such as in anthropology, sociology, and history. In most situations, it is unproblematic that it is possible to convey different meanings with the same word, and the same meaning with quite different words and expressions. The meaning of words and sentences is generally made sufficiently precise by other elements in a relevant setting. However, such ambiguity at the centre of a discipline's self-interpretation as a science can contribute to a lack of sufficient clarity with regard to scientific tasks, operations, and desirable results.

There is a certain inflation in the use of the word "theory" in sociology. A content analysis of social-scientific journals would probably show that the word is most often used by our tribe. My hypothesis is that a shadow scientism in contemporary sociology explains much of this infatuation with "theory". In several situations, it would be better to choose words that are closer to practical research operations, for instance, to discuss the (re)construction of concepts and creation of typologies instead of theory 3 and theory 15. It would also be wise to talk more often about "analysing"; or use "analysing" and "theorizing" as synonyms, as I do here. I suppose that for many sociologists, the word "analyzing" more easily provides associations with something specific that is located in social space and historical time.

Words, not only concepts (meanings), are important in our thinking and for clarity in discussions. There is always a danger of linguistic inflation and the supposition that a new word is the same as a new concept. Lyngstad (2009) documented 47 different meanings of "capital" in contemporary sociology and noted that there is no theoretical benefit in discussing "social capital" instead of "trust". Merton warned against "misleading terminology": "the vocabulary of concepts fixes perceptions, thought and associated behavior" (1968: 146). We should therefore discard misleading words and develop new ones that more precisely denote our operations and research phenomena.

Such a respect for words was a recurrent theme for Charles Peirce:

> Man makes the word, and the word means nothing which the man has not made it mean. But since man can think only by means of words or other external symbols, these might turn round and say: "You mean nothing which we have not taught you, and then only so far as you address some words as the interpretant of your thought". In fact...men and words reciprocally educate each other....
>
> Quoted from HABERMAS, 1978: 332

Theoretical Sociology as a Kind of Empirical Research

A descriptive typology that is suited for the analysis of sociologists' actual use of the word "theory" can be made longer, even much longer. However, let us only look at two more examples that are close at hand in light of this chapter's focus. Sociologists sometimes characterize articles such as Merton's on theoretical sociology (1968, Part I) or several of Boudon's articles (as 1996) as being "theoretical". A theorist using the meaning of theory 18 is thus basing his or her argument on existing scholarly contributions. Academics who practice in this way are not doing empirical research; rather, they "theorize". A related conception of "theory" was presented by Aubert and Vale (1973: 96), who commented on "what most often goes by the name of sociological theory", namely "meta-theory, a theory of the logical and semantic relations between the terms and concepts used in analysing social reality". They utilize concepts such as "inter-action, norm, value, and role" and mention Merton's (1957) analysis of role sets as an example. This approach can be designated as theory 19.

The last two conceptions are inadequate descriptions of what authors such as Merton and Boudon actually did in the contributions mentioned here. Firstly, articles and books are real things, empirical entities, that are located in a socio-cultural reality. We have to do with phenomena that can be described and analyzed as other entities. Academic publications are generally primary empirical material within subfields such as the sociology of science, the sociology of knowledge, and the history of sociology. For the sociology of science, it is normal to regard "theorizing" as a type of ordinary action and interaction in the field of science, which is one of the essential institutions of modern society. Merton's (1970) doctoral dissertation on the scientific revolution was based partly on an analysis of a large number of published articles. Bannister's (1987) book on the emergence of scientism in American sociology is an empirical study based on what historians call "existing" sources or "primary" sources, such as scholarly publications. My own analysis (Kalleberg, 2015) of academic plagiarism is based on primary empirical sources, published reports, articles, and books.

Secondly, Merton's (1957) analysis of status (position) and role-set is not only about logical and semantic relations between concepts, which were used later in empirical analysis. It is already an analysis of social reality that is focused on the ordinary phenomena of positions (statuses) as bases for role-sets. Consequently, Merton's analysis of status is a type of empirical contribution. It is useful to distinguish between three types of empirical studies, based on (a) new data, such as interviews, (b) a synthesis of existing empirical studies, and (c) reconstructive studies (see Kalleberg, 2007: 147–152, 2010: 185–186.). Merton (1957) is not based on new data from the field nor on the synthesis of existing contributions. It is a reconstructive empirical study. What we need to generate new and better insights is not always more data and evidence. Sometimes authors and readers have more than enough data and experience, and what we need are better concepts, typologies, perspectives, models, and interpretations. Then, we can engage in reconstructive empirical studies.

Contributions such as Merton's on theoretical sociology and Boudon's (1994) on the social explanation of false beliefs in science and society are based on ordinary empirical material. We do not have to theorize in an empirical void. Studies in this field, therefore, have to be organized in the same way as in other fields of research, applying the same types of *research designs*. Thus, we need to properly conceptualize research design.

I opened this chapter with a model of the four basic operations of research design: asking, data collecting, analysing (theorizing), and answering. The most important element is the research question. Questions provide direction for the other main elements in a project: relevant data types, appropriate analytical strategies, and possible answers. In most research, there is widespread agreement on the primacy of questions. It is easy to back up this claim with insights from the theory of science, based, for instance, on the critical rationalism of Popper (1968) or insights from hermeneutics, such the importance of the "logic of question and answer" (Gadamer, 1989: 369–379). This widespread agreement makes it appear strange that empirical studies of questioning are such an underdeveloped empirical field. In sociology, and in social science generally, there is a discrepancy in the large amount of collective work on data collection and theorizing and the tiny amount of work on the construction of good research questions (see Lindblom, 1990: 266–269). There are few published studies on strategies for questioning, and few on the basic skill of asking questions during interviews.

We need a typology of legitimate research questions and the research designs that they direct. Elsewhere, I have argued that in sociology, and other social sciences, there are two basic types of legitimate research questions, descriptive-explanatory and normative (Kalleberg, 2009, 2005). Under the umbrella of descriptive-explanatory questions, there are different types of sub-questions. Descriptive questions result in the *identification* and *documentation* of actual states of affairs, such as typical actors and procedures in the field studied. Another type is to ask *comparative* questions about phenomena in social space and historical time to discover similarities and differences, stability, and change. For instance, we may ask why German, American, British, French, and Japanese universities are organized in such different ways (Clark, 1995). We could also ask *explanatory* questions, for instance, why institutions are different, or why something has changed or has not changed.

Questions concerning identification, documentation, comparison, and explanation should not be misconceived as theory 6 questions. The identification (Merton, 1959: xiii–xv, 1987: 2–6) and description of phenomena, comparisons, and explanations, all require an understanding of why partly autonomous actors are located in a social space and historical time. *Homo sociologicus* is a self-determining rational actor in that action and inaction are based on all types of opinions and always in context. Data are already theorized by the empirical objects themselves, and there is two-way communication between science and the area of study, a state of affairs unknown in the natural sciences (see Habermas, 1988: 92–95, 117–119, 143–146; Giddens, 1976: 144–148; Kalleberg, 2005: 146–150). Reasons are generally not fully explicated. Actions can lead to unintended results and can be aggregated and transformed in ways no single actor could imagine. This is a basic reason why we are fascinated by Weber's analysis of the Protestant Ethic and the Spirit of Capitalism ideal types. The findings may of course be invalid, both as false opinions about the facts of a situation and as immoral evaluations of phenomena.

When asking normative research questions, we evaluate social phenomena that are identified and documented as well as potentially compared and explained. Evaluations are based on value standards, for instance, concerning the efficient use of scarce resources or the degree of democratization or social discrimination (based on gender, ethnicity, age, etc.). An article by Boudon

(1996) illustrates some of these points. The article focuses on the explanation of collective beliefs, both valid and invalid ones. One of the examples concerns psychological experiments with physicians and their estimations that a person has a certain disease (see Boudon, 1996: 129–132). A majority of the physicians were wrong in the same way, claiming that the probability was very high. Obviously, this is a critique of the opinions in the field. Boudon's interest is to analyse and criticise the explanatory behaviour of social scientists. Psychologists seek external *causes* and neglect *reasons*. They assume that a hunter-gatherer frame of mind may have been mysteriously transmitted through the millennia, distorting the statistical reasoning of well-educated contemporary physicians. Boudon provides a more plausible explanation without introducing mysterious black boxes. It is an explanation that is based on the posing of questions and the reasoning of actors, some of them implicit and some of them wrong. Psychologists can be led astray by the scientistic presupposition that a genuine scientific explanation must be formed in terms of external causes, similar to what is done in a discipline such as chemistry. They are led astray by presupposing that they have to pose and answer theory 6 questions.

One subtype of evaluative questions can be identified as *constructive*. They involve the question of what actors can and should do to improve their situation. The word "can" refers to feasibility, that something is possible in the real world. The word "should" refers to desirability, that an alternative is better than the existing one. Such questions are regularly posed in evaluations, but they can also direct basic research, such as Dahl's (1985) study of economic democracy. The reason for constructive questions is that criticism of a social reality that cannot and should not be changed is sterile in the long run. If it can and should be changed, we also have a scholarly responsibility to pose and answer constructive questions to demonstrate that.

Constructive questions direct constructive designs. In such designs, the same types of data (qualitative and quantitative) and analytical (theoretical) categories (such as concepts, typologies, perspectives) as in other social-scientific research designs are used. There are three types of constructive research designs, indicated by the catch-words *variation* (learning from good and bad examples), *intervention*, and *imagination* (Kalleberg, 1992: 41–52, 1996: 52–55, 2005: 181–186, 2009: 262–266). First, to answer a constructive research question, we should try to learn from good examples. We may for instance be interested in how a school or system of schools should be redesigned to create more stimulating settings for learning. Today, researchers in several nations seek to learn from the Finnish system when posing and answering constructive questions about what to recommend to improve schools in their own societies.

We may of course also learn from bad examples. Such studies do sometimes result in warnings.

Second, we may learn from actual interventions in a socio-cultural field. Then, we can answer constructive questions based on data from such interventions. This type of constructive study is often called action research. I avoid that term because so much that has been placed under this label is not research, but a type of professional developmental work. However, such an approach is perfectly legitimate and can often be more important than simply doing research (Kalleberg, 1992: 6–12, 23–26). Third, we may try to answer constructive questions by performing mental experiments, imagining feasible and desirable alternatives. The task is not to make prognoses about possible futures, which is a descriptive-explanatory task, but to argue that there are feasible and desirable alternatives. Dahl's (1985) study of possible economic democracy can be easily reconstructed along such lines. Dahl knew that there were no existing examples of economic democracies. Therefore, he imagined general traits and conditions. In addition, he engaged in rigorous normative reasoning concerning the requirements for democracy in working life. His main recommendation was to maintain well-functioning markets and connect steering rights for companies with the employees.

A Theoretician's Struggle with His Implicit Constructive Research Designs

Merton's articles on theoretical sociology were written to guide sociology in the right direction on the long path to becoming a mature science. According to Merton's theory 12 of science, sociologists should only ask descriptive-explanatory questions (theory 6). However, he often contradicted his own theory in his own research practice. His articles on theoretical sociology are not, for instance, only descriptive-explanatory but also normative-evaluative. He claims that an approach, a set of operations, should not be identified as "sociological theory", as its author wrongly does. Another example is when he criticizes articles for being based on "basic misconceptions about the sciences" (Merton, 1968: 46–48).

Merton also posed and discussed constructive questions, although implicitly, obscuring them for himself and his readers. His research questions can be explicated as follows: What can and should sociologists do to develop sociology into an ordinary science? To answer such a constructive research question, he was compelled to move within a constructive research design. In this case, he used the most difficult of the constructive designs as his main strategy, that of imagination. He was convinced that at a future stage, sociology would be transformed into an ordinary science. However, he had to imagine that:

> Despite the many volumes dealing with the history of sociological theory and despite the plethora of empirical investigations, sociologists (including this writer) may discuss the logical criteria of sociological laws without citing a single instance which fully satisfies these criteria.
>
> MERTON, 1968: 150

No sociologist could give one single example of a social law that makes it possible to derive a causal hypothesis, present a prediction, test it, and thereby test theory 6. Merton was aware that he had no data on which to base his analysis. There are no data from the future. However, he remained certain of the general answer: Sociologists should in the long run ("ultimately") take "mature" sciences, "such as physics and biology" (Merton, 1968: 140) as their model. Constructive designs of the imaginative type are risky and dispose of utopian answers. Utopianism of different sorts has distorted parts of the sociological tradition. It is easy to find examples in Comte, Spencer, and Marx. This element, also found in Merton's oeuvre, can be appropriately identified as a type of scientistic utopianism on behalf of sociology as a whole.

A standard move in a constructive design of the imaginative type is to also apply strategies from one of the other constructive designs, especially to learn from good examples. This is a move to ground parts of a constructive analysis in existing social realities. Dahl (1985) follows this strategy in his study. To support the feasibility and desirability of his recommendations, he analyzes smaller, existing systems, such as the Mondragon cooperatives in the northern part of Spain. Merton notes that he had found a relevant example. He finished the article on theories of the middle range by claiming that Durkheim's study of suicide was an "approximation" (Merton, 1968: 150). He did not, however, succeed in making a convincing case for Durkheim's study as an "approximation" of theory 6. One of the reasons is that he did not see the tensions in Durkheim's analysis, perhaps because he believed too much in Durkheim's (1895) claims and not on what he actually achieved. One essential problem for Durkheim was the role of individual actors and their motives (reasons) (Lukes, 1973: 220–222). Halbwachs already in 1930 documented that "the regularities established by Durkheim were very largely overthrown in the subsequent period..." (Boudon, 1986: 67).

Based on a series of contributions from the end of the 1970s, for instance, from Boudon (1986, 1998), we have a more realistic conception of sociological explanations. All explanations must include choosing and reasoning actors. Durkheim actually included the reasons of actors in his own research practice, often as implicit presuppositions. Due to his scientistic self-interpretation, he was not able to conceptualize such claims (Boudon, 1995). It should be noted that in a discussion of the classics, more can generally be learned from the actual research practices than from their interpretations of such practices. This is not only the case for Durkheim but also holds for Merton and many of his readers. It is a testimony to the strength of scientism in sociology that generations of sociologists have been able to read Merton's splendid article on self-fulfilling prophecies without noting that it was written from the point of view of a normative sociologist. Consider the following:

> The self-fulfilling prophecy is, in the beginning, a *false* definition of the situation evolving a new behavior which makes the originally false conception come *true*...and perpetuates a reign of error...misleading rumor *created* the very conditions of its own fulfillment...Such are the perversities of social logic.
>
> MERTON, 1968: 477, italics in the original

This phenomenon has also been demonstrated in the work and reception of Marx, Freud, and Weber (Kalleberg, 2007: 153). Philosophers, and even social scientists, have often been seduced by the erroneous theory 12 of classic social scientists instead of learning from their research practices.

Merton also tried to master his difficulties with theory 6 by asking descriptive-explanatory questions. He asked why there were no laws in sociology. His answer to this explanatory question about why something is not the case was that sociology was still immature:

> Between twentieth-century physics and twentieth-century sociology stands billions of man-hours of sustained, disciplined and cumulative research. Perhaps sociology is not yet ready for its Einstein because it has not yet found its Kepler – to say nothing of its Newton, Laplace, Gibbes, Maxwell or Planck.
>
> MERTON, 1968: 47

One argument for such an immaturity thesis has been the large number of possible variables that influence human behaviour as well as the ethical restrictions on doing experiments on human beings. This was a typical move in the 1960s (as Inkeles, 1964: 101; Homans, 1967: 103). Homans was even so sure in his metaphysical belief in scientistic determinism that he was willing to regard the most secure, practical, everyday experiences as illusions, such as our freedom to choose between alternatives (ibid).[1] Such deterministic thinking illustrates Popper's claim (1968: 346) that theological determinism (God's laws) was replaced by naturalistic determinism (the laws of nature) in Western academic thinking.

Given Merton's characteristic sociological realism and his being a sociologist of science, one could have expected that he had critically discussed his scientistic arguments and presuppositions. He could have connected to the growing criticism of the scientistic interpretation of sociology, for instance, as developed by Habermas in 1967 (Merton was fluent in German), by Giddens in 1976, or by Boudon in 1982.[2] A common theme among critics involved analyses of scientism as a determinist worldview – what Boudon labelled "sociologism" (see also Skjervheim, 1958; Habermas, 1984: 111–113).[3] The argument was that causal explanations of a specific kind (theory 6) were not feasible in social science. Giddens summarised this argument by noting that scientistic social scientists waiting for Newton and the discovery of social laws were on the wrong station (Giddens, 1976: 13).

Causal questions and causal analysis in line with theory 6 are inadequate to describe and explain social phenomena. Social processes must be analyzed in terms of reasoning and with partly autonomous actors who are located within enabling and constraining structures, institutions, and traditions. The analytical framework may be called cognitivist because of the importance of reasons (Boudon, 1998, 2010; Kalleberg, 2009). Both the identification, documentation, comparison, and explanation of social phenomena require the documentation and understanding of the reasons of actors, be they true or false, moral or immoral, explicated or merely assumed.

---

1   This was paradoxical. We have to do with a rather extreme criticism of everyday individuals from a self-declared, value-free sociologist. - In some quarters today, there is a feeling that the complexity problem is in the process of being solved (see for instance Butz & Torry, 2006: 1898). This has revived expectations about becoming able to fulfill theory 6 requirements, giving new vitality and visibility to traditional scientism and hope for a "causal turn" of the theory 6 type.

2   Merton can be described and explained like other actors being mistaken, be they researchers or not. We would have to focus on reasons and reasoning, and for instance identify what Boudon (1992: viii) calls Simmel-effects, where "the explicit line of argument is contaminated by hidden a priori notions," for instance that explanations have to be causal (theory 6).

3   The Norwegian social philosopher Hans Skjervheim was the first (1958) to introduce such arguments into the international discussion about the recently institutionalized social sciences (see Habermas, 1984: 111–113).

Important Questions and Methodological Contextualism

Our primary challenge as researchers is to ask important questions and make way for new knowledge and worthwhile insight.[4] That requires us not only to ask questions that are of interest from a disciplinary standpoint but also to pose societally relevant questions that are of interest to researchers outside the discipline (Aubert and Vale, 1973: 75–77). Sociology can and should be explicitly developed both as a descriptive and as a normative discipline. Both descriptive and normative research designs result in the same humble end-products through documentation and argumentation *pro et contra*, i.e., words on paper.

What type of substantive questions should then guide us as a research discipline? I present five reflections on this question related to subject matter, data types, analytical perspectives, social relevance, and the collective responsibility for the construction of relevant questions. I discuss the issues as seen from research universities. These institutions have a special responsibility for the development of sociology as a discipline and for the transmission of such an ambition to new generations of sociologists. This is not cryptic advice to dissuade engagement in productive interdisciplinary work. It is rather an effort to identify that which can make our discipline relevant in a multi-disciplinary world that is in need of greater interdisciplinary cooperation.

Guidance can be received from the specific subject matter of a discipline. However, what is the subject matter of sociology? We do not have a sector in a modern society on which to focus, as is the case for economists, political scientists, and education and media scholars. Sociologists conduct research on all sectors of modern society. In this respect, we are similar to historians, archaeologists, anthropologists, and human geographers. However, we are different from these disciplines because we generally focus on contemporary phenomena and on modern societies but do not emphasize underlining location as a core analytical dimension. We identify the relationships among different sectors, institutions, and roles, such as work and family. What happens in one subsystem is influenced by and influences other systems. We should maintain and develop this broad orientation and do more to benefit from this traditional disciplinary breadth.

Some disciplines have developed central elements in their scholarly identity by focusing on certain types of data. Typical examples are economics and the use of quantitative data, anthropology and qualitative data, historians

---

4   I allude, of course, to Max Weber's lecture in 1919, on "Science as a Vocation" (1919/1989: 18). In the original, he expresses the point like this: "...dass das, was bei wissenschaftlicher Arbeit herauskommt, wichtig im Sinn von "wissenswert" sei".

and existing data sources. Other disciplines have focused not only on data but also on how to generate them. Qualitative data and fieldwork are essential elements in the identity of anthropological research. Sociologists should continue to use both qualitative and quantitative data, maintaining a balance between the data types. With regard to qualitative data, we should stimulate more fieldwork and more archival studies to broaden and strengthen the data bases of our studies.

In my opinion, a general analytical, or theoretical, perspective is at the core of sociology as a science. Half a century ago, Mills (1959) labelled this approach "the sociological imagination". Such an imagination takes a triple perspective that requires social phenomenon to be questioned and analyzed with regard to three dimensions: individual actors, the larger social context, and its location in historical processes. It is individuals who act based on their definitions of situations and always in a social and historical context. Obviously, this perspective is much older than the linguistic expression "sociological imagination", as demonstrated by classical contributions from Montesquieu, Adam Smith, de Tocqueville, Marx, Durkheim, and Weber. This perspective could perhaps be even more appropriately called *methodological contextualism*. Much of what is called "theory" by sociologists can be seen as valuable contributions to such a general, open, analytical perspective, such as theory 3 (concepts), theory 5 (empirical generalizations), theory 8 (general social theory), theory 9 (classics), theory 11 (general insights), theory 13 (synthesizing), theory14 (explanation of puzzling phenomena), theory 15 (typologies), theory 16 (Ritzer), and, of course, theory 17 (Marx, Weber, Mills). The openness of the perspective makes it explicit that the intellectual drive stems from the questioning of social reality, not from a causalist theory 6, which expects us to fill holes in context-insensitive, deductive-nomological systems. Methodological contextualism leads us toward the analysis of situated individuals and institutions; theory 6 ambitions lure us in the direction of decontextualized knowledge. To actively use methodological contextualism in the construction of questions is challenging and fruitful for any sociological community.

A *totalizing perspective* was characteristic of the classics, such as Tocqueville, Marx, Weber, and Durkheim. They analyzed the new societies that emerged in the northwestern corner of Europe and in North America as specific modern societies with particular problems and prospects. This perspective has been maintained as a characteristic of sociology. "Alone among the disciplines of social science sociology has retained its relations to problems of society as a whole", Habermas rightly notes (1984: 5). Practitioners of this orientation in our time include Parsons, Merton, Habermas, Luhmann, Rokkan, Eisenstadt, and Mann. This type of work should be stimulated, whether in the form of historical-comparative macro studies or micro studies that are related to larger trends and institutions. One example of this type of work can be seen in analyses of the specific Nordic models of society and in studies of the transformations that are now taking place in Europe. A third could be the topic of multiple modernities, for instance, those focused on the compatibility of Islam with the institutions and cultures of modern societies that are characterized by market economies, democratic governance, rule of law, freedom of religion and belief, freedom of expression, and independent institutions in civil society.

A *historical perspective* was also characteristic of the classics, but it is underdeveloped in contemporary sociology. This lack undermines the intellectual potential of sociology. We can maintain a productive division of labour in relation to the historians, but we nevertheless must analyse the present as history. It is difficult or impossible, for instance, to fully understand the success of the Scandinavian models without understanding the importance of a long Protestant tradition in these cultures. Some of the most fascinating studies in sociology belong to the category of historical sociology, represented for instance by Merton, Tilly, Mann, Habermas, and Skockpol. The use of archives also represents a possibility for critical studies that is underutilized by sociologists. Archives that are opened after 30, 40, or 50 years can make it possible to base descriptions, explanations, evaluations, and alternative pasts on a solid empirical foundation. An interesting example is the work of the so-called revisionist historians, who profit from the Israeli tradition of freeing all types of documents after 30 years (Shlaim, 2009). Their work has contributed to new definitions of the Israeli-Palestinian and Israeli-Arab conflicts. Such work could also have been done by sociologists. It is easier to obtain excellent data about serious conflicts some years after crucial events. Archives are underutilized by sociologists as data sources for grounded, descriptive, and normative studies.

The *individualizing, actor-oriented perspective*, which identifies specific or typical actors in a situation, is essential to understanding the field that is being documented and analysed. This is also the case when we try to understand broad historical transformations, such as the emergence of modern capitalism. In his classic book on the Protestant Ethic, Weber also focuses on specific individuals, such as Benjamin Franklin, to illustrate important, general points. To understand how actors define situations is crucial in producing valid descriptions and convincing explanations. Only individual human beings always act in specific situations and on the basis of a definition of such situations and of course often act on behalf of other people. We do not have macro subjects acting, such as capitalism, Islam, gender or class.

The construction of interesting and relevant questions should be made into a collective, disciplinary task. Scientific work is part of a scientific community that reads, controls, and stimulates each other; this should also characterize the construction of good research questions. A legitimate research question must have a rationale that can be legitimized in the wider community of scholars. Merton talks about "the statement of the reasons that it is worth asking... the rationale states 'the case for' the question in the court of scientific opinion" (1958: xix). As researchers, we should also have an obligation to state these reasons and relate to counter-arguments and suggestions in the relevant scientific community.

Disciplinary influence on the direction of question construction should be based on more than defining sociology as a community of researchers. As with other academic disciplines, sociology is not only a science but also a teaching enterprise, a knowledge base for dissemination and participation in public discourse, and a profession, in the manner of a consultant who works for a client. As a field, sociology is a bundle of such working programs. On the level of the individual sociologist, there is a corresponding fourfold role set, which includes the academic as researcher, teacher, disseminator (public intellectual), and professional expert (Kalleberg, 2010: 199–205, 2014: 259–263). As with any other discipline, these four tasks and activities can be documented, compared, and evaluated as with other empirical phenomena. Norwegian sociology has, for instance, been evaluated both as a science and in terms of education. It has not been evaluated as a means of dissemination or a profession. This should be done, and sociologists should not continue to act as if their discipline is only a science. However, this is not the point of this article; rather, the point is that these other processes of disciplinary inquiry can also stimulate the basic operation of questioning.

Most university academics have experienced how productive impulses can come from teaching and can inspire our research activity. We obtain new ideas when we teach, which includes learning from our students. We may therefore speak about teaching-driven research. This productive interrelationship has been convincingly documented and analyzed as a general phenomenon by Clark (1995). He showed that one of the important conditions that can explain the excellence of American research universities has been their close bundling of teaching and research. Such stimulation can be used more actively today than it has been utilized in many institutions. Those of us who have experienced different types of popularization and participation in public discourses have found that we also learn from those settings and from those with whom we engage in discourse. The same is the case with professional work, for instance, participating in public investigations or working as internal or external consultants. There is a growing body of research that confirms such productive interrelationships (Kalleberg, 2014). In stimulating the disciplinarily driven construction of research questions, we should therefore also make use of the intellectual interplay between sociology as science, teaching, public dissemination, and profession.

References

Aubert, V. and Vale, M. (1973). "Methods and theory in sociology", *International Journal of Sociology*. 3(3/4): 72–109.

Bannister, R.C. (1987). *Sociology and scientism: the American quest for objectivity 1880–1940*. Chapel Hill: The University of North Carolina Press.

Boudon, R. (1982). "Social determinisms and individual freedom", *The unintended consequences of social action*. London: Macmillan.

Boudon, R. (1986). *Theories of social change*. Cambridge, UK: Polity Press.

Boudon, R. (1994). *The art of self-persuasion: the social explanation of false beliefs*. Cambridge, UK: Polity Press.

Boudon, R. (1995). "Should one still read Durkheim's rules after one hundred years? Raymond Boudon interviewed by Massimo Borlandi", *Schweizerische Zeitschrift für Soziologie*. [Swiss Journal for Sociology]. 21(3): 559–573.

Boudon, R. (1996). "The 'cognitivist model': a generalized 'rational choice model'", *Rationality and Society*. 8(2): 123–150.

Boudon, R. (1998). "Limitations of rational choice theory", *American Journal of Sociology*. 104(3): 817–828.

Boudon, R. (2010). "The cognitive approach to morality", Eds. S. Hitlin and S. Vaisey. *Handbook of the sociology of morality*. New York: Springer.

Clark, B. (1995). *Places of inquiry: research and advanced education in modern universities*. Berkeley: University of California Press.

Dahl, R.A. (1985). *A preface to economic democracy*. Berkeley: University of California Press.

Dahl, R.A. (1989). *Democracy and its critics*. New Haven: Yale University Press.

Gadamer, H.-G. (1989). *Truth and method*. 2nd revised edition. London: Sheed & Ward.

Galtung, J. (1969). *Theory and methods of social research*. Oslo: Universitetsforlaget.

Giddens, A. (1976). *New rules of sociological method: a positive critique of interpretative sociologies*. New York: Basic Books.

Habermas, J. (1988) [1967]. *On the logic of the social sciences*. Cambridge, UK: Polity Press.

Habermas, J. (1978). *Knowledge and human interests*. 2nd edition. London: Heineman Educational Books Ltd.

Habermas, J. (1984). *The theory of communicative action*. Vol. 1. Cambridge, MA.: The MIT Press.

Homans, G. (1967). *The nature of social science.* New York: Harcourt, Brace & World.

Inkeles, A. (1964). *What is sociology? An introduction to the discipline and profession.* Englewood Cliffs, N.J.: Prentice Hall.

Kalleberg, R. (1992). *A constructive turn in sociology.* Report 19. University of Oslo: Department of Sociology.

Kalleberg, R. (1996). "Forskningsopplegget og samfunnsforskningens dobbeltdialog", Eds. H. Holter and R. Kalleberg. *Kvalitative metoder i samfunnsforskning.* ["Research design and the double dialogue in social research", Qualitativ methods in social reseach]. Oslo: Universitetsforlaget.

Kalleberg, R. (2005). "Chapters 1–7, 11–12", Eds. F. Engelstad, C.E. Grenness, R. Kalleberg and R. Malnes. *Introduksjon til samfunnsfag. Vitenskapsteori, argumentasjon og faghistorie.* [Introduction to social science. Scientific theory, argumentation and intellectual history]. Oslo: Gyldendal Akademisk.

Kalleberg, R. (2007). "A reconstruction of the ethos of science", *Journal of Classical Sociology.* 7(2): 137–160.

Kalleberg, R. (2009). "Can normative disputes be settled rationally? On sociology as a normative discipline", Ed. R. Boudon. *A life in sociology.* Vol. 2. Oxford, UK: The Bardwell Press.

Kalleberg, R. (2010). "The ethos of science and the ethos of democracy", Ed. C.J. Calhoun. *Robert K. Merton: sociology of science and sociology as science.* New York: Columbia University Press.

Kalleberg, R. (2014). "The role of public intellectual in the role-set of academics", Eds. C. Fleck and A. Hess. *Knowledge for whom? Public sociology in the making.* Surrey: Ashgate Publishing Company.

Kalleberg, R. (2015). "Plagiarism as violation of law in Norway. On inappropriate juridification of research ethics", Eds. N.H. Steneck, M.S. Anderson, S. Kleinert and T. Mayer. *Integrity in the global research arena.* Forthcoming. New Jersey: World Scientific Publishing Company.

Lindblom, C. (1990). *Inquiry and change: the troubled attempt to understand and shape society.* New Haven: Yale University Press.

Lukes, S. (1973). *Émile Durkheim: his life and work: a historical and critical study.* Harmondsworth, UK: Penguin Books.

Lyngstad, T.H. (2009). "Fri flyt av kapital? En kommentar til begrepsbruk i sosiologi og annen samfunnsvitenskap", *Sosiologisk tidsskrift.* ["Free flow of capital? Commenting on the use of concepts in sociology and other social sciences", Journal of Sociology]. 17(03): 261–271.

Merton, R.K. (1970) [1938]. *Science, technology, and society in seventeenth century England.* New York: Howard Fertig.

Merton, R.K. (1957). "The role-set: problems in sociological theory", *British Journal of Sociology.* 8(2): 106–120.

Merton, R.K. (1959). "Notes on problem-finding in sociology", Eds. R.K. Merton, L. Broom and L.S. Cottrell, Jr. *Sociology today: problems and prospects*. New York: Harper Torchbooks.

Merton, R.K. (1968). Part I "On theoretical sociology", "The self-fulfilling prophecy", *Social theory and social structure*. 3rd enlarged edition. New York: The Free Press.

Merton, R.K. (1987). "Three fragments from a sociologist's notebook: establishing the phenomenon, specified ignorance, and strategic research materials", *Annual Review of Sociology*. 131(1): 1–29.

Merton, R.K. (1996). *On social structure and science*. Chicago, Ill.: University of Chicago Press.

Mills, C.W. (1959). *The sociological imagination*. New York: Oxford University Press.

Mintzberg, H. (1979). *The structuring of organizations: a synthesis of the research*. Englewood Cliffs, N.J.: Prentice-Hall.

Popper, K. (1968). *Conjectures and refutations: the growth of scientific knowledge*. London: Routledge and Keegan Paul.

Ritzer, G. (2008). *Sociological theory*. 7th edition. Boston: McGraw-Hill.

Shlaim, A. (2009). *Israel and Palestine: reappraisals, revisions, refutations*. London: Verso.

Skjervheim, H. (1959). *Objectivism and the study of man*. Oslo: Universitetsforlaget.

Weber, M. (1989) [1919]. "Science as a vocation", Eds. P. Lassman, I. Velody and H. Martins. *Max Weber's "Science as a vocation"*. London: Unwin Hyman.

CHAPTER 7

If Not, Why Not and What If: Asking Counterfactual Questions

Göran Ahrne

Why Ask Counterfactual Questions?

A counterfactual is a proposition stating what would have occurred had something not been the case: what would have happened and what would the consequences have been if someone else had secured power or another event had not occurred? According to many historians, the asking of counterfactual questions and the writing of counterfactual histories have become increasingly common and accepted in the discipline in the past twenty years. The most common counterfactual discussions in history relate to war, e.g., the declarations of war or the outcomes of war. One typical counterfactual question asks what would have transpired had the crown prince of Austria not been shot dead in Sarajevo in July 1914: would World War I still have broken out? Other common questions revolve around Adolf Hitler, Nazism and World War II. Regarding the questions of war and peace or the outcomes of battles in a war, the alternatives appear to be unusually obvious; the answer is either war or peace, and there is typically one winner and one loser. In the case of war, counterfactual alternatives are easily recognisable.

As recently as thirty or forty years ago, counterfactual reasoning was not widely accepted in the academic discipline of history. The well-known historian of the Russian revolution, E.H. Carr, suggests that counterfactual thinking is merely playing a parlour game with what might have been (see Weinryb, 2009: 109; cf. Sørensen, 2004: 178). Nevertheless, historian Elazar Weinryb notes that at the beginning of the 21st century, historiographical counterfactuals "seem to be flourishing" (Weinryb, 2009: 109). The general explanation that Weinryb provides for this shift is "a new scepticism towards more general theories and the post-modern critique of grand narratives" (Weinryb, 2009: 110).

In sociology, however, the notion of counterfactual reasoning has attracted little attention, likely because of the character of sociology as a discipline. Sociology tends to be more abstract and less interested in individual events and narratives than historical research. Further, sociologists have clearly not been particularly interested in questions regarding war and peace and the outcomes of wars. Issues regarding war and peace are largely suppressed in sociological theories (Joas and Knöbl, 2013).

Another explanation for the lack of discussion and interest in counterfactual reasoning in sociology is that numerous sociological theories have been rather deterministic, suggesting that social development only moves in one direction. Two dominant theories, modernisation theory and Marxist theory, granted little latitude with regard to counterfactuals because such questions were not considered to be productive. In modernisation theory, counterfactual events were at best regarded as cultural lags. In Marxist theory, counterfactuals such as nationalism or ethnicity were regarded as expressions of false consciousness or hegemonic power that represented obstacles to the anticipated development rather than real alternatives.

At present, the theoretical landscape of sociology is different, offering a broad variety of theories of various types; however, few theories make assertions concerning the direction of social development. A typical expression of this situation in sociological theory is Piotr Sztompka's book, *Society in action*, published in 1991. In this book, social development is above all regarded as "the intermeshed plurality of events". Social change is not

> ...a uniform and unidirectional process, but may change direction, course and speed. It is not viewed as approaching any fixed final goal, but is open-ended and contingent, allowing for alternative scenarios.
>
> SZTOMPKA, 1991: 71

To me, such a description can only be understood as an invitation to counterfactual thinking. As Norwegian historian Øystein Sørensen has suggested, counterfactual reasoning becomes interesting in open historical situations. Such situations are characterised by the existence of at least two potential alternative outcomes with different consequences. This approach also implies that although there are and have been several potential outcomes, the majority of these possibilities have not been realised (cf. Sørensen, 2004: 163).

Counterfactual thinking is relatively common in everyday life. When individuals reflect on their lives, they consider why certain events transpired in a certain way or why life did not meet one's expectations; this reflection encourages counterfactual thinking. Everyday life is replete with missed opportunities and chances that never appear again. Human beings easily imagine that matters could have been different, and one can compare one's situation with that of relatives or friends: if I had not fallen ill on that occasion, if I had not missed the train, if I had chosen another school, if I had not been at the right place at the right time, if I had known what I know now, etc. However, individuals may also blame misfortune and believe that they were the victims of accidents that destroyed their opportunities or altered their course of lives for better or worse.

When theorising about social development, however, sociologists have devoted little attention to such circumstances; events can have different outcomes, and there are alternative ways that things might have been. It is likely easier to think counterfactually concerning smaller social entities such as families, social movements or organisations. Families may experience misfortune and live at the wrong place at the wrong time, as do organisations of various types. However, certain organisations such as political parties or businesses may be fortunate if these organisations happen to be established at an opportune moment. Moreover, states also miss certain opportunities when events could have gone in another direction. For example, a state may lose an opportunity for development because of personal conflicts between politicians. Certain countries may have been at the right place at the right occasion whereas others have not, and it is uncertain whether the latter countries will choose the same route as the former. The social development of a certain state (a "society") or part of a state may take unexpected turns, for better or worse; for example, if oil is discovered in a territory, a state may become involved in a war or may be exploited by tourism.

Although current sociological theories appear to be broad and general, they are often specific in terms of time, place and subject matter. A theory that departs from what has transpired in Europe or in the United States over the past fifty years may have little to contribute to describing the course of events in Asia or in Africa in the coming fifty years.

To theorise about what could have occurred and to assess the generalizability of theories, we must practice theorising as a methodology and perform theoretical operations to combine alternative theories that have something to say about different possible paths that a particular development might have taken. To construct a sociological theory, it is not enough to explain why something happened; one must also explain why something else (that was possible) did not. At present, I believe that it is often valuable to ask counterfactual questions to combine insights and propositions from different theoretical alternatives.

In sociology and the social sciences in general, theories are rarely either true or false; instead, theories are merely different. Rather than being opposites, theories emphasise different factors and processes that lead to divergent outcomes. Sociological theories are highly dependent on their context. For example, although there are numerous theories to explain inequality, none of them is applicable in all situations. Instead, their relevance depends on the context. The most general purpose in applying counterfactual reasoning is to demonstrate that social constructions are more fragile and accidental than we generally presume. There are numerous ways in which social conditions could have been different.

A Realism of Possible Worlds

Counterfactual thinking is not particularly well developed in sociology, perhaps because sociologists generally follow a single theoretical perspective and are rarely interested in comparing theories. We adopt a particular theory and attempt to explain as much as possible even if we are aware that the theory does not explain everything. When the notion of counterfactual reasoning is mentioned, it is usually done in a general way to indicate that "other arrangements were, are or will be possible" (Tilly, 1998: 37). References to counterfactuals are used to indicate that social development is not deterministic; however, the question of how to apply counterfactual reasoning in an analysis is not typically discussed. In this chapter, my aim is to begin such a discussion. To gain inspiration and ideas toward this end, I will first present one of the most developed methodological and philosophical discussions regarding the relevance of counterfactuals.

American philosopher David Lewis (1941–2001) published several books and articles on the use and status of counterfactual thinking in science in general. His first book, *Counterfactuals*, was published in 1973. His second book, published in 1986, is entitled *On the plurality of worlds*, which is also his expression for discussing counterfactuals. In this later book, he devotes substantial energy to responding to some of the criticism that was raised against his first book, while also further developing his perspective. The discussion in the second book demonstrates that it is controversial to consider counterfactual events and possibilities.

Lewis defends his interest in counterfactuals as follows:

> I believe that there are possible worlds other than the one we happen to inhabit. If an argument is wanted, it is this. It is uncontroversially true that things might be otherwise than they are. I believe, and so do you, that things could have been different in countless ways. But what does this mean?.
>
> LEWIS, 1973: 84

In his later book, he explains: "There are ever so many ways that a world might be; and one of these many ways is the way that this world is" (Lewis, 1986: 2). Other worlds are unactualised possibilities (ibid: 5).

He summarises his approach as follows: "I therefore believe in the existence of entities that might be called 'ways things could have been'. I prefer to call them possible worlds" (Lewis, 1973: 84). Lewis' ambition is to develop a type of theory concerning such "possible worlds" and to examine the ways in which this approach could be applied in scientific reasoning. He describes his approach as "a realism of possible worlds" and suggests a counterfactual assertion as "an invitation to consider what goes on in a selected counterfactual situation; which is to say, at some other possible world" (Lewis, 1986: 20–21). In addition, "the other worlds provide a frame of reference whereby we can characterise our world" (ibid: 22). Lewis suggests that the notion of a plurality of worlds is a highly serviceable hypothesis, which is a good reason to believe that it is true (ibid: 3).

In response to an individual who wonders what this is all about, Lewis says:

> I can only ask him to admit that he knows what sort of thing our actual world is, and then explain that other worlds are more things of that sort, differing not in kind but only in what goes on at them. Our actual world is only one world among others.
>
> LEWIS, 1973: 85

Later, he adds that all "possible worlds" have the same logic and arithmetic as our world (ibid: 88). This assertion has nothing to do with science fiction:

> If worlds were creatures of my imagination, I could imagine them to be any way I liked, and I could tell you all you wish to hear simply by carrying on my imaginative creation. But as I believe that there really are other worlds, I am entitled to confess that there is much about them that I do not know, and that I do not know how to find out.
>
> LEWIS, 1973: 88

In his later book, he further notes: "I have no use for impossible worlds on a par with the possible worlds" (Lewis, 1986: 7).

Another question concerns the number of possible worlds and asks why these worlds represent a "plurality of worlds". In his later book, Lewis addresses this question: "The worlds are many and varied…There are so many other worlds, in fact, that absolutely *every* way that a world could possibly be is a way that some world *is*" (Lewis, 1986: 2).

Possible worlds are isolated from one another, and there are no spatiotemporal relations between them. Nor can we say that these worlds are distant from one another or nearby; they are simply different in certain respects,

although they are "of a kind with this world of ours", and the differences between them are not categorical (ibid: 2).

The particularity of this set of all possible worlds is simply that what occurs in them does not occur in our world. Events transpire differently in those
worlds, but not in strange or mystical ways. If we could discover events that
were occurring in them, we would be able to understand. Such events might
even have occurred in our own world, if not... Although the possible worlds are
different from our world, it is their similarity with our world that makes such
differences interesting and possible. By virtue of this similarity, we can regard
them as possibilities (and not as impossibilities) and not preposterous. If the
differences are excessively large, they are also less interesting. To determine
how interesting it is to compare our world with another possible world, we
must consider such similarities and differences as follows:

> Overall similarity consists of innumerable similarities and differences
> in innumerable respects of comparison, balanced against each oth-
> er according to the relative importance we attach to those respects of
> comparison.
>
> LEWIS, 1973: 91

Lewis recognises that it is not always easy to discuss such similarities and
differences. His point is that it is relevant whether these difficulties are "ill
understood" or "vague", and he concludes that the distinction is a matter of
vagueness. For example, regarding the difference between blue and green,
Lewis suggests: "The border between blue and green is not well fixed, so blue
and green are both vague. But their relation to each other is fixed: one begins
where the other leaves off, with no gap and no overlap" (Lewis, 1973: 92).

The discussion of similarities and differences is not unique to comparisons
between possible worlds. We will encounter the same problem, for example,
if we wish to compare cities with one another. Lewis cites the example of a
comparison among Los Angeles, San Francisco and Seattle. Although it is obvious that Seattle resembles San Francisco to a greater extent than it resembles
Los Angeles, the degree to which this assertion is reasonable depends on what
is most important in this comparison, e.g., the climate, public transportation,
architecture or another factor (ibid: 92).

Moreover, Lewis notes, this vagueness also applies to counterfactual
conditions:

> The truth conditions for counterfactuals are fixed only within rough lim-
> its; like the relative importance of respects of comparison that underlie

the comparative similarity of worlds, they are highly volatile matter, varying with every shift of context and interest.

LEWIS, 1973: 92

By examining Lewis's arguments we can understand counterfactual analysis as
a type of comparative research or case studies of possible worlds, with differences from our world. However, these differences are not differences in kind;
a given event could also have occurred in our world. There are also similarities
between our world and the possible worlds. Counterfactual conditions are not
creatures of our imagination or utopias.

However, the world in which we live is only one of these possible worlds.
From this perspective, we can obtain a (wider) frame of reference for understanding the world in which we live. Through this type of comparative research,
we can discuss what circumstances would have been required in our world
for a situation that occurred in another possible world to have transpired in
ours, or what the obstacles to this situation to occurring in our world would be,
for better or for worse. The suggestion that another world is possible does not
necessarily imply that things are "better" in that world; it is possible that they
are simply different. If something was possible there, why was it not possible
here? Moreover, if something is possible here, why is it not possible there? It
is far from certain that the explanation of why something was not possible in
our world is identical to the explanation for its impossibility in another world.

The critical aspect of this type of comparative analysis is how one comes to
understand the other worlds and what one can know about them. How can we
know what other worlds we will observe and use in our comparison? Which
counterfactuals are meaningful and interesting? It is in this respect that theoretical operations may be useful, and we can apply theorising as a methodology to discover possible worlds.

From the beginning of our research, we should be generous in accepting
ideas and conceptions of possible worlds to provide rich material with which
to make our comparisons. However, we must also explain why comparisons are
interesting and avoid the inclusion of impossible worlds, i.e., worlds created
out of sheer imagination, in our comparisons.

In the following discussion, I formulate three counterfactual questions that
differ with respect to how obvious and decided the counterfactual moment is
and whether the alternatives are evident. The first question, "if not", is intended to demonstrate that the decisive moment and the alternatives are comparatively well understood. The majority of the discussion will then concern what
determined the outcome and the likelihood that the consequences would have
been different.

The second question, "why not", begins from a situation in which the outcomes are different but the worlds appeared relatively similar. The question here thus focuses on determining what triggered a differentiation and when it began.

The third question, "what if", is more abstract and therefore more of an analytical exercise. This question concerns what the consequences would be if something in the present world did not exist. A potential aim of asking such a question is to disclose the character and function of a certain institution that is taken for granted and to discover alternatives.

If Not?

Numerous recent discussions and illustrations of counterfactual reasoning in history build on case studies of various sequences of events in wars. Wars appear to have explicit alternatives and winners and losers; moreover, it is comparatively easy to identify decisive moments or moments that could have made a difference. A war is typically perceived as a struggle for power, and it is assumed that the party/army that wins will obtain power and thereby the ability to determine future development. If one army had not won a certain battle, another army would have had the opportunity to change the outcome (at least for a certain period). Øystein Sørensen's book, *Historien om det som ikke skjedde, kontrafaktisk historie* (History about what never happened, conterfactual history), provides a number of such examples: the Battle of Salamis in 480 B.C., the Battle of Poitiers in 732 and the Great Armada in 1588. He also discusses the possibilities of a failed American Revolution in 1777 and the possible alternatives in Norway in 1814.

Another historian, Ian Kershaw, reflects on the readiness to perceive outcomes as necessary:

> In retrospect, what took place seems to have been inexorable. In looking at the history of wars, perhaps even more than at history generally, there is an almost inbuilt teleological impulse, which leads us to presume that the way things turned out is the only way they could have turned out.
> KERSHAW, 2008: 6

Kershaw's book, *Fateful choices: ten decisions that changed the world, 1940–1941*, presents ten case studies of decisions taken by political or military leaders during the beginning of World War II, such as Hitler's decision to attack the Soviet Union or Roosevelt's decision to wage undeclared war. In Kershaw's analysis, a war is regarded from the perspective of decision-makers (military leaders or politicians), examining how events evolve depending on a number of decisions that were not obvious, for which the available information was insufficient and the decision often irrational. However, a decision implies that there are choices, and the decision and its consequences could have been different (Kershaw, 2008: 6; cf. Brunsson, 2009; Ahrne and Brunsson, 2011). If there had not been alternatives with different consequences, we would not be interested in pronouncing certain decisions as more important and significant than others. Without considering counterfactual conditions, we are "unable fully to ascertain the significance of what actually did take place" (Kershaw, 2008: 6).

One of the few sociologists to have considered the question of counterfactual reasoning or "what might have happened if" is Max Weber (1949: 164). In an essay titled "Critical studies in the logic of the cultural sciences. A critique of Eduard Meyer's methodological views", Weber discusses how to adequately analyse what he termed "objective possibilities". Weber departs from an example discussed by Meyer, namely the Battle of Marathon. There were two alternative consequences of the outcome of the war between the Persians and the Greeks, either a victory for a theocratic-religious culture or for the free Hellenic circle of ideas. The victory of the Greeks (Athenians) at the Battle of Marathon was a decisive moment because a Persian victory would have had substantial consequences for the development of what is now Europe. As Weber notes, the fact that the Athenian victory in the Battle of Marathon is perceived as decisive is the only reason that we are historically interested in it (Weber, 1949: 171–172).

Weber's discussion concerns how we can make adequate "judgements of the possibility of the two highly divergent alternatives that existed". His suggestion is that we must "decompose the given into components", and in this respect he discusses abstractions in terms of both the isolation and generalisation of different components (ibid: 173). In the next step, we are asked to attempt to determine what would have happened "when a causal component is conceived as excluded or as modified" (ibid: 175).

Weber's methodological reflections on how to make judgements concerning objective possibilities are summarised in the following paragraph.

> The assessment of the causal significance of an historical fact will begin with the posing of the following question: in the event of the exclusion of that fact from the complex of factors which are taken into account as co-determinants, or in the event of its modification in a certain direction, could the course of events, in accordance with general empirical rules, have taken a direction in any way different in any features which would be *decisive* for our interest?.
>
> WEBER, 1949: 180

Subsequently, Weber also discusses the gradations of objective possibility.

In the course of discussing these matters, Weber also mentions other examples from Meyer concerning decisive events in the history of the unification of Germany during the 19th century. However, the most elaborated example is the Battle of Marathon. Weber's own interpretation of this event is not that a Persian victory would have necessarily led to a substantially different development. Such a judgement would, according to Weber, be quite impossible. "Rather is that significance to be put as follows: that a different development of Hellenic and world culture 'would have' been the *adequate* effect of such an event as a Persian victory" (Weber, 1949: 184–185).

War is an extreme form of a struggle for power over a certain territory. To win a war is a means to obtaining that power. However, there are other ways to gain power. In democratic states, power over a certain territory is gained through political elections in which relatively clear-cut alternatives with different consequences are outlined. Moreover, political elections may be objects of counterfactual analysis. For instance, one might ask what would have happened had Al Gore been elected president of the United States instead of George W. Bush in November 2000. Gore received more popular votes than Bush, but Bush became president because he won the state of Florida by several hundred votes, a result that has been contested. With Gore as president, events would very likely have been rather different, not least in Iraq and the Middle East.

Political elections, similarly to wars, are examples of open conflicts concerning power in which the alternatives are relatively obvious. However, power may be decisive, even in situations in which there are no open conflicts, when individuals simply obey without protesting or attempting to change the division of power.

In his book, *Power, a radical view,* Steven Lukes (1974) advances a theory concerning a three-dimensional view of power that has become highly influential. Lukes defines power in line with Weber and several others as, "saying that A exercises power over B when A affects B in a manner contrary to B's interests" (Lukes, 1974: 34). Such a definition implies that we must be able to express what is in B's interest. According to Lukes, this implication entails the consideration of a relevant counterfactual question regarding what B would have done had she/he not been the object of the exercise of power. If A had not exercised power over B, she/he would have done something else. In cases in which there is an open conflict regarding the exercise of power and who will wield it, we are in a better position to observe the interests of B and the relevant counterfactuals because they are, as Lukes suggests, "ready-made". However, "when there is no observable conflict between A and B, then we must provide other grounds for asserting the relevant counterfactual" (ibid: 41).

To identify situations that contain the exercise of power, we must be able to simultaneously identify some type of relevant counterfactual: what would have happened but for the exercise of power. For example, B's actions if no exercise of power were involved can be understood as an unactualised possibility.

Lukes provides no definitive solution to this requirement. In his book, he discusses a case study regarding air pollution for which the relevant counterfactuals appear relatively clear, i.e., preventing air pollution at a specific factory. However, in general, Lukes also notes certain difficulties in justifying relevant counterfactuals (ibid: 46). Nevertheless, he does not believe that it is excessively complicated:

> We are concerned to find out what the exercise of power prevents people from doing, and sometimes even thinking. Hence we should examine how people react to opportunities – or more precisely, perceived opportunities – when these occur, to escape from subordinate positions in hierarchical systems.
>
> LUKES, 1974: 48

In a new chapter in the second edition of his book, he adopts a more philosophical attitude toward the problem of identifying counterfactuals and contends, citing Spinoza, that there are always some types of resistance to power. Further, he criticises Herbert Marcuse and his notion of the one-dimensional man: "Power's third dimension is always focused on particular domains of experience and is never, except in fictional dystopias, more than partially effective" (Lukes, 2005: 150). To observe the exercise of power, we must seek out unactualised possibilities.

Why Not?

A counterfactual is an idea concerning something that could have been realised but never was, an objective possibility that never occurred in our world. When we ask why something did not happen, we proceed from an assertion, perhaps a theory or a casual observation, that it has occurred in some places or in some other possible world, and we attempt to explain why the same thing did not transpire in our world.

We can construct and observe a possible world in which an event did occur, but we must also motivate our interest concerning why it did not happen here, i.e., why we expected it to happen. Even if the reason for comparing different possible worlds were their present differences, our interest would most likely need to be grounded in a perceived previous similarity that made us presume that the worlds could nevertheless be similar. This operation is simultaneously a theoretical one, perceiving what is missing from a theory that may explain one outcome but cannot explain another. The theory may not be entirely incorrect but must be complemented; why is this theory helpful in one possible world but not in another?

When we ask why not, we are unaware of what constitutes the decisive moment that made a difference and do not know when this moment occurred. It is not a question of who won a certain battle or another type of open conflict. We seek to discover when the decisive moment occurred that triggered another chain of events.

One early, well-known example of a study that begins with the question of "why not" is the essay, "Why is there no socialism in the USA?" written by Werner Sombart in 1906. From a general Marxist perspective, it appeared odd that there was no strong socialist party in the most developed capitalist country at the beginning of the 20th century. The core of Sombart's response to his own question is based on an analysis of the political system in the United States and its effects on the political position of the working class. Because of the early development of formal democracy and nearly universal male suffrage in the early 19th century, a rather flexible two-party system had been established. This system differed from the majority of states in Europe, where the socialist parties were also pioneers in the struggle for political rights. In the United States, however, the prevailing two-party system was also able to mobilise many working-class votes (Sombart, 1976).

This explanation for the absence of a socialist party in the USA may, in turn, be used to complement theories that directly explain the socialist parties in European countries from a class perspective. The establishment of political parties cannot be explained by the formation of social classes alone but is also dependent on factors such as the parliamentary systems and the temporality of the establishment of other political parties. When one asks "why not" and not only why, one will be able to observe different objects. The answer to the question "why not" need not be the opposite of the answer to the question "why".

A much later study considers the question "Why is there no soccer in the United States?" (Markovits, 1988). The answer provided is as follows. In the middle of the 19th century, football was played with different and rather fluid rules in public schools and colleges in both England and the USA. Football was organised and codified in both countries in the 1860s but with different rules. For this reason, there was no room for English soccer in the USA despite it being the type of football that became common in nearly the entire world.

The early development of American football prevented the introduction of soccer, which was "crowded out", similarly to the way in which the socialist parties were crowded out by the early democratic development in the United States.

In another example, the question "Why is there no clientelism in Scandinavia?" is perhaps somewhat surprising because there is no theory that would predict the existence of clientelism in Sweden or any other Scandinavian country. This question is examined in a comparative study of Sweden and Greece by Apostolis Papkostas (2001, 2012). The question, however, is motivated by the observation of prior similarities between Sweden and Greece. In the 18th and 19th centuries, there were important tendencies towards particularism in Sweden and towards universalism in Greece, and the countries were more similar at that time than they are at present (Papkostas, 2012: 85). The development of a clientelistic system in Greece cannot be explained by ancient cultural traditions. What triggered the different chains of events in Sweden and Greece is instead related to the relationship between the development of political democracy and the state. In Greece, political democracy, in a sense, developed much earlier than in Sweden, whereas the development of the state apparatus was relatively weak. Conversely, in Sweden, the state apparatus was well developed before democracy was introduced. In Greece, the early political democratisation allowed for clientelistic practices, whereas these practices were hindered in Sweden because of the strong development of the state and its direct relationships with its citizens before the introduction of a parliamentary and democratic political system.

All of these examples may be regarded as comparative studies. The question of why not is raised in these cases by the combinations of similarities and differences. In all cases, the researcher had expected the cases to be similar, but the absence of such similarities led to the question of why not.

However, concerning the processes of globalisation, it is difficult to work with real case studies. When all cases are connected in some manner, and ideas and concepts are available worldwide, it is difficult to identify isolated cases to compare. Therefore, in studies of globalisation, one must discover one's own possible worlds to be able to make comparisons. This is the case, for instance, when John Meyer and Patricia Bromley analyse the worldwide expansion of the concept of "organisation". In their discussion of how the idea of organisation is spread and applied in the contemporary world, these researchers invent a "possible world" as a means of comparison.

> In an alternative world society – one built around central imperial structures, say – the changes we discuss in the rest of this article would take

radically different forms. Overall "organisation" as we know it would be a less central form of social structure.

MEYER and BROMLEY, 2013: 369

In this alternate modern universe, fewer soft law forms of governance and ways of accounting for the value of an activity would exist because the state could, by directive, specify desired outcomes.

MEYER and BROMLEY, 2013: 373

To make their analysis more convincing and interesting, a counterfactual serves as a useful frame of reference and a reminder that the present state of things is not necessary and another world is possible. Although the possible world that Meyer and Bromley consider is not directly a theoretical construction, this world appears to be reasonable and may be accepted by the majority of readers as a plausible alternative.

To analyse the processes of globalisation, I have also found it useful to compare an actual development with another objective possibility or a possible world. In this project, we asked ourselves: why are there no global political parties? This question was provoked by the observation that all types of organisations, from churches and sports clubs to multi-national corporations and professional associations, are becoming global actors. Even numerous families are global. Although global political organisations such as Amnesty International and Greenpeace exist, there are no global political parties.

If we aim to understand the processes of globalisation, we cannot simply consider those actors that succeed in becoming global. To understand what globalisation implies and how it changes social life, we must also understand and observe what is missing from this process and what is lost; we have to ask "why not" and not merely "why".

Our answer is that political parties are inherently local organisations. Nearly all of their activities pertain to local issues, and these parties are engaged in solving local problems for their members and sympathisers. Although liberal or socialist political parties in many parts of the world share the same ideology, they are deeply embedded in local or national political systems and struggles and therefore experience significant difficulties in cooperating with other parties sharing the same ideology through organisations such as Socialist International or Liberal International (Ahrne and Sörbom, 2015). This difference in preconditions between political parties and numerous other types of organisations was not evident before the massive growth of globalisation that has been observed over the past thirty or forty years. In a possible world with global political parties, the differences between the various parts of the world might not be as substantial as they are in our world.

What If?

A third type of question, what if, takes yet another step away from the questions of if not and why not in terms of the visibility of the alternative scenarios. With the question "what if", I wish to highlight a third way of asking a counterfactual question that is more abstract and more of a thought experiment than the previous two questions. However, it is still a matter of constructing another possible world. The motivation for this question is to attempt to determine what would occur if something that is regarded as essential in our world were to disappear: what would be lost, what could come instead, or could we simply do without it? The central purpose behind such a question may be to attempt to identify an aspect of a certain type of institution or organisation that is taken for granted in the present to analyse its role. What does a possible world look like without this institution?

To the best of my knowledge, one of the very few studies that ask "what if" is the 1971 book *Hvis skolen ikke fantes* (If there were no schools) by Norwegian criminologist Nils Christie. The work immediately gained substantial attention throughout Scandinavia and succeeded in shedding new light on the growing school system. A review of this book states that Christie's primary aim was to make readers "start questioning their most cherished beliefs, and in this I think he succeeds" (Johansson, 1973).

To use Weber's words, the method applied by Christie in this book is to decompose what the school actually does into several different components, examining why certain actions are performed by the school system and whether schools could be organised in other ways.

Christie identifies at least three main functions of a school. First, a school provides a place for children to spend their days, a place where they are watched and supervised. This function has become increasingly important over the 150 years that a compulsory school system has existed because children are no longer needed anywhere else.

Another function of schools is to stratify society. In schools, children are graded and classified into different social strata. Because these two functions have increased in importance throughout the expansion of the school system, schools' third function (the transmission of knowledge and skills) is less effective and substantially hampered by the other functions. Many of the officially proposed aims of the school cannot be fulfilled through its present organisation and could be organised in much more effective ways were they not combined with or dependent upon the other functions.

In the absence of the school system, the functions that Christie identified could be performed in other ways. In the book, Christie discusses other possible means of organising and implementing the transmission of knowledge and learning if there were no schools.

Asking "what if" is a means of discussing what could occur if some element in a social structure were excluded, analysing the element's functions and the extent to which these functions could be served in alternative ways. One can easily imagine other similar studies of institutions, including prisons, the military or banks: what would be the outcome if there were no prisons, if there were no armies, or if there were no banks?

Some Conclusions

Counterfactual questions can serve as a theoretical operation to compare theories and to understand how they may strengthen instead of contradicting one another. In the present state of social theory, I believe that counterfactual analysis is a useful method of addressing a situation in which we encounter a number of theoretical approaches. We should not first ask whether a theory is true or false but instead consider under what circumstances the theory would be meaningful and vice versa. Theories are rarely complete; they are typically only partial. Although a theory may be valid in certain circumstances, these circumstances might not be explained by the same theory. The reasons why a theory is valid might be explained by another theory.

When social change is perceived as a series of events instead of evolutionary directions or teleological paths, we need counterfactual reasoning to discuss what possibilities exist and why certain possibilities were not realised. A social event generally includes several components and episodes that may be attached to different theoretical packages. Theories are intertwined in real events. To discuss what could have transpired, we can search for possible worlds using theoretical operations.

In counterfactual analysis, social structures are not totalities; instead, they emerge through the interconnection of parts. Small elements become more important and may have significant consequences. As Weber suggests, we must decompose the given into components and analyse the extent to which the exclusion or modification of a given fact would have changed the course of events. How social elements are connected cannot be taken for granted; we must consider how these elements interact in time and space in varying sequences (cf. Tilly, 1984).

Counterfactual reasoning is not a theoretical operation designed to predict the future or permit change in the world; instead, it is a method for better understanding the world that we currently inhabit. If we are aware that events could have been different, but are not, we will obtain a better understanding of why things are as they are than if we believe that things could not have been different. In addition to knowing why things are as they are, we also know why things are not different. One theory may explain why something occurs, whereas another theory may explain why something else did not occur. We must rely on both theories to understand the present situation.

References

Ahrne, G. and Brunsson, N. (2011). "Organisation outside organisations: the significance of partial organisation", *Organisation.* 18(1): 83–104.

Ahrne, G. and Sörbom, A. (2015). *The organization of global politics.* Forthcoming 2015.

Brunsson, N. (2009). *The consequences of decision-making.* Oxford: Oxford University Press.

Christie, N. (1971). *Hvis skolen ikke fantes.* [If there were no schools]. Oslo: Universitetsforlaget.

Joas, H. and Knöbl, W. (2013). *War in social thought: Hobbes to the present.* Princeton: Princeton University Press.

Johansson, L. (1973). "Review of Hvis skolen ikke fantes", *Acta Sociologica.* 16(1): 65–67.

Kershaw, I. (2008). *Fateful choices: ten decisions that changed the world, 1940–1941.* London: Penguin Books.

Lewis, D. (1973). *Counterfactuals.* Oxford: Blackwell Publishers.

Lewis, D. (1986). *On the plurality of worlds.* Oxford: Blackwell Publishing.

Lukes, S. (1974). *Power: a radical view.* London: The Macmillan Press Ltd.

Lukes, S. (2005). *Power: a radical view.* 2nd edition. The original text with two major new chapters. Basingstoke: Palgrave Macmillan.

Markovits, A.S. (1988). "The other American exceptionalism – why is there no soccer in the United States?", *Praxis International.* 8(2): 125–150.

Meyer, J.W. and Bromley, P. (2013). "The worldwide expansion of organisation", *Sociological Theory.* 31(4): 366–389.

Papakostas, A. (2001). "Why is there no clientelism in Scandinavia?", Ed. S. Piattoni. *Clientelism, interests and democratic representation: the European experience in historical and comparative perspective.* Cambridge: Cambridge University Press.

Papakostas, A. (2012). *Civilising the public sphere: distrust, trust and corruption.* Basingstoke: Palgrave Macmillan.

Sombart, W. (1976). *Why is there no socialism in the United States?*. New York: M.E. Shape, Inc.

Sztompka, P. (1991). *Society in action: the theory of social becoming*. Cambridge: Polity Press.

Sørensen, Ø. (2004). *Historien om det som ikke skjedde. Kontrafaktisk historie*. [History about what never happened. Counterfactual history]. Oslo: H. Aschehoug & Co.

Tilly, C. (1984). *Big structures, large processes, huge comparisons*. New York: Russell Sage Foundation.

Tilly, C. (1998). *Durable inequality*. Berkeley, L.A.: University of California Press.

Weber, M. (1949). "Critical studies in the logic of the cultural Sciences. A critique of Eduard Meyer's methodological views", Trans. and eds. E.A. Shils and H.A. Finch. *The methodology of the social sciences*. New York: The Free Press.

Weinryb, E. (2009). "Historiographic counterfactuals", Ed. A. Tucker. *A companion to the philosophy of history and historiography*. Oxford: Wiley-Blackwell.

CHAPTER 8

Abduction – Assessing Fruitfulness and the Construction of Scientific Concepts

Roar Hagen

Introduction

Is there a specific logical inference that leads to the discovery of new phenomena? Abduction claims to be exactly that – the only research logic that enables scientific discovery. Possessing a method for discovering new knowledge would certainly be something of an "epistemological dream" (Wolenski, Sintonen and Niiniluoto, 2004: 205). However, scepticism prevails. The default position is that the function of science is to establish truth for new phenomena but also that discovery itself is not a part of science. The issue that divides the waters is how to conceptualise the role of scientific concepts in the research process.

The classical conception is of science as representation, of mind and science as mirrors of nature (Rorty, 1979). Empirical reality exists "out there", and the task of science is to present an accurate picture or theory "in here". Science operates like a searchlight, revealing things beyond the horizon or below the surface – ultimately, a surface of ignorance and superstition. The researcher operates like Columbus and discovers new continents, organisms, particles or a new type of solidarity. This received view is not limited to the natural sciences. Qualitative research may also produce its own type of positivism (Hagen, 2002). There is a different ontology of the social – meaning versus things – and because the research objective is different, the methods must be different. However, the relation to reality is the same. Traditional presentations of qualitative research methods assert that studies can capture the meaning humans ascribe to things (Snape and Lewis, 2003; Denzin and Lincoln, 2013). In both cases, the task of scientific concepts is to register and report, and induction is the favoured research logic.

This positivist stance is epistemologically naive. At present, it is widely accepted by both natural and social scientists that empirical observations are already imbued with concepts (Cassirer, Bachelard, Peirce, Popper, Kuhn, Parsons, etc.). There is no empirical observation without concepts, and science can only observe those things for which it has a concept. Scientific concepts therefore play an active role in scientific discovery. To register new phenomena, science requires new concepts, and to understand how discoveries are made, we must comprehend how science creates concepts and applies them to empirical research.

There are two main positions regarding this double relationship. Reichenbach (1938) and Popper (1959) famously distinguish between the context of discovery and the context of justification. According to these authors, only the latter belongs to science, and Popper entirely attributes creativity to the idiosyncrasies of the researcher who derives the new idea or concept. From this perspective, creativity cannot be combined with logic, and theoretical innovations must occur outside of science. What science can do is deduct hypothetical assumptions concerning reality and test the concept or theory against the data.

Deduction has become a standard procedure in the sciences. However, conceptual analysis is also considered to be a normal and necessary part of the research process. The dominant self-understanding of the contemporary social sciences is a self-emblazoned, post-positivist theory of science (Joas and Knöbl, 2009; Alexander, 1985; Aakvaag, 2008). A critique of the positivist epistemology allows for reflection on the function of concepts in the research process. Nevertheless, the post-positivist account of sociological theory appears to encounter severe difficulties in precisely demonstrating how scientific concepts relate to empirical research. While there is an abundance of literature on empirical research methodologies, there are few methods for the construction of scientific concepts. Those that do exist are confined to a particular theoretical perspective or tradition, such as grounded theory. The research logic of abduction might be helpful in achieving this goal of obtaining an improved understanding of the function of scientific concepts in the research process.

A Third Research Logic

The notion of a third type of inference in addition to induction and deduction has a long history in science and is presumably first found in Aristotle. The recent scientific discourse relies heavily on Charles Sander Peirce, who first coined the term abduction. At the core of this discussion is a particular quotation from Peirce. Abduction, Peirce asserted, differs from deductive and inductive inferences. It moves from an explanation-requiring observation to an explanation-yielding hypothesis through the following pattern (Peirce, 1960: 117):

> The surprising fact, C, is observed;
> But if A were true, C would be a matter of course,
> Hence, there is reason to suspect that A is true.

Deduction, and/or possibly induction, establishes the surprising fact C, but how does science discover the phenomenon A that would account for C and make it part of the known universe, something normal? This task requires a research logic of its own. In some instances, Peirce called it abduction and in others, retroduction, without making a clear distinction between the two. In the subsequent scientific discourse, certain researchers have settled on abduction (Swedberg, 2012; Josephson and Josephson, 1994; Bertilsson, 2007) and others on retroduction (Glynos and Howarth, 2007; Bhaskar, 1979; Harré, 1972) to explain how science discovers and establishes the truth of new phenomena. Norman Blaikie (2007), for his part, treats abduction and retroduction as two different logics of discovery. He regards abduction as being specific to the social, while retroduction tends towards the natural sciences.

Thus far, no consensus has emerged regarding what abduction or retroduction implies for the research process with respect to scientific operations or "theorising". Perhaps, obtaining a research logic for scientific discovery is ultimately merely a sweet dream? My belief, however, is based on the assumption that making discoveries is a regularity, and scientists create concepts to make discoveries. To abduct, in a sense, is a matter of course. Nonetheless, we lack the concepts to describe and therefore have sufficient awareness of how we conceptualise. Instead of deeply engaging with the specific literature on abduction or retroduction, I will attempt to observe the processes social scientists follow when they create conceptual frameworks that inform empirical research.

My argument will be that abduction and retroduction are two distinct research logics that denote two different sets of scientific operations and that both are necessary to make discoveries. To explain C, we require a new concept for the phenomenon A, and abduction concerns creating new scientific concepts (Hagen, 1999, 2006). However, obtaining the new concepts is a necessary but insufficient condition for making scientific discoveries. We must apply the new concept in the empirical analysis and "test" it against reality. The research logic of retroduction guides this component of the research process, together with induction and deduction.

We must distinguish between the phenomenon A and the scientific concept of A. Scientific concepts are not true or false, but more or less fruitful, more or less conductive to making statements concerning empirical phenomena that can be either true or false. The quotation from Peirce above confounds the two research logics, and the subsequent theoretical discourse has been unable to disentangle the two aspects of the research process they denote. However, for the various operations of the research process to proceed in a rational manner, the different research logics must be clearly distinguishable. The aim of this chapter is to both separate and relate the two to each other, although the focus is on abductive reasoning. To accomplish this task, we must take issue with certain epistemological and ontological conventions found in current theories of science.

Limitations of Post-positivism

Our task is to understand how scientists make discoveries and the role that scientific concepts play in that endeavour. How do we achieve this aim? Certainly not simply by reading the scientific literature. That approach would lie within the confines of the mirror perspective on science. Knowing that scientific concepts enable empirical observations, we can assume that they can also be obstacles. We might then read, for instance, the post-positivist literature in an attempt to identify those concepts that make it difficult for practitioners of this perspective to observe actual abductions performed by other social scientists.

A promising data source for this investigation comes from Jeffrey Alexander (1985) via Hans Joas and Wolfgang Knöbl (2009). Alexander's work is the last substantial attempt at disclosing a theoretical logic in sociology. Joas and Knöbl (2009) build on Alexander's research and are more reflective and ambitious in evaluating and synthesising theories than comparable textbooks, which are more descriptive. It is also widely used in courses on sociological theory.

According to these authors, sociological theory is situated between two external environments – the metaphysical and the empirical. Closest to the metaphysical environment is the most abstract element of sociological theory, the ontology of the social. Closest to the empirical environment are the most concrete elements, observations. All of the other elements of theory are ordered along this continuum of degrees of abstractness.

Theory as a means of relating empirical and metaphysical environments stretches in both directions and can approach, but never ultimately reach, either. At each end, there is a severance. This distance between the system and environment is fundamental. By distancing itself, sociological theory establishes autonomy with respect to both empirical research and the philosophical tradition. Distance allows for creativity and constitutes the post-positivist dimension of science. If science could directly link to the environment, scientific events would be caused by events in the environment, and there would be no freedom. How, then, does sociological theory use its space of freedom to address its own elements?

Both Alexander (1985) and Joas and Knöbl (2009) experience difficulty in precisely explaining how the different elements of the research process relate to one another. Their epistemological position is one of declared vagueness. The core of post-positivist epistemology is that it is impossible to make empirical observation in the absence of theory or concepts. Consequently, it is *also* "impossible to draw a strict dividing line between the levels of theoretical and empirical knowledge" (Joas and Knöbl, 2009: 10–11). Empirical research is impossible without theory, and empirical and theoretical research presuppose one another. However, they cannot say how.

Instead, Joas and Knöbl frame the research questions for conceptual analysis in typical philosophical fashion. They contend that the theoretical development of the social sciences can be understood as revolving around three very specific questions, namely: "What is action?"; "What is social order?"; and "What determines social change?" (Joas and Knöbl, 2009: 18). Here, "what" refers not to empirical reality, as in the empirical research question "what is the case", but to the metaphysical environment and an inquiry into the true nature or essence of things. At least implicitly, these authors hold the untenable epistemological position that conceptual analysis can somehow establish direct and unmediated contact with at least the metaphysical environment and reveal, for instance, the true nature of social action.

Presumably, conceptual analysis can proceed independently from empirical research. Significantly, observation is believed to be closest to the empirical environment, whereas general presuppositions concerning social reality are at the greatest distance from the empirical.

Epistemological Constructivism

Post-positivism creates space for theoretical reflection within social science. That is an important accomplishment. The limitation of those reflections on theory subsumed under the term "post-ism" is that they end in confusion with respect to what is theoretical and what is empirical. But must we accept "the ultimate impossibility of drawing a clear dividing line between empirical and theoretical knowledge"? That depends on what we mean by the word "clear", which ultimately returns us to the concept of observation.

Presumably, the distinction would be clear if we were to discover a method to sort the data according to whether they match reality, independent of theory. Clarity, apparently, implies that it would be possible for an observer to have unmediated access to the empirical environment. Post-positivism admits that this situation is impossible, but it also cannot conceive of another possibility. Post-positivism, therefore, has not transcended but remains informed by and tied to positivism in its conception of observation. This is expressed in figure 8.1, which places observation closest to the empirical environment, as if observation were established by sense impressions.

Currently, the rival view, which conceives of observation not as representation but as construction, is ascending. The critique of positivist epistemology can be extended when we understand that the dependence of empirical observations on theory is not a fault or problem; on the contrary, theory is the condition that enables empirical observations. It is because one is blind that one can see, to borrow a phrase from Niklas Luhmann (1990). Without a blind spot, one literally cannot see anything. In other words, the observing system constructs what it sees. Reflection on epistemological issues leads to an *epistemological constructivism*: Reality is in the eye of the beholder.

We may now provide a new and formal definition of observation as distinction. According to Spencer-Brown (1969) and Shiltz (2009) observation is the unity of distinction and indication. A distinction divides the world into marked and unmarked states. The observer uses the distinction to indicate something that becomes observable. The other side of the distinction remains occluded. Moreover, the distinction itself is unobserved: The observer cannot simultaneously use and observe the distinction. To observe an initial distinction, one needs another distinction, a so-called second-order observation. The second-order observation is used to observe the first observation and to identify the distinction that grounds it. This second-order observation also cannot observe

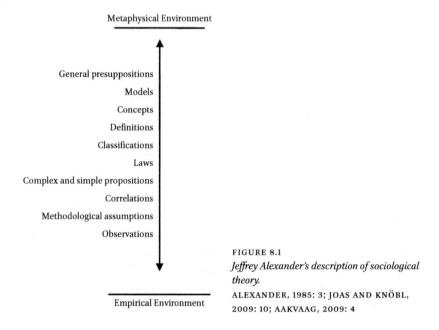

FIGURE 8.1
Jeffrey Alexander's description of sociological theory.
ALEXANDER, 1985: 3; JOAS AND KNÖBL, 2009: 10; AAKVAAG, 2009: 4

itself and has its own blind spot. This observing of observations requires time and perhaps a third-order observation.

The view that every observer creates its own world does not imply a denial of the existence of an independent external reality, merely that the observer has no direct access to it. The claim for this constructivist concept of observation is not "match", but "fit" (Glasersfeld, 1995: 114). Epistemological constructivism is not identical to idealism. Rather, ideas – and even consciousness – become external to an observer, and the observing system creates a more-or-less accurate picture of them. It is precisely this distinction between reality and the observer's construction of that reality that is conductive to our task of creating new foundations for social science.

We may now ask *how* the observer creates an image of the world – by which distinctions? What type of construction is scientific knowledge; how are theories of societies developed and how can we determine if a theory is more or less fitting? To answer such questions, we must shift from epistemological to *methodological constructivism* (Hagen and Gudmundsen, 2011; Hagen, 2006), from a philosophical account of how knowledge is possible to analysing how science observes reality, and establish guidelines for deconstructing and constructing theories concerning society.

Theories of Society and General Theory

Science is a special type of observer that claims empirical truth for its observations. As with any observer, science does not have direct access to the environment. A researcher cannot eschew a theoretical framework and instead observe and compare one or more theories directly from the perspective of reality. Observation already implies scientific concepts. Science, therefore, must observe its relationship to the environment through itself. Science employs scientific theory and concepts to make empirical observations and applies scientific theory and concepts to observe its empirical observations. To obtain this ability, sociology has developed the distinction between *general theory* and *theories of society*.

Theories of society concern social phenomena and have empirical references. They may address a part of society or attempt to account for all things social. In any case, the theory makes statements about the world that can be judged as empirically true or false. General theories, however, are systems of concepts, in the sense that the concepts refer to and define one another. Scientific concepts are not true or false but more or less fruitful. The distinction between general theory and theory of society replaces the distinction between metaphysical and empirical environments. Science only has one external environment, which is reality.

There are several suggestions for how to create order and classify theories. Gabriel Abend (2008), for instance, identifies seven basic types. My proposal does not replace these other ways of discussing theory. The goal is to observe the distinction between theories of society and general theory within existing classifications. As an alternative to theories of society, one could speak of a diagnosis of the present or theories of modern society in opposition to theories of pre-modern or postmodern societies. A theory of society can concern the entirety of society, all stages and social developments, an aspect of society, or even miniscule accounts of encounters between small numbers of individuals. In any event, the theory addresses society, its statements are either true or false, and the theory can be tested against social reality. In brief, a theory of society has empirical references. This is a characteristic of three of the seven types of theories in Abend's (2008) classification.

General theory is a more contested concept. Its poor reputation is in part due to its association with "the general law paradigm", because it is based on the ontology of naturalism, but also because it is a result of Talcott Parsons' striving for a single general theory for sociology. However, the suggested alternative of middle-range theories also appears to fail to solve the problem. Every theory is a generalisation, and every empirical observation is an abstraction. Instead of distinguishing between more-or-less general theories of society, I suggest considering whether a theory is more or less *comprehensive,* and this approach has attained wide usage. We may then reserve "general" for the most general theoretical construct – i.e., general, not as a question of degree, but as the universal; namely, the system of scientific concepts. The concept of action should apply to all empirical investigations of actions, and the concept of system should cover every empirical observation of social systems that fall under this particular definition of action and system. Scientific concepts and theories are the object of study in three of the four remaining types in Abend's classification, whereas the final type has a fundamentally normative component associated with social and not necessarily sociological theory.

In sociology, theories are assigned names, and these personalised theories are often combinations of both types of theory. Anthony Giddens' (1984) structuration theory is his general theory that is applied to empirical research and generates a more-or-less comprehensive theory of modern society. Both Luhmann and Habermas created conceptual systems and applied these general theories to empirical studies. Fararo (2001) demonstrated how an analytical perspective, school or theoretical tradition may place varying degrees of emphasis on either type of theory. Parsons did both, whereas Homans' contribution was primarily to general theory and had little to offer to a theory of society. Michael Mann (1986) contributed extensively to a comprehensive theory of society but assigned little weight to the presentation and discussion of the central concepts.

Abduction – General Theory and Conceptual Analysis

The distinction between general theory and theory of society enables both the observation of empirical reality and the self-observation of science. But how does general theory more precisely relate to empirical research, and how are theories of society used to inform the construction of scientific concepts? My suggestion is that the process of constructing concepts is guided by the research logic of abduction and follows the steps indicated in the quotation from Peirce presented at the beginning of the chapter.

The first step is observing the surprising fact C. Surprise is only possible because one has expectations. In the case of science, this situation can arise because the existing systems of concepts enable the researcher to generate data concerning a phenomenon that cannot be accounted for within the same conceptual framework. Allow me to provide two examples. Suppose that we are viewing a television program on mycology. The mycologist and the reporter are inspecting the forest floor. Suddenly, the mycologist bends down and exclaims, "Look, here is a new specimen". The reporter and the public, of course, see nothing in particular.

The second example comes from my own research. I observed that individuals refer to collective consequences when they offer reasons for their actions. For "lay people", such behaviour is common, and it is a frequent element in public discourse. Only the trained sociologist can regard this behaviour as an anomaly, as sociological theory only provides two reasons for action: self-interest and a normative orientation (Hagen, 1999). The consequences of an action for a group or for society do not play a role in the sociological explanation of actions that produce collective goods.

In both cases, the researcher cannot explain – or understand – the observation and must now turn away from the empirical analysis, examine the general theory in greater detail and scrutinise the conceptual toolbox. The mycologist returns to the laboratory with his sample to perform tests and consult the literature. The next step in abductive inference is, according to Peirce, to establish the phenomenon A, which if it were true, would make C a matter of course. We surmise, however, that Peirce, in the quotation presented above, mistakes two scientific operations for one. We must distinguish between creating the new concept A and establishing the truth of the phenomenon to which it refers. The first operation of constructing concepts, again, consists of several sub-operations, and each can be designated by a particular concept that is helpful in organising the conceptual analysis.

The basic inventory consists of *framework, model, epistemic obstacle, residual categories, rationale* and *ontology*. The framework is general theory applied to a particular empirical research project. The research design includes the use of scientific concepts to develop a model of the phenomena to be investigated. The surprising and unaccounted for observation C actualises the distinction between model and phenomena, and the researcher realises that the model is deficient. To understand why, one must analyse or decompose the model, and the distinction between model and framework is helpful for this deconstruction. The framework consists of the concepts employed to develop the model and, eventually, of all other concepts applied in the empirical analysis of the actual phenomenon.

The framework is also a general theory. The conceptual framework no longer denotes particular things or social phenomena, as when applied in the model, and can be regarded as a system of concepts. One recognises that the framework does not comprise the concepts of phenomenon A that would explain C. Scientific concepts are often characterised as the toolbox of a discipline, and the tools used to account for the A that would explain C are lacking. The metaphor of toolbox, however, might be inadequate to describe how the tools presuppose one another and can only be jointly applied in a certain order. Concepts define one another. This systematic character of the general theory is key to conceptual analysis.

Several criteria are applied in the evaluation of conceptual systems: volume or scale (indicating the number of concepts composing a general theory), logical consistency, economy (parsimony), aesthetics and fruitfulness. I will focus on fruitfulness because this criterion most directly connects general theory to empirical analysis. It is also the least developed. Although it is often held that scientific concepts are not true or false, but more or less fruitful, the literature on how to determine fruitfulness is scant. However, the following appears to be clear: Fruitfulness refers to problems in the empirical analysis resulting from the conceptual framework. Concepts that make the empirical analysis difficult are less fruitful, whereas concepts that solve problems encountered during the empirical analysis are more fruitful.

To isolate and locate both types of candidates, we can consider concepts in terms of epistemic obstacles and residual categories or concepts. Because concepts enable empirical observations, they might also hinder empirical research. By creating the term *epistemic obstacle*, Gaston Bachelard intended to

locate concepts that impede empirical analysis (Tiles, 1984). Residual categories are preliminary concepts and constructions that replace or compensate
for such obstacles (Alexander, 1987). Concepts are considered residual because
their introduction is made ad hoc, without complete logical integration into
the system of scientific concepts. Talcott Parsons (1968), for instance, sought to
identify a normative orientation of action in the works of authors as diverse as
Durkheim, Weber and Pareto and then developed this residue into the central
component of his concept of the unit act.

This example indicates where the roots of epistemic obstacles can be
located – namely, in ontology. If the logical structure of the general theory is
impeccable, the obstacle is located at the end of the logical chain. General assumptions serve to ground the theoretical edifice. Thus, the ontology of the
social supplies the foundation for sociological theory. Ontology is foundational
because it supplies the rationale for relating concepts to one another and to
empirical research. The selection of basic assumptions has consequences for
and informs the definition of concepts at higher levels of the logical structure.
Changes made to the general presuppositions reverberate throughout conceptual system and offer a different approach to social inquiry.

Creating Ontologies of the Social

The list presented above should apply to conceptual analysis in both the natural and the social sciences. The topic here, however, is society, and sociology
commonly regards society as consisting of individual human beings and their
actions. Theories differ concerning whether individuals are able to exercise
control over their action to be rational or non-rational and to distinguish between types of rationality. How are such general assumptions regarding the
social constructed?

According to Joas and Knöbl's (2009) post-positivist account, sociological
theory exists on a continuum between the two environments of the metaphysical and the empirical. In this model, the ontology of the social is the furthest
from and unrelated to empirical research. The approach is philosophical inso-
far as it contends that the theoretical discourse revolves around non-empirical
"what" questions: *What is action?* and *What is social order?* These questions
invite a theoretical discourse concerning the deeper meaning of things. Joas
(1996), for instance, holds that creativity is the essence of being human. Contributions to the theoretical discourse in social theory can now be ordered
according to the extent to which a theory takes creativity into consideration.
Consequently, creativity is the topic of the penultimate chapter in Joas and

Knöbl (2009), which organises the interpretation of social theory backwards from this vantage point.

However, Hobbes, Parsons, Luhmann and many others address questions concerning social action and order not in the sense of what action and order are but *how* the social order emerges. The question of how social order is possible is a counterfactual, hypothetical question used to scrutinise the concepts that are employed in theories of society. There is always some type of order to any society, and the question is not how this or that particular society emerged. The counterfactual question invites a thought experiment in which the researcher can introduce different concepts of, for instance, action and can contemplate how they enable empirical research to explain social order.

The challenge for a social ontology is to combine choice of action, social order and change. When addressing these three questions, sociological theory is caught in a series of dilemmas: voluntarism versus determinism, action versus structure, subjectivism versus objectivism and micro versus macro. These are true dilemmas because, whichever choice one makes, it will create problems for the empirical analysis.

One begins, as Parsons (1968) does, with the intention of creating a general theory of voluntary action; specifically, Parsons begins with a critique of the utilitarian tradition. He does so not because the concept of utility misrepresents the true nature of human action but because utilitarianism can explain neither choice nor order. When everything is reduced to utility, there is only one standard and no choice. According to Parsons, only different normative orientations of actions allow for true alternatives.

With respect to the question of order, utilitarianism and contract theory overextended the concept of rationality. Parsons believed that society was too complex to be the result of conscious human design. As we know, Parsons solved the problem of order by assuming that individuals have internalised meta-norms that determine decisions between lower-level norms. The critics were quick to note that this theoretical move replaced voluntarism with structuralism. Individual choice of action had to be sacrificed to explain social order. To explain the norms and cultural values that inform action and create order, Parsons referred to their function in society, namely that of reducing complexity and creating order.

Parsons' general theory was critiqued for implying determinism and functionalism and for its failure to explain change in the empirical analysis. To compensate for these deficiencies, different versions of the individual human actor are "brought back in". These new theories of action, for their part, experience difficulties in explaining order. To avoid this oscillation in theoretical reasoning, Niklas Luhmann (1995) demands a radical change in the ontology of the social and suggests that sociology should assume that society consists *not* of individual human beings, and *not even of actions*, but only of communications.

The rationale behind Luhmann's proposal is that, when sociology conceives of society as consisting of individual human beings, reductionism is a logical consequence. Typically, patterned social relations are explained by individual preferences, internalised norms or values that determine choice of action and generate social order. To avoid reductionism and enhance its explanatory power, Luhmann (2012) suggests that sociology should assume a society of social systems composed of communications. However, Luhmann's social systems appear to acquire properties typical of social actors with the ability to observe, select, operate and act.

The important matter here is not who is right and who is wrong; all of the examples provided above are examples of conceptual innovation or abductions. This discussion does not concern what action and order truly are but instead concerns fruitfulness, a concept's potential for solving problems encountered during empirical analysis. There are many other abductions in sociology, such as Habermas' concept of communicative action, Giddens' structure duality, Archer's (1995) morphogenetic sequence, and so forth.

Retroduction

Abduction is a common theoretical operation but only brings us halfway to discovery. We now have one – or several – concepts that can be applied to a phenomenon A, but we do not yet have the phenomenon A that would explain the observation C. Concepts are, as stated above, not true or false, but more or less fruitful. Their degree of fruitfulness can only be established through empirical analysis. Abduction is not a research logic of necessity but of possibility (Bertilsson, 2007). *It might be so* as established by abductive reasoning.

We, of course, cannot literally have access to social phenomena. What we can do is employ the new concept and rationale to construct a model of the phenomena we are investigating. I suggest that this transformation of the new concept into a model that can be applied in empirical research can be distinguished as the *research logic of retroduction*. Retroduction is accorded different interpretations in the literature. Perhaps the most well-known is presented by Roy Bhaskar (1979).

Bhaskar bases his conception of retroduction on an ontology of a social reality with three domains: the empirical, the actual and the real. A surprising pattern of events is observed at the empirical level, and the task is to construct a model of the unobservable structures and mechanisms that explain them.

The distinction between surface and depth, between empirical data and the causes or reasons that explain them, is useful for our purpose.

However, it is difficult to accept the epistemology of Bhaskar's ontology. For Bhaskar, the empirical domain is experienced directly through the human senses. In methodological constructivism, the empirical is a scientific creation, as are the other levels. They are useful distinctions to observe an external reality that remains hidden. It is sufficient to have two levels. Bhaskar's distinction between surface and the hidden levels of reality is merely a variant of the common and useful scientific convention of distinguishing between the case and what lies behind the case (Luhmann and Fuchs, 1994). This distinction corresponds to the two standard empirical research questions: What is the case? and What is behind the case? The first is answered by a description, and the second, by an explanation.

The order of the questions seems to reflect properties of reality. Description precedes explanation because it is more concrete and closer to the empirical environment, whereas explanation is more abstract and depends on theory. This understanding concurs with the post-positivist reformulation of the mirror perspective on science. We now know that matters are not so simple. Description is also dependent on concepts.

Moreover, in a sense, explanation comes first. The task of retroduction is to employ the new conceptual framework to create a model of the phenomenon A that would explain C and make the latter a matter of course. A new model must be constructed that integrates conceptual innovations by applying the new rationale implied in the revised general assumptions. From this model, one deducts hypotheses to test it, and induction is applied to substantiate the model or theory. In practical research, these different steps operate in a circular fashion in which abduction is attempted in retroduction and experiences from empirical research feed back into the process of concept construction.

Summary

For this to and fro between the various operations of the research process to proceed in a rational manner, they must be clearly distinguishable. The aim of this chapter was to make a contribution in that direction. To accomplish this task, I was forced to take issue with certain epistemological and ontological conventions found in current theories of science.

Advocates of post-positivism accept that empirical observations are permeated by concepts and thus dissociate themselves from positivist epistemology. Nevertheless, they continue to believe that at least some aspects of external reality enter the social system of science. Reflection on scientific concepts proceeds as philosophical inquiry concerning the true meaning or essence of social matters. This procedure introduces a one-way approach in which there is no feedback from empirical research to concept construction or this relationship is occulted.

In contemporary approaches to social inquiry, four research logics are associated with particular ontologies and isolated from one another. In Blaikie's (2010, 2007) words, they become different research *strategies*. Retroduction is based on a realist ontology and leans towards the natural sciences but can also be applied to the social sciences, as in Bhaskar's ontology of a reality with three domains. In the contemporary literature, the abductive research strategy is grounded on an ontology of social phenomena created by social actors. Lay language is assumed to play a substantial role. Following Blaikie (2007: 91), abduction denotes the process of moving from lay descriptions of social life to scientific descriptions of that social life.

Both realism and social constructivism remain subject to the understanding of science as a mirror representing things as they truly are. For Bhaskar, the empirical domain is experienced directly through the human senses. Intersubjectivity serves a similar function in social constructivism by enabling the social researcher to access the life-world of lay people. Both believe in an environment to which they, in part, have direct and unmediated access. This is reminiscent of positivist epistemology and inhibits reflection. The scientific discourse concentrates on truth – empirical or metaphysical – when the relevant question should concern fruitfulness.

The consequence is that one cannot provide methods for constructing scientific concepts. It is striking how little guidance Blaikie (2007) finds in the literature concerning how lay language can be transformed into scientific concepts or advice on how retroductions can be made. This accords with the continuum model of science developed by Alexander (1985) and applied by Joas and Knöbl (2009). There are distinctions, but it is impossible to be clear on how one proceeds from empirical observations to general assumptions and vice versa.

As long as sociology holds that general assumptions should reflect the true nature of the social, conceptual and empirical analysis will remain isolated from one another, as will the various approaches to social enquiry. Each defends its particular ontology of the social, and there is no commons standard by which to evaluate them. This foundationalism might also explain why general sociological theory cannot resolve its own dilemmas. Scientific examination of the most general assumptions only becomes possible when the researcher acknowledges that the empirical, social action, inter-subjectivity and lay peo-ple are merely concepts. Scientific concepts do not reveal deeper meanings but are invented by science to enable observations of the environment, and they can be evaluated as more or less fruitful in this respect.

As we have seen, we also observe this alternative tendency in the social sciences. Researchers distinguish between general theory and theories of so-ciety and use problems encountered during empirical analysis as a basis for reflection on and observation of scientific concepts. My intention was to build on and develop this alternative tendency, emphasising that both tendencies might be found within the same "theory" and even the same authors.

Conclusion

Science claims truth for its observations and, to defend such claims, is perhaps inclined towards a positivist epistemology. In this image of itself as a mirror, science cannot recognise its own contributions or understand that truth is a scientific creation. The different post-isms are not free from this influence and therefore have become promoters of vagueness or even relativism. My rem-edy for these ills is to embrace epistemological constructivism and accept that there are no exemptions from self-reference.

Science has no direct access to the environment, be it by reduction to brute-sense data, inter-subjectivity or disclosure of the essence of things in philo-sophical speculation. Every observation has a blind spot. We can exploit this insight to create theories of society that are more fitting, if not an actual match. Within this methodological constructivism, the research logic of abduction is no dream. We also learn that no individual research logic leads to scientific discovery. All four research logics (deduction, induction, retroduction and ab-duction) are necessary and collaborate to generate new knowledge.

Disconnected from any particular ontology, the different research logics can be applied in combination to address different aspects of a research process that is circular. Abduction involves creating concepts. Retroduction guides the next step of constructing models based on the theoretical framework. Deduc-tion and induction make empirical conjectures and test and substantiate the model with respect to the data.

Each logic fulfils a function in the overall process of making scientific discoveries. Not all of them are actualised in every research project. Every discovery depends on concepts, but not all of them depend on altering the conceptual framework, and only those that do are abductions. If the model is adequate, deduction or induction might suffice. Models can be refined and new ones created through retroductive reasoning using existing frameworks. If the general theory of sociology is found wanting, the research logic of abduction must be employed to create new concepts.

References

Aakvaag, G.C. (2008). *Moderne sosiologisk teori.* [Modern sociological theory]. Oslo: Abstrakt forlag.

Aakvaag, G.C. (2009). *Frihet og demokrati i den sosiologiske diskursen om det moderne.* [Freedom and democracy in the sociological discourse about the modern]. Oslo: Unipub.

Abend, G. (2008). "The meaning of theory", *Sociological Theory.* 26(2): 173–199.

Alexander, J.C. (1985). *Theoretical logic in sociology.* Berkeley, CA.: University of California Press.

Alexander, J.C. (1987). *Twenty lectures: sociological theory since World War II.* New York: Columbia University Press.

Archer, M.S. (1995). *Realist social theory: the morphogenetic approach.* Cambridge: Cambridge University Press.

Bertilsson, M. (2007). "Pragmatism rediscovered: the relevance of Peirce for social science", Ed. P. Baert. *European pragmatism.* London: Open University Press.

Bhaskar, R. (1979). *The possibility of naturalism: a philosophical critique of the contemporary human sciences.* Brighton: Harvester Press.

Blaikie, N. (2007). *Approaches to social enquiry.* Cambridge: Polity Press.

Blaikie, N. (2010). *Designing social research: the logic of anticipation.* Cambridge: Polity Press.

Denzin, N.K. and Lincoln, Y.S. (2013). *Collecting and interpreting qualitative materials.* Los Angeles: Sage.

Fararo, T.J. (2001). *Social action systems: foundation and synthesis in sociological theory.* Westport, CT.: Greenwood Press.

Giddens, A. (1984). *The constitution of society: outline of the theory of structuration.* Cambridge: Polity Press.

Glasersfeld, E.V. (1995). *Radical constructivism: a way of knowing and learning.* London: Falmer Press.

Glynos, J. and Howarth, D.R. (2007). *Logics of critical explanation in social and political theory.* New York: Routledge.

Hagen, R. (1999). *Rasjonell solidaritet.* [Rational solidarity]. Oslo: Universitetsforlaget.

Hagen, R. (2002). "Positivismekritikkens positivisme", *Sosiologisk Årbok.* ["Positivism among the critics of positivism", Sociological Yearbook]. 7(1): 1–30.

Hagen, R. (2006). *Nyliberalismen og samfunnsvitenskapene: refleksjonsteorier for det moderne samfunnet.* [Neoliberalism and social sciences: reflection theories of the modern society]. Oslo: Universitetsforlaget.

Hagen, R and Gudmundsen, A.C. (2011). "Selvreferanse og refleksjon: forholdet mellom teori og empiri i forskningsprosessen", *Tidsskrift for Samfunnsforskning.* ["Self reference and reflection: the relationship between theory and empirical data in the reserch process", Journal for Social Research]. 52: 459–489.

Harré, R. (1972). *The philosophies of science: an introductory survey.* London: Oxford University Press.

Joas, H. (1996). *The creativity of action.* Cambridge: Polity Press.

Joas, H. and Knöbl, W. (2009). *Social theory: twenty introductory lectures.* Cambridge: Cambridge University Press.

Josephson, J.R. and Josephson, S.G. (1994). *Abductive inference: computation, philosophy, technology.* Cambridge: Cambridge University Press.

Luhmann, N. (1990). *Konstruktivistische Perspektiven.* [Constructivist perspectives]. Opladen: Westdeutscher Verlag.

Luhmann, N. (1995). *Social systems.* Stanford, CA.: Stanford University Press.

Luhmann, N. (2012). *Theory of society.* Stanford, CA.: Stanford University Press.

Luhmann, N. and Fuchs, S. (1994). "'What is the case?' and 'What lies behind it?' The two sociologies and the theory of society", *Sociological Theory.* 12(2): 126–139.

Mann, M. (1986). *The sources of social power. A history of power from the beginning to A.D. 1760.* Cambridge: Cambridge University Press.

Parsons, T. (1968). *The structure of social action: a study in social theory with special reference to a group of recent European writers.* New York: Free Press.

Peirce, C.S. (1960). *Pragmatism and pragmaticism; scientific metaphysics.* Cambridge: Harvard University Press.

Popper, K.R. (1959). *The logic of scientific discovery.* London: Hutchinson.

Reichenbach, H. (1938). *Experience and prediction: an analysis of the foundations and the structure of knowledge.* Chicago: University of Chicago Press.

Rorty, R. (1979). *Philosophy and the mirror of nature.* Princeton: Princeton University Press.

Schiltz, M. (2009). "Space is the place: *the laws of form* and social systems", Eds. B. Clarke and M.B.N. Hansen. *Emergence and embodiment: new essays on second-order systems theory.* Durham: Duke University Press.

Snape, D. and Lewis, J. (2003). "The foundation of qualitative research", Eds. J. Lewis and J. Ritchie. *Qualitative research practice: a guide for social science students and researchers.* London: Sage Publications.

Spencer-Brown, G. (1969). *Laws of form.* London: Allen & Unwin.

Swedberg, R. (2012). "Theorizing in sociology and social science: turning to the context of discovery", *Theory and Society.* 41(1): 1–40.

Tiles, M. (1984). *Bachelard, science and objectivity.* Cambridge: Cambridge University Press.

Wolenski, J., Sintonen, M. and Niiniluoto, I. (2004). *Handbook of epistemology.* Dordrecht: Kluwer Academic Publishers.

CHAPTER 9

Theorizing through Comparative Case Studies

Mette Andersson

Introduction

This chapter brings the two themes of theorizing and small-N comparative analysis together in focusing on how qualitative comparative research designs may offer a rich ground for theorizing, avoiding tendencies of determination based in specific theoretical and epistemological programs. As such its aim is to contribute to sociological discussion about heuristics and techniques for improving our theoretical imagination (Abbott, 2004; Layder, 2005; Swedberg, 2012). The challenge to build sociological knowledge by avoiding both paradigmatic approaches where research evidence only confirms the initial theoretical framework, and research that not relates to existing general and substantive theory from the start, is central in this respect.

A "qualitative comparative case design" does in the further refer to a qualitative research design where a small number (e.g., up to five) of cases are included. In addition the notion, as used here, implies that inclusion of more than one case is found necessary in order to test and/or explore initial research questions in a manner that goes against a tendency to verify earlier theory. Depending on whether the research in question can be linked to a long research tradition or to a new research area, such testing may be positioned along a continuum of explorative and explanatory analysis. Inspired by Bent Flyvbjerg's (2006) strong argument for learning through practical examples, I reconstruct experiences from two earlier qualitative research projects in the field of migration, ethnicity and integration research, both based on a comparison between three cases.

Research project 1 (Andersson, 2005) focused on the identity formation of ethnic minority youth in urban settings in Norway. The project was inspired by general theories on identity, diversity and recognition and by earlier substantive research concluding that the public debate about immigration and integration pushed ethnic minority young adults to reflect on and relate to their status as minority persons. The surmise was that the public debate on integration and immigration in national mass media would impact differently upon young people who were involved in socially desirable activities such as studies or sport, than on people involved in negatively depicted activities and groups such as city strolling (hanging around in the urban space) and gangs. My working hypothesis was thus that the images created of immigrants through mass media would impact on young adults' identity formation, but that the various social arenas where people spent much of their time, would mediate the impact of stereotypes in different ways. The research methods consisted in qualitative life-history interviews with 40 participants in three voluntary youth contexts (a student association, a sports organization and the city stroller and gang context in the inner city) and short-time field-work in and out in two of the three contexts.

In *research project 2* (Andersson, 2008), a different strategy was followed. Here, the research aimed at exploring how the increasing number of non-white elite athletes representing Norway in international competitions interacted with images of national identity and race. This project was informed by substantive research on race, national identity and globalization undertaken in other countries with different colonial and racial histories than Norway. Social theory on transnationalization and globalization was also an important backdrop for the project. The data production was centered around 13 non-white elite athletes, and the data included interviews with these athletes (some were interviewed several times), interviews with coaches, interviews with sports journalists in major newspapers and TV-channels, interviews with representatives of various minority organizations, as well as content analysis of media coverage of the elite athlete informants in the project and some observation at sport events. Also in this project three contexts were chosen for the recruitment of informants. The selection of these three contexts was the result of different criteria than in the first project. Here, all key informants should belong to the sport "elite", in this setting meaning that they represented the Norwegian national teams in their respective sports. The three sport contexts; football, track and field, and basketball, were chosen according to criteria of media coverage and the number of visible minority elite athletes in the national teams. As will be described later, this project had no clear idea about different theoretically constituted cases from the start.

In both projects, comparison across different cases was essential for the results. But the selection of cases, the reformulation of existing concepts and theories, and the generation of new theoretical ideas and concepts developed differently. The two projects are used to describe and discuss central concerns of comparative case research and theorizing at different stages of the research process: (a) research questions, selection of cases and comparative analysis; and (b) theorizing. In the following discussion and in the conclusion, prerequisites and problems involved with generating and/or expanding on theoretical concepts from comparative studies of this kind are presented.

Theoretical Inspiration and Departure

This chapter is inspired by how theorists of the middle range – such as Erving Goffman (1959, 1963), Robert K. Merton (2007), and James Scott (1990) – in some of their theoretical constructions utilize cases from a wide reservoir of own and others' empirical research. The concepts and middle-range theories proposed by for instance Goffman, are valuable precisely because they have been developed from observing social interaction in very different contexts, variously based on others' research, his own empirical observations, or literary examples. They continue to remain intuitively "good to think with" and are well suited to assist researchers in developing creative research designs. Examples of concepts deriving from this tradition are Goffman's concepts of "impression management" and "stigma" (Goffman, 1959, 1963) and Scott's concepts of "hidden and public transcripts" and "infrapolitics" (Scott, 1990), referring to power constellations on a bigger scale. The last author has done intensive ethnographic work on poor agrarian workers in specific locations. In his later theory of resistance and hidden transcripts among the dominated, he builds on this work but substantiates the theory by referring to other empirical cases such as slaves and blue-collar workers, living in different countries and in different time periods, as well as to literary examples illustrating the theoretical points.

The type of middle-range theorizing discussed below, overlaps partly with the research strategy abduction as defined by Norman Blaikie (2004), and in line with Roar Hagen's chapter in this book. In short, the abductive research strategy starts by exploring actors' own practices, meanings and ideas about the world. It builds on Weber's "verstehen" approach and Alfred Schütz' social phenomenology, both claiming that researchers needs to get hold of actors' meanings in order to theorize about the social world. Other authors on middle-range theorizing criticize grounded theory and much abductive research for not including a broad specter of theories and concepts from the start of the research process and for a too narrow focus on micro-level processes. Derek Layder (2005), for instance, holds this position and argues that "orienting concepts" (partly resembling Herbert Blumer's "sensitizing concepts" (Blumer, 1954)) based on existing substantive and general theory are essential in order to "crank start" the process of theory development (ibid: 102). Orienting concepts, thus, are seen as necessary heuristic devices to develop theorizing. In this regard they play a role within a wider repertoire of heuristic concepts as described in Richard Swedberg's chapter in this book.

From a different angle, focusing on how theoretical development is fostered by internal critique between different positions in the social sciences, Andrew

Abbott (2004) describes five main methods which respectively are devoted to different forms of explanation, and to different positions in methodological and ontological debates. Ethnography, for instance, is associated with interpretivism, constructionism and contextualism. And standard causal analysis is associated with positivism, individualism, realism and non-contextualism. Abbott argues that what he names "small-N analysis" denies the reality of many of the debates defining the other methods, and that the only clear position among small-N analysts is that they are contextualist and aim to "square the methodological circle by combining situated and transcendent knowledge" (Abbott, 2008: 58). Abbott's argument is that this "more relaxed" methodological position facilitates theorizing that not is limited by frames inscribed in for instance the grounded theory program or in standard deductive analysis. Abbott's argument reminds of similar arguments from other case study researchers (e.g., Vaughan, 2008) who insist that comparative case studies are well suited both for verification and discovery of theory.

This chapter does not allow for a thorough presentation and discussion of themes related to theorizing and comparative method as discussed by case study researchers themselves. Among such themes of relevance to the ongoing argument in this chapter are discussions about what a case is and how a case can be defined (cf. Ragin and Becker, 2008; Platt, 1999), whether and how one can generalize from case studies (cf. Gomm, Hammersley and Foster, 2000), and the debate about whether case studies in general and comparative case studies in particular should be seen as informed by qualitative method or not (cf. Yin, 2003; Eckstein, 2000; Ragin and Amoroso, 2011). As the main focus in this chapter is on describing how different comparative research designs led to different routes of theorizing, references to the internal debates among case study researchers will be introduced when relevant to the argument at hand.

The position advanced in the further is that small-N comparative analysis, as Abbott argues, is a methodological design aiming "to keep the interpretive and narrative subtlety of ethnography and narration but to add to these an analytical strength that echoes standard causal analysis" (Abbott, 2008: 58). This implies that such methodological designs aim at analyzing differences within and between cases, but also similarities across cases, typically referring to theoretical constructs at different levels of generality. The focus on ethnography in small-N case analysis does not exclude other kinds of data or methodological techniques from being valuable in the construction of, and comparison between cases. What it does mean, is that the main methods are qualitative, consisting of for instance one-to-one interviews, group interviews, observational data and text analysis. Quantitative evidence, based on existing publications, statistics, etc. is important to the extent that it aids the definition of cases as well as the comparative analysis of the qualitative data. In what follows, I turn to the practical examples, showing how the two projects introduced briefly in the introduction took different routes in regard to initial theoretical inspiration, case selection, comparative analysis and theorizing.

Research Questions, Case Selection, and Comparative Analysis

The construction of research questions is closely connected to the amount of existing research knowledge and substantive theories in the domain of interest. At the time when my projects were initiated, there was almost no Norwegian research on these themes. The formulation of concrete research questions in the two projects was informed by a closer reading of specific theories, varying according to the level of abstraction and scope. Whereas research *project 1* was inspired by general social theory about identity, recognition and interaction, as represented through the works of authors such as Charles Taylor, Paul Ricoeur, Alfred Schütz and Erving Goffman, *project 2* was more informed by international substantive research and bottom-up theorizing in the domains of racism, national identity and sports. These different theoretical departures (level of generality) resulted in different types of research questions in the two projects. *Project 2's* research questions were informed by an explorative strategy close to the empirical ground, and the questions were basically descriptive in nature, as in the following research questions: "Which expectations do ethnic and religious minority groups raise toward minority athletes as representatives of ethnic and religious minorities in Norway?" and, "how do the athletes view their role as public minority representatives?" The research questions in *project 1* focused on how the identity formation of immigrant youth in Norway was informed by macro-debates about immigration and by the voluntary youth contexts in which they spent much of their leisure time. These questions were less informed by substantive research in this area (from other countries) and more by a general curiosity about how ascriptive identities and external categorization informed reflections and action in various social settings.

In both projects, there were arguments for involving a few, different cases from the start. For *project 1*, theoretical arguments were the most important. As cases typically points to cases of something, and therefore often "come wrapped in theories" (Walton, 2008: 121), there is always a danger to reproduce earlier research results in the case selection process. A critical reading of earlier one-case studies of young people in ethnic minority groups in Norway revealed that minority youth typically were framed as "ethnic cases". Wanting to explore the impact of ethnicity in relation to other dimensions of identity in a broader process of identity formation meant that including cases outside of conventional ethnic minority settings (i.e., family, intra-ethnic network, neighborhood) was seen as necessary for the research design. Earlier sociological research and theory on stratification and deviance was central in the decision to select cases from youth arenas with different status in society. Student organizations, inner-city sport clubs, and inner city youth gangs were thought to provide different entries to reflections and ideologies concerning ones position as an ethnic minority young person in Norway. The selection of the three cases in project 1 resembles the logic of theoretical sampling as championed by Glaser and Strauss (Glaser and Strauss, 1967; Dey, 2004; Thomas and James, 2006). Whereas Glaser and Strauss argue that theoretical sampling is a *result* of empirical analysis, the cases in project 1 were selected *before* the data production took place.

The first step of analysis of data in this project was to compare individual life-histories within each of the three chosen cases. Here, comparison aimed at producing rough categories that could be used to analyze difference between individual life-histories, but also to provide an account of sameness in social processes and cultural patterns recognizing each case. The second step was to compare between the three cases, and through this comparison, three ideal types describing different social identities were constructed. These were based on a more abstracted and holistic comparison. An initial formulation of a concept of "identity work", as will be described in the next section, was formulated as a consequence of this comparison. In *project 1,* thus, the heuristic device of *ideal types* was used to build social identity types characterizing each of the three chosen cases, and through this comparison the initial cases were theorized as specific versions of social identities.

For *project 2* on elite athletes, race and national identity, other concerns for case selection were central. Here, the aim was to focus the study around a number of non-white elite athletes visible in the public space, through printed mass media and television. The challenge from the start was to recruit such key informants. A mix of concerns regarding the number of non-white athletes in elite sports and different sports' respective media coverage led to the selection of key informants from three sport contexts: football, track and field and basketball. These sport contexts were not initially thought of as cases for comparative analysis. In this project, practical reasons were more important than theoretical arguments for the selection of key informants from three sport contexts. It was first later in the analysis, aided by the orienting concept "non-whiteness", that three cases for qualitative comparative analysis were constructed.

Also in this project a two-step procedure of comparison prevailed. The first step of analysis was to compare the experiences and thoughts of the 13 elite athletes in regard to the orienting concept "non-whiteness" (a process more closely be described in the theorizing section). In the same period interviews with other informants from the media and civil society organizations were conducted. Gradually, as the data showed that there were different orientations to non-white elite athletes in the three sports, a more conscious search for more data and historical trajectories of the three sports in Norway came to inform the analysis. Through comparison of data from different viewpoints inside and outside the three sports contexts, the initial contexts for sampling were reformulated as cases of Norwegian "sport worlds" and the second step of analysis focused on comparison between these sport worlds.

Whereas project 1's cases in the second step of comparison in one sense resembled the initial cases, although more empirically informed and specific, project 2's cases came out as broader and less clearly defined cases first after the initial analysis. Case scope (size) and the level of theoretical ideas employed in the initial and further construction of cases through analysis, differed. On a more aggregate level they resemble two different types of cases: The first type of case has a theoretical anchoring from the start, clearly resembling a "family of cases" anchored in a broader theoretical landscape. This type of case is constructed as a version of a broader aggregate category such as "ethnic minority youth", "social identity", "voluntary organization", "addict", "interaction sequence" etc. The main point is that the case is seen as a specific version of a broader theoretically informed category. A comparative case design based on this type of case partly resembles a deductive strategy aiming to test or to explore a hypothesis through several different cases. The second type of case refers to cases associated with grounded theory and one-case community or field studies. Here, a case typically refers to a broader field of practice or community, such as the sport field, the academic world and so on. Cases constructed in order to resemble wider fields or communities with their own logics of competition, interaction or conflict, points to a more holistic, and macro-inspired definition of a case. A comparative case design of this type typically operates with fuzzier boundaries between the cases.

Theorizing

Both projects were informed by an abductive research strategy focusing on grounded comparative theorizing as the end product of analysis. As already mentioned, the case selection process in project 1 was done before the analysis started. In project 2, however, the cases for comparison were constructed after the initial data were produced, and new data were sought according to

Glaser and Strauss' logic of theoretical sampling. These different analytical trajectories have implications for theorizing, and more specifically in regard to whether comparative analysis only can discover, and not verify or test theory as Glaser and Strauss hold. Vaughan (2008) is one among several researchers who critiques the idea that verification and discovery of theory cannot go on simultaneously from an explicit case study approach. Vaughan argues, in contrast to Glaser and Strauss, and in line with other approaches to middle-range theorizing (Layder, 2005), that the findings from grounded case analyses should be compared with earlier theories, models, or concepts in order to subject the latter as well as the former to challenge and change. Furthermore she argues that such theoretical comparison and testing is strengthened when comparative case analysis includes diverse groups and when researchers compare findings between different levels of analysis.

Vaughan's point is that verification and discovery of theory happens simultaneously through comparative case analysis. My argument, however, is that *the extent to whether one of these processes dominates depends on how clearly the cases are theorized in the first hand.* In order to show this, some detail about the concepts and theories elaborated must be presented. In project 1, general concepts and the theories they were part of, such as identity formation and recognition, worked as orienting concepts guiding the comparative analysis across the three cases. An inductive analysis informed by these general concepts led to the construction of three empirically substantiated ideal-typical social identities: "the liberal multiculturalist", "the ethnic entrepreneur", and the "foreigner". The spatio-temporal horizons characterizing the typical actors in the three cases were central for the construction of the ideal-types (a detailed description of the ideal-types is found in Andersson, 2005). The next step of theorizing was to construct a model of "identity work", a model depicting that identity work was a continuous process informed by three identity modes corresponding to three levels of the social: categorical identities referring to the macro-level, social identities referring to the meso-level and personal identities referring to the micro-level. "Categorical identities", a term taken up from Craig Calhoun (1995) (who had taken it up from Harrison White) referred to identities ascribed to aggregates of individuals having no more in common in general than that they could be distinguished by categories such as gender, ethnicity, or class. "Social identities" in contrast referred to grounded forms of identity based on face-to-face participation in concrete social contexts such as student organizations, gangs and sport clubs. The third concept included in the model, "personal identities" was informed by Charles Taylor's (1995) and Paul Ricoeur's (1992) theories stressing the normative and reflexive character of individual identities, where personal identities were seen as changing over time in regard to normative horizons, but yet having a certain solidity to them. The development of a model of identity-work was the result of the interplay of two processes: 1) abstraction based on the ideal-typical identities found through comparative case analysis and (2) the testing of general identity theories, modifying some of the concepts and the linkages between concepts in earlier theoretical models. One example of such testing is how Charles Taylor's specific theoretical model on the politics of recognition in multicultural societies (Taylor, 1994) was scrutinized against the data. In this model, Taylor argues that the recognition of minorities in multicultural societies depends on whether these societies recognize the ethnic and cultural specificity of minority groups. Although Taylor cites Mead as inspiration for his interactional model of recognition, he does not (as he does in his more general theory of human agency (Taylor, 1995)) distinguish between recognition processes at the micro-, meso- and macro-level. Misrecognition, in Taylor's model, means that the ethnic identities of minority groups not are recognized as the constitutive dimension for minority groups' inclusion in the broader society. The comparative analysis across three Norwegian cases of identity formation among ethnic minority youth did not support Taylor's model. A central reason for this, I argue, is that his model of recognition and misrecognition conflates processes taking part at different levels of the social, using the macro-level political society as a lens for a general theory of recognition and misrecognition. The result of comparative analysis in project 1 suggested that misrecognition at the micro- and meso-levels was more related to the lack of recognition of complex identities than of ethnic or cultural identity as such. The strategies of recognition employed across the three ideal-typical social identities varied substantially, with one of them, built on the Pakistani student association, being closest to Taylor's model of ethnicity as constitutive for identity. More striking, however, was a general aim to deconstruct ethnic identity and stress multiple identity dimensions. Identity formation could be better explained by a model of identity work stressing how social identity grounded in different social contexts mediated categorical and personal identities. Theoretical comparison with other models of identity formation, such as Taylor's specific model of the politics of recognition, was thus constitutive for building the model of identity work.

The development of the concept of "other-time" was another result of theorizing in project 1. This concept illustrated how minority young people in the late teens and early twenties developed a new temporal horizon linked to the national space. This temporal horizon was characterized by abstract, moral reflection on their status as different from the ethnic majority within the national space, and it invoked a re-consideration of earlier judgments and thoughts regarding minority-majority interactions in their own lives and beyond. Earlier in life their temporal horizons were framed within the social arenas and spaces where children and youth spend their time (school, family, friends), and their position as minority was negotiated in regard to these concrete arenas. In this part of the analysis the ideal-types were "forgotten" and new analytical constructs, in this case focusing explicitly on the dimension of temporality, were developed.

To summarize the theorizing in project 1, it was characterized both by testing and revising theories and by developing theoretical models and concepts. The theoretically informed selection of diverse groups for comparison in the initial research design, helped advance the theorizing beyond ethnicity theories to a more general model of identity work. The theorizing was mainly directed at the meso interactional level, although the macro- and micro level were included in the theoretical constructs.

Project 2 took another route from the very start. The initial selection of cases was not theoretically informed, but became so in the course of analysis. This relates both to the explorative design of project 2, and to the descriptive, "what" type of research questions in the project. From the start, the orienting concept "non-white" was central in guiding my focus on instances where difference from the white majority was noticed in regard to sport. This concept was initially defined as "...a category referring to persons who visually, and occasionally also by name, clothing and/or reference to religion, depart from the average white Norwegian". Gradually, due to the growth of the empirical material and the variety of empirical sources, a broader understanding of non-whiteness in regard to specific "sport worlds" constructed around different sports practices and ideologies, was developed.

Project 2 worked with substantive theories and research results from similar studies in other countries as the major background. As mentioned, also globalization and transnationalisation theories were central, and these become gradually more central in the course of analysis. Two general concepts were developed through scrutinizing such theories in tandem with the empirical comparison across the three cases: "identity logic" and "capital logic". The capital logic draws on competition, on getting the most for the least, whereas the identity logic is more stable and does not resemble a zero-game logic. These concepts helped to understand how non-whiteness was interpreted in regard to sport practices and cultures in the three sport worlds. The spatial scope for understanding the relationship of identity and capital logics was glocal, referring to how images and realities from global sports interacted with local Norwegian sports worlds. In both of the projects, the case comparison, and linked to it the widening of the reference to non-white to sport worlds, was constitutive for the theorizing process.

In the football case (specifically clear in the context of the elite clubs), a globalized capital logic pressing towards the import of cheaper and better players from the south worked partly in tandem with an identity logic designating "our" black players as contrasted with other teams "imported" ones. In track and field, the identity logic depicted non-white star athletes as both Norwegian and as part of a global black elite dominating the sport in distinct disciplines such as sprints and long-distance running. The capital logic here predicted that more non-white sprinters and long-distance runners at the national team would increase national glory in international competitions. Yet, the undercurrent or silent knowledge told that the dominance of non-white athletes in track and field internationally, should not infer upon white Norwegians a feeling of non-accomplishment and the idea that they would never be successful anyway. Non-whiteness was ambiguous or double-edged in this context, with more complexity involved than in the more straight-forward football context. In basketball, the relationship between identity and capital logics played out differently. Here, a new professional basket league, constructed after the model of North-American NBA, demanded the import of two foreign players at each team in the elite series. Many of these players were black North-Americans. The prestige of the NBA in international basketball, the association of black players to the NBA and the tendency to listen to rap music among players in this sport, together contributed to a positive identity logic associated with transnational blackness. Thus, Norwegian non-white players were seen and saw themselves as enhancing the identity logic associated with basketball on a broader international level. The capital logic demanding the import of foreign players in the sport, thus, strengthened the identity logic associated with this sport.

The two concepts used to analyze how non-whiteness interacted with national and team identities in different sports, were in project 2 not scrutinized in regard to other theories of identity and capital, such as for instance Bourdieu's multidimensional capital theory. One reason for this was that Bourdieu's field and space concepts traditionally have been used within a national framework, whereas my analysis suggested that the incorporation of a global level was fundamental in order to understand the relevant processes. Another reason was that the development of these concepts came more as a surprising result of analysis. In retrospect, it is clear that the crafting of two general concepts and their relationship in regard to sport more generally definitely could have been more developed in this project. The comparative research design contributed to interesting and original findings of a more explorative than explanatory nature.

Discussion and Conclusion

The theorizing process in these projects was marked by a mix of context-sensitive and transcendent theorizing illustrating Abbott's argument that small-N case studies have a more "relaxed" methodological position aiding creative theorizing (Abbott, 2008). Blaikie's abduction strategy, associated with social constructionism and largely based on Schütz' social phenomenology and his model of theorizing (as anchored in actors' first-order constructs and then theorized by the researcher as second-order constructs) does not fully cover the theorizing process in these projects. The abductive strategy "begins by exploring through everyday language the knowledge that social actors use in the production, reproduction and interpretation of the phenomena under investigation" (Blaikie, 2004: 100). In both of the projects, the actor's point of view was central as a departure for understanding social processes in larger social units and relationships between such units. Yet, the projects were also informed by various theoretical approaches from the very start, in utilizing "orienting concepts" at different levels of generality as informing analysis.

An important question in regard to theorizing more generally is when to stop reading earlier theory and when to start developing ideas from your own empirical analysis. The use of too much established theory can hinder theoretical imagination and further theorizing, in the same way as marginal knowledge of existing theory in the field, can prevent theorizing and development of existing theory. Although project 1 from the start had more theoretical ideas at play, the theory used here was of a general, and relatively open character. In the theorizing process, theoretical models from these general theories were reconstructed and the interplay between general concepts and comparative analysis proved fruitful. The construction of ideal-types characterizing the typical social identities recognizing the three cases did in one sense reproduce the initial case design. A further consequence of this could be that theorizing stopped at the level of aggregate descriptive characteristics of each case. In building further on the ideal-types, and abstracting their characteristics in regard to more general spatial and temporal aspects characterizing interaction contexts and identity work, they proved useful in further analysis. If I had concentrated only on one case in this project, such more general theoretical insights would have been less founded in the empirical ground. The comparison between very different cases was here essential for theorizing.

Project 2 developed more as an explorative, bottom-up analysis, guided by the orienting concept of non-whiteness. Here, theorizing stopped at an earlier stage than in project 1. The cases developed through analysis as "sport worlds" were larger in scope and less theoretically informed from the start. The prerequisite of the comparative case analysis in this project was that I found new and interesting relationships, and developed the two heuristic concepts of identity and capital logics. The dynamic of capital and identity logics, here seen as middle-range concepts, proved relevant to understand how non-whiteness was interpreted differently in the three sport-worlds. These concepts were not formalized as parts of a broader theoretical model or a network of concepts aimed at explanation. They "popped up" as a consequence of comparative analysis, and remained on the level of heuristics.

In projects informed by, but not necessarily restricted by, the abduction strategy, theorizing is typically seen as a continuing process, open for change, revision and never quite finished. Comparative case method, at least most versions of it, aims at transcendent explanations substantiated by testing on different cases (often "extreme cases" or very different cases). The research design here labeled qualitative comparative case design can be seen as a bridging of these two methodologies. As this chapter has shown, concrete research designs are complex, take different routes in theorizing, and are seldom identical with the ideal-typical versions of research methodologies and strategies described as tools in methodology books.

As many case study researchers comment on, there is always a danger of losing depth when playing with too many cases in one project. Discussions between case study researchers often focus on how to balance in-depth ethnographic detail with the generalizing and/or theorizing potential of many cases (cf. Eisenhardt, 1989; Dyer and Wilkins, 1991; Eisenhardt, 1991; Schofield, 2000; Yin, 2003; Bryman, 2004; Ragin, 2008). My experience has been with a number of comparative case studies employing qualitative methods and with a restricted number of cases involved (3 or 4). In these studies, comparison across cases has facilitated theorizing, but the benefit of more than one case needs to be thoroughly balanced with careful qualitative analysis across units within one case. Small-N comparative analysis is well-adapted to avoid theory determination of empirical findings, given that the cases are well selected or developed. The theorizing potential of comparative case studies depends on which type of cases one chooses, and not the least the variation between the cases. In contrast to much method advice on how to do (often national) comparative studies; to make sure the cases are as similar as possible, I would advise for more diversity and difference in case design. This is crucial when one agrees with Abbott in the aim to "square the methodological circle by combining situated and transcendent knowledge".

References

Abbott, A. (2004). *Methods of discovery: heuristics for the social sciences.* New York: W.W. Norton & Company.

Abbott, A. (2008). "What do cases do? Some notes on activity in sociological analyses", Eds. C.C. Ragin and H.S. Becker. *What is a case? Exploring the foundations of social inquiry.* Cambridge: Cambridge University Press.

Andersson, M. (2005). *Urban multi-culture in Norway: identity formation among immigrant youth.* New York: Edwin Mellen Press.

Andersson, M. (2008). *Flerfarget idrett: nasjonalitet, migrasjon og minoritet.* [Multicolor sports: nationality, migration and minority]. Bergen: Fagbokforlaget.

Blaikie, N. (2004). *Designing social research: the logic of anticipation.* Cambridge: Polity Press.

Blumer, H. (1954). "What is wrong with social theory?", *American Sociological Review.* 19(1): 3–10.

Bryman, J.P. (2004). *Social research methods.* Revised edition. Oxford: Oxford University Press.

Calhoun, C. (1995). *Critical social theory: culture, history and the challenge of difference.* Oxford: Blackwell.

Dey, I. (2004). "Grounded theory", Ed. A. Bryman. *Social research methods.* Oxford: Oxford University Press.

Dyer, W.G. Jr. and Wilkins, A.L. (1991). "Better stories, not better constructs, to generate better theory: a rejoinder to Eisenhardt", *Academy of Management Review.* 16(3): 613–619.

Eckstein, H. (2000). "Case study and theory in political science", Eds. H. Gomm, M. Hammersley and P. Foster. *Case study method.* London: Sage.

Eisenhardt, K.M. (1989). "Building theories from case study research", *Academy of Management Review.* 14(4): 532–550.

Eisenhardt, K.M. (1991). "Better stories and better constructs: the case for rigor and comparative logic", *Academy of Management Review.* 16(3): 620–627.

Flyvbjerg, B. (2006). "Five misunderstandings about case-study research", *Qualitative Inquiry.* 12(2): 219–245.

Glaser, B. and Strauss, A. (1967). *The discovery of grounded theory.* London: Sage.

Goffman, E. (1959). *The presentation of self in everyday life.* New York: Doubleday.

Goffman, E. (1963). *Stigma: notes on the management of spoiled identity.* New Jersey: Prentice Hall Inc.

Gomm, R., Hammersley, M. and Foster, P. (eds.). (2000). *Case study method.* London: Sage.

Layder, D. (2005). *Sociological practice – Linking theory and sociological research.* London: Sage.

Merton, R.K. (2007) [1947]. "On sociological theories of the middle range", Eds. C. Calhoun, J. Gerteis, J. Moody, S. Pfaff and I. Virk. *Classical sociological theory*. Malden, MA.: Blackwell Publishing.

Platt, J. (1999). "What can case studies do?", Eds. A. Bryman and E.G. Burgess. *Qualitative research*. London: Sage.

Ragin, C.C. (2008). "Introduction: cases of 'What is a case?'", Eds. C.C. Ragin and H.S. Becker. *What is a case? Exploring the foundations of social inquiry*. Cambridge: Cambridge University Press.

Ragin, C.C. and Becker, H.S. (2008). *What is a case? Exploring the foundations of social inquiry*. Cambridge: Cambridge University Press.

Ragin, C.C. and Amoroso, L.M. (2011). *Constructing social research*. 2nd edition. Los Angeles: Sage/Pine Forge.

Ricoeur, P. (1992). *Onself as another*. Chicago: The University of Chicago Press.

Schofield, J.W. (2000). "Increasing the generalizability of qualitative research", Eds. R. Gomm, M. Hammersley and P. Foster. *Case study method*. London: Sage.

Scott, J.C. (1990). *Domination and the arts of resistance. Hidden Transcripts*. New Haven: Yale University Press.

Swedberg, R. (2012). "Theorizing in sociology and social science: turning to the context of discovery", *Theoretical Sociology*. 41(1): 1–40.

Taylor, C. (1994). "The politics of recognition", Ed. D.T. Goldberg. *Multiculturalism: A critical reader*. Oxford: Blackwell.

Taylor, C. (1995). "What is human agency?", *Philosophy and the human sciences. Philosophical papers 2*. Cambridge: Cambridge University Press.

Thomas, G. and James, D. (2006). "Reinventing grounded theory: some questions about theory, ground and discovery", *British Educational Research Journal*. 32(6): 767–795.

Vaughan, D. (2008). "Theory elaboration: the heuristics of case analysis", Eds. C.C. Ragin and H.S. Becker. *What is a case? Exploring the foundations of social inquiry*. Cambridge: Cambridge University Press.

Walton, J. (2008). "Making the theoretical case", Eds. C.C. Ragin and H.S. Becker. *What is a case? Exploring the foundations of social inquiry*. Cambridge: Cambridge University Press.

Yin, R.K. (2003). *Case study research: design and methods*. London: Sage.

CHAPTER 10

Explanatory Practices in Sociology: An Overview

Willy Martinussen

Introduction

Explanation is one major task requiring theory. The question I ask is "Where in the vast and multifarious field called 'sociological theory' may we find general answers to our 'why' (or 'how come?') questions concerning a documented social pattern or regularity?" I answer this question by presenting examples of the eight main types of explanations I encounter in everyday sociology, highlighting the theories constructed or used by the research workers. This is not a typology of theories, then, but of modes of explanation.

To explain a social pattern is to account for its stability or change. This accounting typically involves explicating the processes that lead to the reproduction of the pattern or to its remodelling or death. When a social process is specified and documented and then interpreted as an exemplar of a more general sociological theory, at least some of us feel that a satisfactory explanation has been produced. A complete sociological explanation, then, is a complex set of four elements:

- the point of departure: a documented social regularity or pattern of stability or change that one wishes to specify and understand;
- a theory concerning the process(es) that may account for the observed reproduction of or change in the pattern;
- a specification of one or more hypotheses or a model of the process, which is then confronted using some type of empirical material; and
- an evaluation of the theory in light of this confrontation.

This somewhat loose specification is obviously more comprehensive than the concept of a deductive-nomological explanation, which often is presented as the ideal in the natural sciences. Moreover, the relationships among the four elements may occasionally be blurred: Theory and method may not be entirely distinct; theories may be expressed as statistical models; the reporting of results may be intertwined with evaluations of theories, etc. Such problems will not be addressed here. My discussion of examples will concentrate on the first two elements mentioned above.

Sociological theories have been described in several ways. In this chapter, I will classify them along two conflict dimensions, which have been the targets of heated debates in the discipline. The most basic of these is perhaps the agency-structure dispute, the nature of which involves understanding individual action and interaction (Jenks, 1998: 8–33). At the extremes of this continuum are found the epistemological positions of constructionism and structuralism. The second dimension that is relevant to my presentation concerns the understanding of smaller or larger societal patterns: should they be regarded as complex social wholes with their own logics, or are they merely the sum of the atoms (actions, interactions, individuals, groups, organisations, institutions, etc.) of which they are composed? Disagreement over such questions at the meta-theoretical level is often called the "holism-atomism controversy".

Explanatory theories on the "structure" side of the structure-agency continuum typically concern social life *conditions*, their interrelations, and their consequences. On the "actor" side, the theories focus on the *intentions* of social actors, the interactions of which they are a part, and the social patterns in which they result. Occasionally, the explanations related to these sides are distinguished as causal and intentional explanations, respectively. *System* theories concern smaller or larger sociocultural patterns with some degree of internal cohesion, whereas atomistic theories concern the *sum total* of individual behaviour. Several theorists (Alexander, Bourdieu, Collins and Giddens, among others) have attempted to bridge the gaps across the axes on a more general level (Ritzer, 2008: 373–420).

In day-to-day research, one must typically select some part of what might be called the explanation chain, while only hinting at processes in the other parts of it (there are quite a few similar accounts, e.g., Hedstrom and Swedberg, 1998: 21–23; Skog, 2006: 72–82). This chain is illustrated in the figure below. An arrow indicates one or more social processes. Note that individual action is a central component of this chain.

In the researcher's mind, the explanation he or she provides may include the whole chain, and several famous sociology studies are combinations of the types of explanation outlined below. However, in the majority of research projects, it is typically only possible to investigate one or two of the connections, while making (tacit or explicit) assumptions concerning the rest. System theoreticians make assumptions regarding individual actions, actor theoreticians concerning the systems, and so forth. They all make assumptions concerning related psychological, biological, ecological and historical processes.

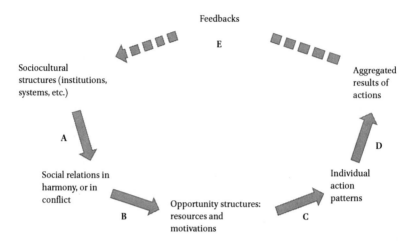

FIGURE 10.1   *The sociological chain of explanation.*

The figure above may be regarded as one possible specification of the holism-atomism continuum. Using this chain as our point of departure, four modes of explanation that I believe are often found in everyday sociological research are distinguishable:

– *meaningful behaviour explanations*, which reveal how social patterns are the aggregated results of individual actions and the immediate conditions and motives of those actions (arrows C and D);
– *opportunities explanations*, which regard regularities and patterns of action as the results of individuals' evaluations and access to resources of various types given by the situations in which they exist (arrows B and C);
– *communities explanations*, which hold that sociocultural patterns are reproduced or change as results of the relationships and interactions between individuals who act in the positions they occupy in the social systems to which they belong (arrows A and B); and
– *systems explanations*, which seek to demonstrate that social systems or some part of them are reproduced or change as a result of their internal relations and dynamics (arrows A and E).

Each of the four types may be based on either a structure-oriented theory or an actor-oriented theory. This provides us with the eight forms of explanations that will be discussed in this chapter. The choice of terminology will be justified during the discussion. In the fourfold meta-sociological space outlined above, the eight modes of explanation might be situated in a manner approximated by the figure below.

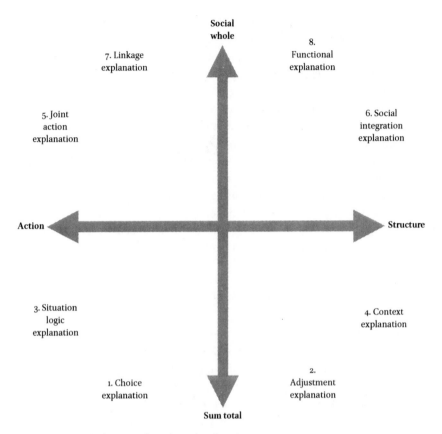

FIGURE 10.2   *Eight types of sociological explanation.*

The discussion of the eight forms of explanation is organised as follows: I begin by presenting the meaningful behaviour explanations. They comprise the two combinations that lie at the aggregation end of the part-whole continuum (one intentional and one conditional, assigned the numbers 1 and 2, respectively). I then move "upwards" to the system end of this continuum, depicting the two combinations on each side of the action-structure divide at each step. For each type of explanation, I discuss a main example, highlight variations by mentioning other examples, and conclude by suggesting the social processes explaining it, theories concerning such processes, and how the explanations may be investigated empirically. Certain types of explanation may "share" a theory. The examples are *not* selected because I believe all of them are well documented empirically.

The main examples are drawn from studies conducted by researchers who are supposedly well known by most sociologists. Consequently, many examples are not recent. The theorists include Emile Durkheim, Robert Michels,

Robert K. Merton, Pierre Bourdieu, Raymond Boudon, Candace West and
Donald Zimmerman, and Kingsley Davis and Wilbert E. Moore. I might have
selected more telling examples from among newer studies or local studies that
I know well, but doing so would require substantially more space to present
the studies.

Before beginning my discussion of examples from the world of sociological
research, I would like to emphasise that the excerpts I present do not in any
way constitute comprehensive or representative reports of the works of the
classical or more recent sociologists I have selected. For instance, Pierre Bourdieu's theory of the reproduction of educational inequality covers the whole
chain, despite my only referring to its aggregation component. The elements
I have selected may not come from the main strand of their research or thinking. Moreover, in this overview, there is insufficient space in which to present
or discuss the empirical basis of their work.

Meaningful Behaviour

A substantial number of sociological explanations take as their point of departure the notion that social patterns of development, reproduction or change
are the sum total of individual actions in different social groups and categories. In this type of study, one often observes that the major component of
groundwork and reporting lies in gathering data, analysing data, and specifying the aggregation processes, whereas theory development and use plays a
more humble role. The basic model is that individuals, with varying degrees
of awareness, seek to make the best of the situation in which they find themselves. On the "action" side of the structure-action continuum, this idea means
that individuals to some extent explicitly compare their various alternative
actions in specific situations and select the one that renders the best outcome, given the costs involved. On the "structure" side, actions are regarded as
learned and automatic to a much greater extent. However, routine, everyday
behaviour (based on convictions of one sort or another) may be as meaningful to the individuals involved as careful rational choices. I have named these
two types of explanation "choice explanations" and "adjustment explanations",
respectively.

Choice Explanation

The basic concept in choice explanations is that differences in goal-oriented
choices of actions among individuals, social groups, social organisations, nations, social categories such as men and women, generations, etc. aggregate to

larger-scale patterns of stability or change. What makes the choices meaningful is typically the notion of rationality, in one form or another.

One of the well-known examples in sociology is the literature on the differences in educational careers between young men and women belonging to different social classes or strata. Raymond Boudon (1974) performed one such study. Boudon's question pertains to why the social class inequalities in educational attainment are reproduced across generations. His general answer identifies the decisions made by the youths when they are forced to choose their future work lives and the cost-benefit analyses they perform in these situations. Youths from the lower social strata evaluate their alternatives differently from their counterparts in the higher strata, in accordance with the choices of their parents and peers. These apparently rational behaviours, in turn, aggregate to the results observed in educational statistics. In subsequent studies, this theory has been modified, studied extensively, and even formalised (Breen and Whelan, 1994).

There are alternative explanations, and when it was presented, Boudon's theory led to a heated discussion in France, with Pierre Bourdieu as his main adversary. As I will note shortly, Bourdieu's alternative hypothesis assigned decisive importance to the differences in *habitus* between social classes. Other alternative hypotheses identify differences in faculties or economic and cultural resources or opportunities between social strata.

It is not difficult to find studies from other areas of social life exhibiting the same characteristic. We may mention the stepwise filtering out of suspects by carefully weighted decisions in the judicial chain, resulting in the overrepresentation of lower-class persons in prisons. Studies of the use of religious rituals by non-religious persons in connection with weddings and funerals represent another example. This pattern is frequently explained by referring to rational action theory, noting that, for various practical reasons, the religious supply of ceremonies is the easiest and least expensive alternative.

A number of general social-scientific theories concerning choice behaviour exist. Typically, these theories are of the rational actor type, although the concept of rationality has been subject to substantial debate and modification over the years. They come in packages named "rational choice theory", "decision making theory", "resource conversion theory", "cost benefit theory", "value maximising theory", and the like (historical overview in Collins, 1994: 121–180, 301–304). They are to a large extent employed in studies of distributions of some type or another and constitute the theoretical element in macro-sociological investigations of whole or partial populations.

George C. Homans, who attempted to integrate the notion of rational behaviour and stimulus–response theory in psychology, was one of the earliest sociologists who presented a coherent theory of this type. Other well-known proponents of exchange and rational choice theories are Peter M. Blau, James Coleman, and Jon Elster. The weight in the empirical investigations is placed on the perceptions and preferences leading to choices, which result in specific actions. It is in these processes that an explanation emerges.

Adjustment Explanation

Choice explanations and adjustment explanations have much in common but differ in regard to the use of theories. Adjustment explanations hold that internalised differences in individuals' responses to the social conditions they experience create patterns of social stability or change. The groups and categories to which individuals are attached render individual behaviour meaningful. They do what they have been socialised to do: They imitate their parents, or peers, or other persons important to them, or they follow expectations or norms that are central in the social systems to which they belong. In Max Weber's words, a substantial share of our actions are affective or traditional, not goal oriented.

Pierre Bourdieu and his colleagues employ one version of this type of explanation when they study the same pattern of inequality in educational attainment that Boudon studies. The basic notion is that children and youth in the different social classes develop different *habituses* that render some of them better equipped than others to succeed in our modern competitive societies. Their parents' position in the class system offers new members of society unequal access to economic, cultural, and social capital, and the control of cultural capital is particularly decisive in determining what type of education they are able to complete and wish to pursue, and thereby which occupations they may hold in later life. To a large extent, these perceptions and attitudes are subconscious, habitual, and more or less consistent. As a strong tendency, however, one result of class-differentiated socialisation is that children select educations that keep them in the same social class as their parents (Bourdieu and Passeron, 1977).

Among other adjustment studies in sociology are examples such as the quality of life studies conducted in many countries. They describe the distribution of access to goods regarding various social indicators such as health, wealth, education, housing, working conditions, opportunities for political influence, etc. and explain variations in their distribution by demonstrating how they are interrelated, how resources in one area may be converted to well-being in another, the existence of supportive or antagonistic circles among them, and so forth.

The theories applied in such studies include processes such as consistency seeking, conformity pressures, learning, ritualism, imitation, mimicking the successful, generalisation of resources, and the interplay of stimuli and responses. In other words, adjustment explanations often employ theories from social psychology, combined with notions concerning differential socialisation or cultural and structural pressures of various sorts. A case in point is one of the most frequently cited experiments, conducted by Stanley Milgram (1974) and repeated subsequently in other versions, which demonstrates how easily individuals obey authorities despite having good reasons not to do so. It may also be noted that Homans' theory suggested above can be assigned both an adjustment interpretation and a rational action interpretation.

The basic structure of the explanatory model in adjustment explanations is much the same as in choice explanations. Instead of choices, however, the features of note are orientations, values, psychic resources, personal capabilities, and so forth. Instead of perceptions and preferences, the objects of study include the general personality traits of the type that Bourdieu labels "habitus", or what Anthony Giddens indicates by his concept of practical consciousness.

This type of aggregation analysis also often requires large quantitative studies (preferably over a certain time span), with data from existing public or private sources or survey research of various types. In addition, intensive studies on the development of particularly interesting habituses have been performed.

Opportunity Structures

The core of the explanations explored thus far can be linked to the notions of rational and habitual action. This is somewhat unfair to Boudon and Bourdieu because their works are both multifarious and complex. By concentrating on other aspects of their reasoning, their research on educational inequality might also have been used as examples of the types of explanation observed when introducing the notion of opportunity structures. In this type of explanation, external limitations and access to resources become more important.

The question now is the following: what *social* factors lie behind the differences in individuals' values and wants and their choices and adjustments? One answer is that social patterns are often the results of the possibilities for action and interaction offered by the sociocultural structure in which the action is taking place. We shift the explanatory weight from individual decisions and faculties to the material, structural and cultural circumstances that channel individual motivations and behaviour. These circumstances may be regarded as either situational elements or conditions of action connected to the roles the individuals occupy.

Situation Logic Explanation

In this type of explanation, the sociologist regards social patterns as results of the relationships between actors in specific situations and the actions that appear rational given that situation. When many individuals face similar situations and the majority of them choose the same solutions, a social regularity emerges. The description of the situation will often contain specifications of the actors' interests and power resources and the resulting strategies they follow. A simple and well-known example of this type of analysis is the supply and demand theory in economics, which is applied in one market situation or another.

Our main example, the correlation between crimes for profit and urbanisation, has been a favourite theme among criminologists in the area of situational crime and its prevention (see e.g., Clarke and Felson, 1993). The proponents of the "criminality game", as many other criminologists/sociologists refer to it, seek to find answers to the question of why there is a strong correlation between urbanisation and the frequency of crimes for profit. Their central contention is that such behaviour emerges in differing situations based on the relationships among four sets of factors: the effectiveness of informal social control, the resources of the formal control apparatus, the reactions of the public, and the supply of material goods in the community. All actors involved make decisions based on evaluations of the situation and the other actors, and the strategies selected are more frequently to the benefit of the perpetrators the more urbanised the neighbourhoods are.

There are several studies that appear to confirm such an explanation of varying criminality rates. In Sweden, for instance, Olof Dahlbäck has conducted advanced studies demonstrating that the theft rate increases with increasing urbanisation and decreasing strength of social ties. These factors work together, and Dahlbäck's interpretation is that the associations may be considered a result of decisions to steal when conditions are favourable (Dahlbäck, 1998).

In addition to the theories outlined in the presentation of choice explanations, the obvious type of theory to be mentioned here is exchange theory and its variant, game theory (Ritzer, 2008: 280–318). Decision-making theory is another candidate. These types of theories are applied extensively in political science, often concerning collective actors in various settings. Additionally, Erving Goffman's ideas concerning impression management may be relevant in studies of how situations develop. A third theory in this vein is Fredrik Barth's expositions of "generative processes", which has shaped much of Norwegian and international social anthropology (Barth, 1966).

We observe situation logic explanations at all social levels, and the empirical studies comprise all types of studies: experiments, observations, surveys, the use of existing statistics, historical studies, and so forth. They presuppose that human beings attempt maximise or at least optimise their values, given their "rationality horizon". The explanations consist of descriptions of the situation that the actors experience, explications of the actors' reasons for their actions, and demonstrations of how they act in line with their interests. The actions often may be regarded as aspects of more extensive lapses of interaction. The explanations often include simple or more extensive documentation of how the actions result in social regularities or other patterns. In this way, social reality is constructed by social exchange and rational action.

Context Explanation

Context explanations maintain that structural and cultural circumstances channel individuals' actions and behaviour, and because the circumstances are mostly relatively stable, they thereby reproduce social patterns. By the same logic, when circumstances change, the social patterns also change. Some of these circumstances derive from individuals' roles (sex roles, age roles, occupational roles, family roles, etc.), whereas others derive from the groups and communities (including organisations, nations, etc.) to which they belong.

Because many social systems at times may have conflicting norms or interests, their members experience cross pressures and strains. This is a crucial point in Robert K. Merton's theory of the distribution of deviant behaviour (Merton, 1957). Merton asks why an inverse relationship between social status and crimes for profit exists in the USA. He finds the answer in a combination of individuals' opportunity situations and the dominant cultural values concerning success. When means and ends are incongruent – as they, nearly by definition, are in the lower social strata – a stressful situation occurs. For certain citizens, the solution to this situation is to commit crimes. For certain individuals, deviance is an adaptation to the national culture, when the economic context prohibits other routes of action. The aggregate result is the existing pattern of criminality.

This stress theory was further developed by researchers such as Albert Cohen, Richard Cloward, and Lloyd Ohlin, who specified several types of blocked opportunities and investigated them empirically (Cloward and Ohlin, 1960). Of course, there are also a number of alternative and supplementary explanations of criminal behaviour, some contextual, some of other types. Among other issues, they emphasise the socialisation to subcultures, differential associations, or the stigmatisation of deviant groups.

A vast number of studies explain action and interaction patterns by characteristics of the context in which individuals are placed. The context may be characterised by the structural and cultural opportunities or the blocked opportunities that individuals experience. Contextual factors may comprise social pressures or cross pressures or the expectations individuals perceive and the values and norms they have internalised. An example is Oscar Lewis' analysis of the culture of poverty in Mexico City and other places (Lewis, 1959). As a contrast, a Norwegian study of generational differences demonstrated that, as the historical context changes, new generations change their evaluations and expectations accordingly, occasionally in opposition to their parents' socialisation efforts (Almås, Karlsen and Thorland, 1995).

According to such explanations, the processes at work may be subsumed under the headings of structural and cultural coercion. They include the resource distribution, socialisation, social pressures and cross pressures, overt social inclusion and exclusion, alienation, and so forth. Role theory includes some of these processes. Additionally, Erving Goffman's theory of frames and framing may be mentioned in this respect. The processes may be investigated by the complete spectrum of sociological methods. However, as these processes are typically modelled at the individual level, they are often quantitative and apply a multivariate analysis of some type. In quantitative studies, perceptions, needs, wants, and attitudes comprise the intermediate variables that are included to grasp the processes at work.

Communities

A central idea in sociology is that all individuals depend on the groups and networks to which they belong and require the support and directions that they are given in these communities. The explanations of social action and interaction focusing on this idea generally consist of accounts and interpretations of cultural and social structures, usually with less quantitative documentation than in the studies considered thus far. The main idea is that humans, as essentially social beings, act in accordance with the expectations and pressures they experience in the various groups and organisations to which they belong, while simultaneously exerting their own influence on the on-going interaction. The result may be in-group conformity and out-group hostility, with both cases leading to social differentiation and specific structural and cultural patterns.

I denote the framework that gives a society (or any social system) its shape "the sociocultural structure" to emphasise that not only its division of labour and hierarchical order but also its culture are central aspects of it. When individuals act as occupants of various positions and roles in the communities to which they belong, they behave differently because the positions are defined by certain possibilities for action and certain values, norms and understandings.

Of course, the sentences above express the tension between structural and intentional modes of thought. Anthony Giddens' solution, his concept of the duality of structure, implies that the over-individual socio-structures afford individuals certain possibilities of action while simultaneously enabling them to act in competent ways in the groups and organisations to which they belong. Structure and actor are mutually conditioning. The two types of explanations in this section each focus on one of the sides of this duality. Our two main examples are thus quite different. West and Zimmerman emphasise the intentional side of human interaction, whereas the example from Emile Durkheim's work focuses on the consequences of social integration itself and how social structure affects individuals' tendency to commit suicide.

Joint Action Explanation

The concept of joint action stems from Herbert Blumer (1969). The point of departure for action explanations is that in everyday interaction, individuals' understandings of social reality and their own positions in said reality regularly lead to certain actions rather than others. Moreover, the mutual processing of their actions results in common norms and styles of behaviour. As a typical example of such an analysis, I have selected Candace West and Donald Zimmerman's analysis of how children and youths become gendered beings (West and Zimmerman, 1987). Gendered norms and behaviours are conspicuous traits of social institutions worldwide.

West and Zimmerman seek to explain the stability of existing sex roles and gender-specific inequalities over generations. They find their explanation in the day-to-day interactions of those involved in the socialisation of children (including the children themselves). Values and norms concerning femininity and masculinity are communicated in nearly all everyday situations, even among those who oppose them on a political level. West and Zimmerman coined the expression "doing gender" to label their account of how gender differences are reproduced in the USA. Subsequently, several studies were conducted of other cultural or relational patterns that are "done" during the course of individuals' day-to-day interactions. Through this type of interaction, one affirms what is legitimate and what is considered deviant. Other processes involved in everyday interactions among parents and children comprise the communication of what is considered right or wrong, as well as tacit negotiations concerning the correct behaviour in all types of situations. The result is that gender differences are reproduced. Much gender research has sought to unveil these types of relations and processes.

Among other well-known examples of this type of research are Howard S. Becker's studies on how gossip and stigmatisation in local communities lead certain youths into criminal environments in which group or gang members develop solidarity and identities as deviants (Becker, 1963). We also find Herbert J. Gans' investigations of how the USA has evolved to conceptualised the poor as "the unworthy needy" by the use of phrases and arguments in the mass media depicting their misery as self-inflicted (Gans, 1995). Furthermore, Fredrik Barth's analysis of value integration in groups and societies resulted from myriad public and private conversations and implied evaluations, which has undergone continuous modifications.

For several reasons, the typical study design in joint action research is a type of participatory observation, followed by a narrative presentation of results. Community studies, organisation studies, small group research, etc. often use observations or intensive interviews. Theory and presentation of results are often intertwined. Erving Goffman's studies are a case in point.

The processes emphasised in joint action explanations include imitation, identity and conformity seeking, identity construction, tacit negotiations, labelling, personal influence, integration, and exclusion, among others. Some of these may be regarded as components of discourse theory. Randall Collins presented a theory concerning ritual chains of interaction, which is central to many studies of joint action. His work on the microfoundations of macro-sociology (Collins, 1981) must be regarded as a classic in this area. The majority of theories employed in joint action explanations stem from the Chicago school and its offspring: symbolic interactionism and ethnomethodology.

Social Integration Explanation

The basic understanding in social integration explanations is that humans are members of various social systems (small and large groups, organisations, regions, nations, etc.) and occupy specific positions in the institutions of these systems, which offer them restricted courses of action in the various situations that compose their lives. Occasionally the values and norms of the systems are conflicting, thereby creating stress and other problems. Clearly, these ideas are not substantially different from those underlying context explanations. However, in integration explanations, system descriptions become more important, and social identity and belongingness play greater roles. The social integration of members of a given community is not a matter of course, and theories of social exclusion may be important in certain social integration explanations.

This last point is important in our main example in this section: Emile Durkheim's explanation of what he (somewhat unfortunately) called egoistic suicide (Durkheim, 1952). By means of suicide statistics from nations and regions in Europe, he sought to study whether suicidal tendencies varied in accordance with how well individuals were integrated into various social groups and networks. His definition of social integration partly included the clarity of the norms concerning moral conduct in a social system and partly the strength of belonging to various social unities. When these circumstances vary, the suicide rate will also vary.

Egoistic suicide is the result of weak social ties. When an individual in such a situation encounters problems, he or she will not receive adequate social support. Single adults, for instance, generally have weaker family ties than others, and their probability of suicide will therefore be higher than that of married persons or formerly married individuals with children. Suicide may be a solution to one's life problems in such situations, which is the reason that Durkheim called such suicides "egoistic". Durkheim also maintains that social integration in general is weaker among Protestants than among Catholics, a fact explaining why suicide rates are the highest in Protestant nations and regions. He also finds that when nations are subject to external threats, social integration in general increases, and suicide rates decline.

Other types of social integration explanations may not involve the personal consequences of variations in types and degrees of integration but instead concentrate on behavioural patterns that affect group stability, effectiveness in organisations, human relations, and many other interpersonal relations. Ideas regarding the consequences of various degrees of integration have been central in network studies of various types. Position in social networks has been demonstrated to influence outcomes as diverse as job chances, illness, happiness, etc. Integration in religious communities has been identified as a source of social capital (Furseth, 2008). Social capital in itself has been regarded as an aspect of social integration, and in *Bowling alone,* Robert Putnam (2000) discussed the negative effects of the decline of communities in the USA. Any type of research method may be used to investigate these types of processes.

The processes most frequently studied in social integration explanations include socialisation, resource mobilisation and conversion, the use of power, informal sanctions, habitual behaviour, role taking, and formal sanctioning. The actions involved in such processes are typically unconscious and unplanned and part of what Bourdieu would label the "practical consciousness". Theories concerning these processes include role theory, power resources theory, alienation theory, social capital theory, reference-group theory and network theory.

Social Systems

In this text, I use the term "social system" in a broad sense, as a common label that can be applied to social groups, organisations, institutions, and societies of various types. This usage may differ from the concept of system in (general) system theories.

Systems explanations regard social patterns as elements of social wholes. The central concept is to analyse the whole or system as a complex set of mutually reinforcing or conflicting components that, to varying degrees, shape a given social regularity. This type of relatively stable social unit may be the result of on-going balances of power, or it can be based on arrangements for common solutions to a given problem. The systems may have developed over a long period, and the reproduction or change they undergo may be protracted and manifold.

The explanatory strategy employed in these studies is to render accounts of important elements and interdependencies in the system as a whole, thereby revealing how the specific pattern to be explained is a built-in or more-or-less necessary part of the whole. The idea is that the system and its elements contain an impetus that drives it in the direction of stability or in the direction of a specific change. The documentation of on-going processes may be quantitative, narrative, or both.

Linkage Explanation

The main concept in linkage explanations is that social relations and structures are interrelated in specific ways that compose larger wholes in which the parts are mutually conditioning. The effects often work across societal levels. The reasons that individuals in different situations act in different manners remain in the background or are built-in assumptions, and the researchers' interest lies in the characteristics of groups, organisations, societies, and so forth, as well as their interrelations and connections. The processes involved include mutual dependencies and reinforcement, market dynamics, built-in pressures, etc.

A classic example of a linkage explanation is Robert Michels' analysis of the tendencies toward oligarchy in political parties, especially the parties on the left that have an explicitly democratic ideology (Michels, 1962). His famous answer to the "why" question involved is this: "Who says organization, says oligarchy". In his book, he specifies this assertion and attempts to document the connections he observes using various methods.

By "oligarchy", he means the recurring pattern in large organisations of domination by elite group(s), despite their egalitarian ideology and the controls implemented to promote it. His explanation is a two-step one, and in both steps, he develops hypotheses regarding causes at the psychological, organisational, and societal levels. The first step is to describe a relatively long list of oligarchic tendencies. The explanation provided consists of the interplay of several factors. At the societal level, Michels stresses the need for a division of labour, which leads to the development of effective organisations, including political parties. At the psychological level, the effects of mass and leader attitudes and skills are investigated. However, amongst the most immediate conditions, certain technical considerations are noteworthy: the impossibility of direct government in the organisation, the need for strategic promptness, the superiority of leaders relative to the incompetence of the members, and the complex composition of the mass membership.

Among other examples of linkage explanations, one is much simpler: Maurice Duverger's study of the interrelation between election arrangements and party systems in democratic states (1954). Another example is the frequent linking of welfare systems and poverty, which have been extensively studied in more recent years. Certain researchers have distinguished among four welfare systems or life-cycle regimes in Western nations and have demonstrated how these sociocultural structures lead to quite different poverty risks among the members of the various nations (Brückner, 1995).

In summary, this type of analysis explains components of a larger social system by demonstrating that they are connected in specific ways. The connections are often results of rational decisions in many of the components. The mutual conditioning processes included in linkage explanations may include of all of the types of processes mentioned in this chapter thus far. Some of them are grouped under the headings of "bureaucracy theory", "governance theory", "market theory", and so forth. In other words, a substantial share of what is placed under the heading of "organisation theory" may be used in linkage explanations. The research methods employed may also be any of those observed in sociology.

Functional Explanation

Functional explanations seek to document how social relations and structures are reproduced or change because they have positive consequences for the social whole of which they are a part. This idea implies an element of feedback, meaning that a functional explanation consists of at least two (or often more) interconnected processes. The understanding is that the pattern to be explained is reproduced or changes because its consequences trigger reactions that have the reproduction or change as their effect. The typical functional explanation is perhaps a combination of a social integration explanation and a joint action explanation.

One of the most well-known and extensively debated functional explanations in sociology is Kingsley Davis and Wilbert E. Moore's analysis of social stratification in modern industrial societies (Davis and Moore, 1945). In summary, their exposition highlights that an enduring pattern in the modern world is the hierarchy of economic positions in larger social systems, which results in an unequal distribution of numerous types of goods and burdens and, thus, of the welfare of the systems' members. We find the factors contributing to this structured social inequality to fall into two complex processes that are linked together: those that secure the recruitment to the various positions and those that motivate the members to participate in the recruitment system.

Wealth and prestige are approximately distributed in accordance with the importance and difficulty of the positions in question. The motivating feedback is regarded as an extensive process of justification, often mediated by important rituals and ceremonies. Feedback mechanisms may consist of indirect exclusions, social distancing, open or tacit negotiations, conformism/ imitation, empathy, subconscious strategies, etc. As is well known, this theory has been criticised extensively and on many accounts.

Another famous functional explanation is William Kornhauser's analysis of the stabilising role of voluntary organisations in modern societies (Kornhauser, 1959). In the same vein, Sverre Lysgård (1967) explained the existence of an informal "workers collective" by its protection of the industrial workers against the insatiable demands of the technical-economic system. Yngvar Løchen (1965) explained a phenomenon observed in the mental hospitals he studied, which he labelled "the diagnostic culture", as necessary to day-to-day problem solving, maintained by the joint actions of staff members acting on the basis of their professional habitus.

The debates on functionalism and functional explanations have persisted for many years, and they have occasionally been quite heated (e.g., Ritzer, 2008: 97–138).

Conclusion

On the preceding pages, I have argued that a substantial number of sociological explanations fall into one of eight basic types. They stem from four general notions regarding what shapes patterns of human actions: the behaviour that individuals consider meaningful, the opportunities of action they encounter, the norms and resources with which they are endowed by their communities, and the characteristics of the social systems of which they are a part. For each of these four ideas are corresponding condition-oriented and intention-oriented versions.

Explanations are nearly always tentative and bypass certain elements in the chain of explanation. Typically, there are no ready-made theories for each type. The theory or theories to be confronted in a specific explanation frequently must be sought by the researcher or constructed during the investigation. On the preceding pages, I have indicated that choice explanations and situation logic explanations are primarily based on rational actor and social exchange theories, whereas joint action explanations and linkage explanations chiefly employ a type of interaction theory. Adjustment explanations and context explanations generally contain elements of a materialist or social ecological theory, perhaps of a neo-Marxist type, or a power resources theory or some other theory involving structural differentiation and coercion. Social integration explanations and functional explanations are generally based on functionalist or neo-functionalist theories.

In the discussions above, explanations are shown to be based on all types of empirical documentations and may have a narrative or quantitative form. Statistical tools may be utilised in all forms of explanations. The intentions and characteristics of social systems may be measured and appear as variables in statistical causal analyses.

The main reason that *combinations* of the two axes in our figure occasionally appear in actual social research is that the explanation would otherwise be incomplete and unsatisfactory. A sociologist attempting to clarify a broad societal pattern must make assumptions regarding the actions and interactions of which the pattern is composed or even document some of them. Regardless of whether this pattern is depicted as a social system or an aggregated phenomenon, the researcher would likely prefer to complete the explanation using theories and justifications from either the constructionist- or the structure-oriented camp. Boudon's rational choice explanation of the inequality of educational attainment, for instance, might be combined with a joint action analysis of conversations among youths and their parents. In the same manner, a sociologist attempting to explain a given pattern of action often wishes to indicate or describe how the actions and interactions are aggregated or constitute an element in a larger social system.

In everyday empirical sociology, two or more types of explanations often ought to be confronted, as in the case of Boudon versus Bourdieu, as mentioned above. Elements of more complex analyses should more frequently be pitted against one another as *alternatives*, regardless of whether they are part of a statistical argument or a narrative one. However, one ought not to forget that these theories and explanations stem from different philosophical and meta-theoretical perspectives that likely cannot be combined at all. This means that providing an explanation nearly always entails presenting the reader or listener with a certain universe of interpretation. Another type of theory and explanation would have offered another perspective and a different understanding.

References

Almås, R., Karlsen, K. and Thorland, I. (1995). *Fra pliktsamfunn til mulighetstorg*. [From a society of duties to a marketplace of opportunities]. Trondheim: Center for rural research.

Barth, F. (1966). "Models of social organization", *Occational papers 23*. London: Royal Anthropological Institute.

Becker, H.S. (1963). *Outsiders: studies in the sociology of deviance*. New York: The Free Press.

Blumer, H. (1969). *Symbolic interaction: perspective and method*. Englewood Cliffs, N.J.: Prentice-Hall.

Boudon, R. (1974). *Education, opportunity and social inequality: changing prospects in Western society*. New York: Wiley.

Bourdieu, P. and Passeron, J.C. (1977). *Reproduction in education, society and culture*. London: Sage.

Breen, R. and Whelan, C.T. (1994). "Modelling trends in social fluidity: the core model and a measures-variable approach compared", *European Sociological Review*. 10(3): 259–272.

Brückner, H. (1995). "'Times of poverty'. Lessons from the Bremen longitudinal social assistance sample", *Research in Community Sociology*. 5: 203–224.

Clarke, R.V. and Felson, M. (eds.). (1993). *Routine activity and rational choice*. New Brunswick: Transaction Publishers.

Cloward, R.A. and Ohlin, L.E. (1960). *Delinquency and opportunity*. Glencoe: The Free Press.

Collins, R. (1981). "On the microfoundations of macrosociology", *American Sociological Review*. 86(5): 984.

Collins, R. (1994). *Four sociological traditions*. New York: Oxford University Press.

Dahlbäck, O. (1998). "Modelling the influence of societal factors on municipal theft rates in Sweden: methodological and substantial findings", *Acta Sociologica*. 41(1): 37–57.

Davis, K. and Moore, W.E. (1945). "Some principles of social stratification", *American Sociological Review*. 10(2): 242–249.

Durkheim, E. (1952). *Suicide: a study in sociology*. London: Routledge and Kegan Paul.

Duverger, M. (1954). *Political parties*. London: Methuen.

Furseth, I. (2008). "Social capital and immigrant religion", *Nordic Journal of Religion and Society.* 21(2): 147–164.

Gans, H.J. (1995). *The war against the poor.* New York: Basic Books.

Hedström, P. and Swedberg, R. (eds.). (1998). *Social mechanisms: an analytical approach to social theory.* Cambridge: Cambridge University Press.

Jenks, C. (ed.). (1998). *Core sociological dichotomies.* London: Sage.

Kornhauser, W. (1959). *The politics of mass society.* New York: The Free Press.

Lewis, O. (1959). *Five families: Mexican case studies in the culture of poverty.* New York: Basic Books.

Lysgård, S. (1967). *Arbeiderkollektivet.* [The workers' collective]. Oslo: Universitetsforlaget.

Løchen, Y. (1965). *Idealer og realiteter i et psykiatrisk sykehus.* [Ideals and realities in a psychiatric hospital]. Oslo: Universitetsforlaget.

Merton, R.K. (1957). *Social theory and social structure.* New York: The Free Press.

Michels, R. (1962). *Political parties: a sociological study of the oligarchical tendencies of modern democracy.* New York: Dover.

Milgram, S. (1974). *Obedience to authority: an experimental view.* New York: Harpercollins.

Putnam, R.D. (2000). *Bowling alone: the collapse and revival of American community.* New York: Simon and Schuster.

Ritzer, G. (2008). *Modern sociological theory.* 7th edition. New York: Mc Graw-Hill International.

Skog, O.J. (2006). *Skam og skade. Noen avvikssosiologiske temaer.* [Shame and damage. Some themes in the sociology of deviance]. Oslo: Gyldendal akademisk.

West, C. and Zimmerman, D. (1987). "Doing gender", *Gender and Society.* 1(2): 125–151.

CHAPTER 11

A Thick Description of Robert K. Merton's Middle Range Theory – Manifest Properties and Latent Ambivalence

Peter Sohlberg

Introduction

In the introductory chapter to this volume, we discussed various approaches to theory, implying an immense variety of theoretical operations. The variety of approaches attests to, on the one hand, a richness of perspectives from which to understand social life and, on the other, the associated problems of trying to provide a systematic and comprehensive account of them. This is a typical situation characterizing the openness and unpredictability of creativity; a creativity with its roots in methodological as well as theoretical innovation. The abundance of books on methodology and their related prescriptions on the practical aspects of conducting research has, however, no equivalent in the literature on theory (cf. Swedberg, 2014). In other words, while we have many explicit prescriptions on research method, a more uncertain situation exists when it comes to theory use. Theories are often treated as iconic and closed world-views rather than knowledge-generating devices (cf. Ch. 1).

In this chapter I will discuss an attempt to systematize sociological theorizing in terms of middle range theory as formulated by Robert K. Merton (1910–2003). Few sociologists have coined, formulated and reformulated as many theoretical concepts as Merton. He may be regarded as one of the most creative sociologists since World War II. His influence, as marked by his ability to construct and reconstruct heuristically fruitful concepts such as *self-fulfilling prophecy*, *anomie* and *opportunity structure*, is often latent and more widespread than openly acknowledged, largely depending on his ability to construct and reconstruct heuristically fruitful concepts. The scope of Merton's oeuvre is massive (cf. Calhoun, 2010; Sztompka, 1986). His theoretical creativity is firmly based on his interest in the "empirical world". This is probably a major reason for the wide programmatic acceptance of his brand of theory – theories of middle range.

Aside from his middle range theories, and to some extent his reformulation of functionalism, it would be surprisingly difficult to give a comprehensive summary of Merton's theoretical contribution. Rarely, if ever, do we refer to

"Merton's theory" in the same way that we refer to "Parson's theory" or "Bourdieu's theory". Additionally, Merton does not get treated to a separate chapter
in Joas and Knöbel's textbook of sociological theory (Joas and Knöbl, 2009),
and he is mentioned, merely in passing, in a few sentences in Jeffrey Alexander's overview of sociological theory (Alexander, 1987). And when Merton is
discussed more comprehensively, as in Jonathan H. Turner's *The structure of
sociological theory*, it is under the rather restricted heading "Empirical functionalism" (Turner, 1991). In George Ritzer's textbook *Sociological theory*, Merton's theoretical contributions are identified as "Robert Merton's structural
functionalism" (Ritzer, 2008: 251 ff). Thus, Merton's theoretical identity seems
rather vague and ambivalent as he is often identified with functionalism, a
theoretical tradition he famously criticized. Here I will argue that the difficulty
in characterizing Merton's oeuvre in a holistic fashion is not solved by referring
to his middle range theory.

The aim of this chapter is to give a "thick description" and discussion of
middle range theories as presented by Merton. I use "thick description" in an
extended metaphorical way as it relates to the interpretation of texts. Clifford
Geertz's idea of the contextual, cultural understanding of social events can be
transposed to texts. This is highly relevant as an interpretative strategy when
reading Merton, as his texts are often ambivalent, vague, and replete with
examples and programmatic statements pointing in different directions.
The outcome consists of multiple layers of text where I take, as a starting point,
the programmatic statements and examples, and then continue with a discussion of their implications for how to interpret Merton's actual practice in
a wider theoretical perspective. This general theoretical perspective is partly a
matter of Merton's programmatic positioning and partly the implications that
result from this. A methodological aspect is that Merton's text, in its complexity and ambiguity, is an interesting case, demonstrating the need to separate
between programmatic statements and their implications, when analyzing
theory.

In terms of disposition, I begin with describing the usual "negative specification" of middle range theory, i.e., what they are *not*. This definition by negation
is followed by a characterization in positive terms of structural/methodologi-
cal and functional properties of middle range theory, according to Merton's
writing. What follows on the basis of this presentation, is a discussion of the
problems with the application of middle range theorizing to theory construction. Finally middle range theorizing is contextualized within the general
framework of Merton's theoretical work. My conclusion is that Merton's theoretical creativity extends beyond the programmatic limits of middle range
theory.

The Middle Way of Theorizing

In the introduction to his famous essay, *On sociological theories of the middle range* Merton complains about the imprecise use of the word theory:

> Like so many words that are bandied about, the word theory threatens to become meaningless. Because its referents are so diverse-...use of the word often obscures rather than creates understanding.
>
> MERTON, 1968: 39

The attempt to codify middle range theory could be seen as a response by Merton to the vagueness of the theory concept in sociology. His theoretical construction and baptizing of "middle range" theories has been influential in the discussion of theoretical strategies in sociology and in other fields. His position has been particularly important in social science as a kind of programmatic standpoint, formulated as a reasonable middle-position between not so reasonable extremes. The one extreme being universal deductive theories in grand scale, and the other extreme low-level inductive generalizations:

> ...the term *sociological theory* refers to logically interconnected sets of propositions from which empirical uniformities can be derived. Throughout we focus on what I have called *theories of the middle range*: theories that lie between the minor but necessary working hypotheses that evolve in abundance during day-to-day research and the all-inclusive systematic efforts to develop a unified theory that will explain all the observed uniformities of social behavior, social organization and social change.
>
> MERTON, 1968: 39

Whatever topic, Merton is meticulous when describing the genealogical network of the development of theories, perspectives and concepts. This relates to his idea of science as a collective effort where the cumulative character is essential for understanding the open and dynamic character of a sound scientific community. When presenting the idea of a general middle range strategy for theory formation, Merton refers to names as e.g., Francis Bacon, John Stuart Mill and Karl Mannheim as examples. Despite obvious differences in articulation and varying historical contexts, Merton claims they all employ a common research strategy consisting of theoretically informed but empirically based studies – the middle way. How should we then understand this middle way? The most common way is by negation.

The Negative Characterization – The Theoretical Other

In the introductory chapter we identified, as a powerful force in theoretical social science discourse, the reactive force, i.e., its positioning in contrast to other, often dominant, positions in the theoretical field. Middle range theory is a good illustration of this kind of positioning. When scholars refer to Merton's middle range theories it is usually in negative terms, by contrasting them with two other kinds of theories: general theories and low level empirical generalizations.

The problem, however, is that a great majority of theories in social science are situated between the extremes of Parsonian general theory and raw empiricism. This main bulk of theories cannot be regarded as homogenous enough to qualify for a particular label as, for example, middle range theories. This seemingly balanced position of middle range theory is more a matter of verbal phrasing than capturing the methodological "essence" of what is labeled middle range theories. As will be elaborated below, being positioned *between* general theories and empirical generalization is not, methodologically, a symmetrical relation.

To conclude this section, the negative characterization of middle range theories does not make the idea of middle range theories particularly substantial. It is also an implicit assumption to be problematized in this chapter that there is a clear-cut theoretical position between the two extremes. Merton does, however, also provide some positive clues of how to identify the middle range quality.

The Positive Characterization of Middle Range Theories

The Ostensive Definition by Examples

Merton's main characterization of middle range theories is done by giving examples of theories along with brief comments on how their properties represent the middle way. Some examples presented by Merton include theories of reference groups, theories of social mobility, theories of role conflict and theories about the formation of social norms (Merton, 1968: 40).

This catalogue of theories seems intuitively reasonable as being something more than mere empirical generalizations and something less than general theories of the Parsonian kind. It is however also conceivable that e.g., theories of social mobility and the formation of social norms could be theoretically integrated in general theories. This is actually the case with theories about the formation of norms, where the functionalist tradition is the best example of a highly general theory integrating a concept of norms as a basic element.

An example of middle range theory from the classic tradition suggested by Merton is Durkheim's work, *Suicide* (Merton, 1968: 63). This may come as a surprise since Durkheim's treatise is complex and general in a way that would not make it an obvious example of a middle way. A less logicical and more pragmatic way of understanding this labeling of Durkheim's work is that it was used as a methodological illustration in Merton's teaching at Columbia (Turner, 2009b: 485). I will come back to the positioning of Durkheim when discussing his methodological strategy.

It remains to be discussed whether the ostensive definitions and examples of middle range theorizing presented by Merton really has a common denominator rather than just a superficial resemblance. In addition to his examples, Merton also provides some positive and substantial characterizations of middle range theorizing. In my presentation of these properties, it is useful to distinguish between structural/methodological characteristics and functional characteristics. The structural/methodological characterization relates to the conceptual structure of the theories and strategies behind their formation whereas the functional characterization has to do with their role and use in social science.

Structural and Methodological Properties of Middle Range Theories

When characterizing middle range theories Merton often refers to logical structure and logical relations and draws analogies between natural sciences and sociology. He states that it is the logical structure that is fundamental for their common identity as theories of the middle range:

> Contemporary sociological theories of the middle range may not uniformly have the cogency or power of such earlier examples of physical and natural science, but they do exhibit the same uncomplicated logical structure.
>
> MERTON, 1957: 110

As mentioned above, Merton's structural characterization of middle-range theories basically states that they are constituted by propositions that are logically interconnected and can be used to derive empirical uniformities. When describing, in another context, theory formation in general, Merton describes the genesis of theory where he highlights the importance of choosing theoretically loaded concepts:

> It is only when such concepts [e.g., gemeinschaft, status, role (my comment)] are interrelated in the form of a scheme that a theory begins to

emerge. Concepts, then constitute the definitions (or prescriptions) of what is to be observed; they are the variables between which empirical relationships are to be sought. When propositions are logically interrelated, a theory has been instituted.

MERTON, 1968: 143

This means that rather than the simple logical structure per se, it is the interrelated concepts that are crucial. Later in this chapter I will get back to the importance of choice of concepts for Merton's theorizing.

The Property of Being "in between"

As we have seen, the metaphorical quality of being "in between" is crucial for the description of middle range theories. Being "between" suggests some dimension of generality, but it is unclear of what this dimension consists. It may in principle refer to, for example, the *structural properties*, i.e., the organizational complexity of the theory; or it may refer to the *generality of the premises*. The premises of Parson's functional requisite analysis, in the form of the AGIL-scheme is, for example, general indeed. The dimension of generality could also refer to the *knowledge-claims* of the theory. For example, rational choice theory is almost universal concerning its knowledge claims, even though its basic structure is simple. Furthermore, the dimension could refer to *the reference in time and space* of the concepts constituting the theory.

In addition to the non-answered question of what constitutes the "generality-dimension", the methodological strategies related to these different levels remains to be discussed. The localization *between* general theories and low-level empirical generalizations does not mean that middle range theories are a kind of *methodological compromise* between the extreme levels. The ideal of middle range theory, regarded as a research strategy by Merton, is highly asymmetrical in relation to restricted empiricism and deductive general theory.

Concerning theoretical operations related to the two extremes, they represent qualitatively separate operations and not a matter of degree along a continuous dimension. In Merton's definition of middle range theories there is an ambiguity when it comes to what kind of actual theoretical operations are involved when constructing them. When discussing the abstract formation and use of theories, a distinction is usually made between inductive and deductive inferences. The question is if middle range theories can be seen as a compromise between the inductive and deductive approaches. Merton is vague on this point, and there are certainly tensions between his programmatic statements, their logical implications, and their actual practice.

Programmatically, Merton seems strongly in favor of the inductive approach, but this is in conflict with his actual practice. The concepts Merton chooses in his theoretical practice are not inductively constructed but are rather chosen from a deductive point of view, i.e., the concepts are at the outset theoretically embedded and not the outcome of inductive generalization.

Concerning the deductive way, it is hard to find cases where Merton gives explicit examples of general theories that in any way could be potentially useful for the formation of middle range theories. He is programmatically skeptical of the deductive utility of general theoretical schemes for theory formation. He states, for example: "it is equally clear that such middle-range theories have not been logically *derived* from a single all-embracing theory of social systems, though once developed they may be consistent with one" (Merton, 1968: 41).

In summary, Merton's standpoint is programmatically in favor of some kind of inductive approach which is theoretically more informed than working hypotheses. He regards it as a "misinterpretation...that systems of thought can be effectively developed before a great mass of basic observation has been accumulated" (Merton, 1968: 46). At the other extreme, he is explicitly skeptical of working deductively downwards from general theories. However, in practice, he works deductively when he chooses theoretically embedded concepts and applies them to an empirical setting.

The metaphor being located *between* empirical generalizations and general theories becomes even more confusing – considering that Merton sees Durkheim's theory of *Suicide* as an example of middle range theorizing. *Suicide* marks an attempt by Durkheim to deductively apply general methodological rules more explicitly formulated in *The rules of sociological method* (Durkheim, 1982). These general methodological principles begin with the identification of social facts. In turn, these facts are, in a most general way, characterized by their externality and their quality of exercising external constraints. Furthermore, these facts should be explained in terms of historical processes and functions. This is a highly deductive strategy and does not in any obvious way contain methodological elements of the middle range. Durkheim's substantial work could generally be regarded as an application of his methodological receipt, i.e., this is actually a case where, contrary to Merton's statement, a specific theory has "been logically *derived* from a single all-embracing theory of social systems" (Merton, 1968: 41).

A problematic implication of Merton's understanding of middle range theories has to do with their relationship with more general theories. On the one hand, he argues that middle range theories could be neutral in relation to more general theories, i.e., there is a potential for them to be embedded in several (even within themselves) conflicting or discrepant general theories:

> comprehensive sociological theories are sufficiently loose-knit, internal-
> ly diversified, and mutually overlapping that a given theory of the middle
> range, which has a measure of empirical confirmation, can often be sub-
> sumed under comprehensive theories which are themselves discrepant
> in certain respects.
>
> MERTON, 1968: 43

At the same time that Merton allows for a looseness between middle range-
theories and general theories, he also emphasizes that middle range theories
should be testable. Viewed from the perspective of a specific middle-range theory, it would seem difficult to envision any further value of the general theory
if it is so loosely connected as to allow embeddedness in several discrepant
general theories.

As we have seen, Merton's idea is that middle range theories should consist
of something more than specific empirical generalizations. Since there is nothing meaningful about the deductive process, according to Merton, a reasonable
interpretation is that middle-range theories should come into being through
some higher order inductive inference and abstraction. It is, however, hard
to identify this kind of reasoning in Merton's text when he discusses theory-
building programmatically. It is one thing is to give examples of middle-range
theories and quite another to demonstrate their construction.

In the few but interesting cases where Merton attempts to demonstrate the
practice of middle-range theory formation, inductive processes are actually
absent, however another aspect seems crucial here.

He uses concepts from natural science like magnetism and atmospheric
pressure, which form specific abstractions, to show how some sort of low-level
metaphorical deduction can be used to demonstrate the cognitive or heuristic
power of middle-range theorizing (Merton, 1968: 40). In Merton's own phrasing, it is a matter of "an image that gives rise to inferences...The initial idea thus
suggests specific hypotheses which are tested by seeing whether the inferences
from them are empirically confirmed" (Merton, 1968: 40). An analogous form
of reasoning is assumed valid for social science of the middle range (e.g., theories of reference groups and role sets).

Merton's view of theory is a rather conventional position and cannot easily
be differentiated from, for example, the hypothetical deductive model. Stephen
Turner discusses Merton's middle range conception in terms of the scientific
ideal existing in Merton's academic milieu. The main criticism articulated by
Turner is that Merton is intrinsically vague, diffuse, and undecided, even beyond ambivalence. Turner introduces what he labels the "Columbia model
of theory construction" as a point of reference when he tries to identify and

clarify Merton's position. Turner regards Merton's formulation of middle range theory as based on this Columbia model. This means that middle range theory, according to Turner, initially included a strategy and a promise:

> The promise of middle range theory was to free us from the problem of many approaches and few arrivals. By concentrating on empirical generalizations based on BASR-type [Bureau of Applied Social Research, my comment] survey results, abducting from them and transferring our theoretical understanding of them to other contexts, then theoretically systematizing these results and consolidating one theory with another, we could get conclusions, or arrivals.
>
> TURNER, 2009A: 205

Turner's assessment of Merton's approach is that this promise was never fulfilled. This verdict is, in my opinion, somewhat too categorical (for a critical discussion of Turner's critique see Sztompka, 2009).

Richard Swedberg (1996: 314) refers to "The Columbia school of sociology", with Merton and Lazarsfeld as its leaders (the conception actually validated by Merton). In this understanding, the Columbia school is almost identical with the common understanding of middle range theory along with its avoidance of raw empiricism and abstract theory and its focus on partial aspects of the social structure or social mechanisms (ibid). In this interpretation, the Columbia school of sociology constitutes, rather than influences, middle range theory.

It is certainly true that Merton's concept of middle-range theories is a fuzzy concept, and it is also true that the examples of middle-range theories mentioned by Merton as potential building-blocks for more comprehensive theories remained isolated building blocks. There are, however, aspects of Merton's theoretical strategies that should not be over-systematized, but could contribute in a piecemeal way to a more general understanding of theoretical creativity.

It is clear that Merton wants to avoid theories as empty analytical schemes, without empirical substance. Following the conventional hypothetical deductive ideal, he also wants theories to be tested. Nevertheless, what about the relationship between a specific middle-range theory and a set of general theories?

The loose logical and empirical ties between a specific middle range theory and possible general theories discussed above are in strong conflict with Merton's programmatic skepticism against deductive reasoning and his positive attitude towards theoretically informed inductive reasoning. General theories could, in consequence with this position, be acceptable only if they are based on inductive reasoning. When Merton describes the preconditions for the advancement of sociological theory, he identifies this strategy as a matter of "evolving not suddenly revealing a progressively more general conceptual scheme that is adequate to consolidate groups of special theories" (Merton, 1968: 51).

Seen in retrospect, Merton's "prophecy" that middle range theories could be developed and later integrated into more general theories following some sort of "inductive" process where the items "generalized" are middle range theories, does not seem to be fulfilled in any case. This can be seen as an important empirical indicator of the problems with Merton's idea of consolidation of more general theories. Stephen Turner even problematizes Merton's sincerity concerning the prospect of middle range theories being extended to more general theories: "In one of his oral histories Lazarsfeld comments that middle range theory was a misleading term since Merton himself didn't believe that there was anything beyond middle range theory" (Turner, 2009: 199).

Whatever the construction and substance or range of middle range theories, their function remains to be discussed.

Functional Characterization of Middle Range Theory

What then are the functions and knowledge claims of middle-range theories? Do middle range theories have a specific application and function that distinguishes them from other kinds of theories? The answer to this question relates to matters of generalization and theoretical heuristics. So far I have referred, nominally, to three levels of generalizations where middle range theories represent the middle way. I have problematized the conception of these three levels as representing a one-dimensional and continuous dimension, but for the sake of argument let us assume that we can identify these levels and that we can also relate them to their knowledge claims.

The knowledge claims of low-level generalizations and inductively formulated working-hypothesis are by definition restricted to the specific time and context in which they are formulated. Their function is mainly heuristic: finding a way to understand the specific patterns observed at a specific time and setting. Beyond the basic description of context-specific patterns, this can be described as low-level abductive reasoning, i.e., making understandable the specific situation studied.

The knowledge claims of general theory, as treated by Merton, are more complicated. Intuitively the answer would be that the knowledge claims are general and consist of identifying universal truths. Interestingly, this is not the typical case with general theories in social science. Taking the case of Talcott Parsons, he formulates general nomenclatures to be transposed as theoretical schemes to empirical cases. The claim of universality concerns not explanations per se but the applicability of these nomenclatures to a variety of empirical settings. Examples of such nomenclatures to be applied in a variety of settings are the pattern-variables and the AGIL-scheme. Merely adapting a specific theoretical scheme to an empirical case does not involve an explanation in the conventional case. Nicos Mouzelis (1995) identifies this problem with the deductive use of general theories when he discusses problems with Parson's operationalization of the AGIL-scheme. Mouzelis' discussion illustrates the extremely important distinction between a theory functioning, on the one hand, as a static, conceptual nomenclature and, on the other hand, as a substantial conceptualization identifying, for example, forces of change and inertia.

Middle range-theory does not constitute an end in itself, and Merton is programmatically very clear about their instrumental value. Beyond representing a point of view, theories should also, according to Merton, be testable and used for further inquiry. When describing the methodological position of middle range theories, Merton emphatically argues against theoretical closure. He writes, for example, about one of his favorite examples of middle range theories, the theory of a role set: "If this relatively simple idea of role-set has any theoretical worth, it should at the least generate distinctive problems for sociological theory" (Merton, 1957: 111). A basic aspect of middle range theories is, according to Merton, their theoretical openness or dynamic character; they should generate new questions and fields of discovery. This instrumental value does however not differentiate them in a clear way from inductively or deductively formed theories in the conventional sense.

Possible Paths of the Middle Way

In the beginning of this text I quoted Merton where he complained about the vagueness of the concept of theory (see Ragnvald Kalleberg's chapter). The question is if Merton's own programmatically formulated concept of middle range theories has met the same fate, and whether it is too often used in a vague metaphorical fashion in order to characterize some reasonable and not too general theory. It seems to derive its rhetorical power from its diffuseness.

The programmatic construction of middle range theories, though famous and widespread as a label, is however merely one part of Merton's rich oeuvre. Alongside his emphasis for the codification of sociological theory, he is also famous for his criticism of (assumed) prevailing postulates in functional analysis and his positive formulation of a strategy for functional analysis. Furthermore he has also identified himself as a structural theorist (Sohlberg, 1999).

The theoretical landscape of Merton's reasoning is interestingly complex or fuzzy. This is somewhat ironic considering his plea for a precise definition of the concept of theory. Merton's theoretical landscape can be characterized as a tension between a highly reactive attitude, profound interest in empirical matters, reluctance of specialization, and seemingly abductive reasoning. The reactive attitude of Merton, whether psychological or not, has to do primarily with his opposition against grand or general schemes in social science, chiefly represented by Talcott Parsons. The reactive attitude is also expressed in his criticism of functionalist reasoning.

Merton's main criticism of general theories seems to be that the strategy of formulating and using general theories is sterile and empirically empty. Another interpretation of his skepticism of general theories is that it is impossible to find any general factor influencing all social events, i.e., there is no "prime mover" in the social world. This interpretation, however, presupposes that Merton's theoretical world-view is oriented towards causal analysis.

In his discussion of "mechanisms of the middle range" Charles Tilly goes somewhat beyond the causal approach in offering an interesting application of middle range theorizing (Tilly, 2010). Referring to the level of Merton's theorizing, Tilly writes about "social processes somewhere between the stratosphere of global abstraction and the underground of thick description" (Tilly, 2010: 55). Tilly's interpretation of middle range theorizing is not primarily oriented towards their level of "between-ness" but rather on their quality as identifying mechanisms behind social processes. Tilly formulates a comprehensive typology with seven varieties of how to explain social processes that include, for example, covering law reasoning, variable analyses, and stage theories. His conclusion is that "beyond epistemology and ontology, mechanistic explanations offer a distinctive, superior grasp of how social processes actually work" (Tilly, 2010: 55). Tilly's interpretation of middle range theorizing overlaps to some extent with Boudon's interpretation of middle range causes (discussed here below). As well, his interpretation of mechanisms might also be understood in a system-theoretical perspective which, as I see it, is more in line with Merton's actual strategies.

In a discussion of Merton's conceptualization of middle range theory, Raymond Boudon interprets Merton's negative attitude towards general theories in the sense that it

> is hopeless and quixotic to try to determine the overarching independent variable that would operate in all social processes or to determine the *essential* feature of the social structure, or to find out the two, three, or four couples of concepts...that would be sufficient to analyze all social phenomena.
>
> BOUDON, 1991: 519

This interpretation of Merton's skepticism against general theories is inter-esting in that it identifies several possible aspects of generality. The quota-tion contains three thinkable and by Merton possibly criticized varieties of generality – general causes of social processes, general features of social struc-ture, and general concepts.

Beginning with the *generality of causes* as the goal of Merton's criticism, this aspect is hardly relevant. The main target of Merton's criticism of general theories is Talcott Parsons, and this criticism has little to do with the general-ity of causes. The crucial point is not that Merton is favoring middle-range causes over Parsons' general causes but rather that both share a relative dis-interest in causes. Parsons is famous for his system-theoretical approach. A main feature of this kind of system-theoretical approach is that the focus is not on causes, whether ultimate or not, but on interrelations. It would be meaningless to say that Talcott Parsons' theoretical nomenclature as expressed in, for example, the AGIL-scheme, is oriented towards finding the ultimate cause of anything. This system-theoretical approach is to a high degree shared by Merton who is well-known for his more empirically oriented form of functionalism.

The next potential candidate for dimension of generality mentioned by Boudon is *feature of social structure*. We could here imagine a dimension where Merton would be interested in features of the social structure of the middle range while remaining critical of its highly general features. This is a more complex interpretation to evaluate than the causal interpretation. On the one hand, it is clear that in his research Merton often focuses on clearly delimited structures and contexts compared to Durkheim's discussion of social struc-ture and its more general properties. This is evident, for example, in Merton's analysis of anomie and the success goal, which is specific only to American social structure. This is one of several examples demonstrating that Merton's orientation towards middle range theorizing is focused on delimited features of a specific social structure. On the other hand, there are also tendencies in the opposite direction where Merton identifies highly general features of social structure, including his point that differentiated social structures lead to conflicts (Merton, 1976). Another example of Merton referring to general features of social structure is when he discusses sociological ambivalence:

> *In its most extended sense,* sociological ambivalence refers to incompat-ible normative expectations of attitudes, beliefs, and behavior assigned to a status (i.e., social position) or to a set of statuses in a society.
>
> MERTON, 1976: 6

There are further problems with identifying Merton's ideal of middle range theorizing with skepticism of working with general *features* of the social structure. This is the case when Merton mentions Durkheim's *Suicide* as an example of middle-range theory. The consistent strategy for Durkheim when discussing social facts like anomie, solidarity, and suicide and whatever social fact is to analyze these phenomena in context of general features of the social structure in an abstracted sense. These features of the social structure in terms of control, integration or solidarity are then contextually related to more specific social facts. Durkheim's deductive and generalist approach stands in sharp contrast with Merton's programmatic idea of middle range theory. Durkheim's strategy is to identify "mechanistic" properties applicable to the study of any social structure.

Merton also theorizes from within a framework of general features of social structure when he criticizes the "prevailing postulates of functional analysis" and formulates his own paradigm for functional analysis (Merton, 1968). Merton's discussion concerning functionalism is easily mistaken for a variety of functional analysis on a lower level (the middle range level) than the version of general functionalism he criticizes. The case, however, is that he adheres to a highly general scheme of functional analysis potentially applicable to any social setting. Merton's contribution is that he tries to make the tools of functional analysis empirically verifiable, not less general. His suggestions of how to verify functional statements, (e.g., calculating net-functions can, however, not be applied to empirical analysis. For a detailed argument on this see Sohlberg, 1999).

Regardless of whether Merton's actual reasoning assumes general features, a reasonable reading of his work would find he is often programmatically critical of strategies that attempt to explain "everything" as well as ones oriented towards finding very basic features of social structures.

The third possible factor of generality mentioned by Boudon as the background to Merton's criticism of general theory has to do with the generality of *concepts*. This aspect, I would argue, is the key to understanding the formation of Merton's programmatic approach, even though the situation is complex.

A basic feature of Merton's middle-range theory has to do with the conceptual dependence on a specific type of features. It is the creative choice of concepts in combination with their transposition to delimited contexts that often identifies Merton's focal points for creative theorizing. Even though the concepts in themselves are general and without indexation (e.g., role and status). they are transposed to specific contexts.

Reification of Middle Range Theory

In Merton's programmatic presentation of middle range theorizing there are several basic problems, ones which I have tried to address with examples. The definition of middle range theory as something "between" inductive general- izations and general theory is at best vague and metaphorical and at worst totally misleading. The negative characterization of middle range theory as *not being* abstract general theory, and *not being* raw empiricism is simply not in- formative enough given that a vast majority of theory in social science fulfills these criteria.

Theoretically, much of the reception of the idea of middle range theory is a matter of conceptual reification; this assumes precision that is lacking when following up with its programmatic construction. This conceptual reification follows a rather common pattern in the discourse of social science theory. A concept (e.g. "discourse", "system", "episteme", "social field") is put forward from which follows the idea, or rather illusion of a relative homogenous entity. Many of the concepts in social science are a matter of dispute and controversy and the fallacy of simplistic reification is thus avoided. Oddly, this does not apply to middle-range theory in that it is generally treated as a rather unproblematic ho- mogenous "entity", deriving its identity as the sensible avoidance of extremes.

The assumption of conceptual "homogeneity" is one of the main reasons for ambiguities, fuzziness and vagueness in theoretical reasoning. A basic dimen- sion of relevance for creating this kind of conceptual problem has to do with the relationship between conceptual formation and ontological matters. With the linguistic turn, social science and philosophy became occupied with how "matters" could be done with language, without discussing the restrictions of the linguistic reality (see Willy Guneriussen's chapter). The "construction of X" could illustrate this problem:

Assume that X *has properties* P_1, P_2, P_3, etc. Assume that we by X refer to a specific, well-known "concrete" phenomenon possible to identify by an osten- sive definition, independently of properties P_1, P_2, P_3. It would then usually be regarded as testable whether X really has these properties or not. Moreover, the existence of X would not be in doubt but would be the starting-point for searching the qualities of X. What possibly could be questioned is whether X has these qualities or not.

On the other hand, assume that Y is *defined by* having properties P_1, P_2, P_3, etc. There is then no guarantee that there actually exists some entity or phenomenon having these characteristics, even if Y was substantiated by a name. In Swedish we have the expression "tulipanaros" (tulip-rose) referring to a non-existing "entity" whose existence is constituted only by its name. A name specifying a concept followed by a set of proposed qualities does not necessarily mean that any bearer of the set of qualities exists. This is, to a high degree, applicable to middle-range theory.

What historically can be understood as a relevant distancing strategy of Merton towards grand theorizing in the 19th century spirit, where the role of the social scientist should be to formulate a general and all-encompassing theory, should not be taken as a concrete formula for theory formation. If this interpretation would be accepted, along with the further assumption that Merton's theoretical oeuvre can be subsumed under the label middle range theory, it becomes totally misleading. Fortunately, Merton does not follow his own prescript when actually theorizing.

Merton's Theorizing beyond Middle Range Theory

It is evident that it is hard to give a general and substantial characterization of Merton's theoretical contribution. When Piotr Sztompka characterizes Merton's general position, he does so by describing four general themes: a classicist theme (search for simplicity and coherence), a cognitivist theme (search for empirical confirmation and objectivity), a structuralist theme (interest of social contexts) and finally an ironic theme (interest of paradoxes and complexities) (Sztompka, 1986: 4 ff). This almost stylistic characterization by Sztompka goes well beyond middle-range theory. So too does Merton's codification of functional analysis and his orientation towards a structural analysis (cf. Sohlberg, 1999: Ch. 7).

Even if Merton is inconsistent in his discussion of middle-range theory, and even if his actual theorizing not is illuminated by the application of this concept, I do not consider this a major problem. As I have argued, middle range theory is mainly a rhetorical concept used against the general system-approach of Parsons. It would be unfair, however, to restrict Merton's criticism of general theory to only Parsons, even if Parsons is the most influential and problematic target of Merton's criticism. Well-versed in the history of science, Merton compares the quest for overarching and comprehensive systems in social science with the outdated search for total systems in philosophy:

> To concentrate entirely on a master conceptual scheme for deriving all subsidiary theories is to risk producing twentieth-century sociological equivalents of the large philosophical systems of the past, with all their varied suggestiveness, their architectonic splendor, and their scientific sterility.
>
> MERTON, 1968: 51

An Example of Merton's Deductive Reasoning – Social Structure
and Anomie

So far I have presented several examples of Merton's skepticism towards deductive reasoning and the potential use of general theoretical schemes; his
main argument being that nothing substantial can be derived from abstract
and general schemes.

It is thus ironic that one of the best examples of Merton's theoretical creativity is his deductive application of a general theoretical framework in *Social
structure and anomie* (1938, 1968). In this article/chapter Merton applies Durkheim's over-all perspective, where general properties of the social structure
are used as a framework for understanding social phenomena. Even though
Merton is, programmatically, very critical of abstract deductive reasoning, this
kind of abstract deductive reasoning is actually the starting point of his highly
substantial and creative application of the Durkheimian approach, whom he
also acknowledges (Merton, 1968: 215).

His specific approach to anomie could be described as a deductive down-
scaling of Durkheim's general theory of anomie. This deductive application
means, first of all, that Merton "downscales" Durkheim's general normative
structure to a matter of a specific normative structure, i.e., the general
norm of economic success in the u.s. along with the further premise that
individual economic failure depends on unsatisfactory motivation and effort
from the individual. Furthermore, Merton is not satisfied with Durkheim's
rather general understanding of the consequences of the anomic situation
at the individual level as some sort of general conflict or tension. Merton
rather identifies a set of individual strategies of how to handle the conflict
between the accepted norms of economic success and the non-existent
legal means by which to achieve this goal. These strategies are not inductively and empirically established but are instead a methodological matter
in the manner of a thought experiment, and an exercise in theoretical
categorization.

To summarize, Merton's approach to anomie is a clear case where he deductively uses Durkheim's highly general theory of anomie and substantiates or
operationalizes it in a specific case. The normative structure as an abstraction
is substantiated by a specific historic situation with a commonly shared success goal. The "anomic situation" is substantiated by the discrepancy between
this success goal and the non-existent legal means by which to approach it.
Finally, the consequences of the anomic situation are substantiated by the different individual strategies by which to handle this conflict between norms
and possible paths of behavior.

The fact that Merton's specific application of the general structural scheme
in the North-American setting is on a "lower level" than general theory in the

Parsonian sense is generally taken as indicative of a middle-range theory. The important point is, however, that the starting point of Merton's theorizing consists, in this case, of some very general premises which are not really in line with the middle range idea. This is made clear in the following statement where Merton writes:

> our primary aim is to discover how some *social structures exert a definite pressure upon certain persons in the society to engage in non-conforming rather than conforming conduct.*
>
> MERTON, 1968: 186

Merton's discussion in *Social structure and anomie* is thus a very good illustration that deductive reasoning from general "axioms" – not established by middle range reasoning – can be highly productive and substantial. This means that Merton's general criticism of general theory seems to miss the target, and the proof of this is actually delivered by Merton himself. The problem seems not to be a matter of generality of the theory in itself but has to do with the deductive operationalization process.

A key to Merton's theoretical creativity has to do with what seems to be a kind of abductive reasoning. The difference being that Merton seldom, in Peirce's sense, begins with a particular state of affairs to be explained, choosing instead to begin with the concepts. I have already discussed his description of the genesis and structure of theories, beginning with concepts and their interrelations. Merton's ability to coin or construct fruitful and generative concepts is exceptional. The fascinating fact is that these concepts are not systematically derived from theoretically informed inductive reasoning from empirical findings, i.e., middle range reasoning. We saw in an earlier quotation that Merton explained the relative immaturity of the social sciences by their lack of sufficient observations. Rather than being the outcome of some inductive generalization the concepts in Merton's framework are a consequence of soft deductions from general theories – a path not in line with Merton's programmatic strategy. This ironic situation could be regarded as a good illustration of the unintended consequences of theoretical operations.

References

Alexander, J. (1987). *Twenty lectures: sociological theory since World War II*. New York: Columbia University Press.

Boudon, R. (1991). "What middle-range theories are", *Contemporary Sociology*. 20(4): 519–522.

Calhoun, C.J. (ed.). (2010). *Robert K. Merton: sociology of science and sociology as science*. New York: Columbia University Press.

Durkheim, É. (1982). *The rules of sociological method: and selected texts on sociology and its method*. London: Macmillan.

Joas, H. and Knöbl, W. (2009). *Social theory: twenty introductory lectures*. Cambridge: Cambridge University Press.

Merton, R.K. (1957). "The role-set: problems in sociological theory", *The British Journal of Sociology*. 8(2): 106–120.

Merton, R.K. (1976). *Sociological ambivalence and other essays*. New York: Free Press.

Merton, R.K. (1968). *Social theory and social structure*. Enlarged edition. New York: The Free Press.

Mouzelis, N.P. (1995). *Sociological theory: what went wrong?: diagnosis and remedies*. London: Routledge.

Ritzer, G. (2008). *Sociological theory*. 7th edition. Boston: McGraw-Hill.

Sohlberg, P. (1999). *Mål och mening i samhället: funktionalistiska program i samhällsvetenskapen*. [Ends and meaning in society: functionalist programmes in social science]. Uppsala: Acta Universitatis Upsaliensis.

Sztompka, P. (1986). *Robert. K. Merton. An intellectual profile*. Basingstoke: Macmillan.

Sztompka, P. (2009). "The assault badly misses the mark: (comment on Stephen Turner)", *Philosophy of the Social Sciences*. 39: 260–265.

Swedberg R. (1996). "Analyzing the economy: on the contribution of James S. Coleman", Ed. J. Clark. *James S. Coleman*. London: Falmer.

Swedberg, R. (2014). *The art of social theory*. Princeton and Oxford: Princeton University Press.

Tilly, C. (2010). "Mechanisms of the middle range", Ed. C. Calhoun. *Sociology of science and sociology as science*. New York: Perseus Books.

Turner, J.H. (1991). *The structure of sociological theory*. 5th edition. Belmont, CA.: Wadsworth Publishing Company.

Turner, S.P. (2009a). "Many approaches, but few arrivals: Merton and the Columbia model of theory construction", *Philosophy of the Social Sciences*. 39(2): 174–211.

Turner, S.P. (2009b). "Shrinking Merton", *Philosophy of the Social Sciences*. 39(3): 481–489.

Index